STRANGER CITIZENS

T0340673

Stranger Citizens

*Migrant Influence and National Power
in the Early American Republic*

John McNelis O'Keefe

CORNELL UNIVERSITY PRESS

ITHACA AND LONDON

First published 2021 by Cornell University Press

Library of Congress Cataloging-in-Publication Data
Names: O'Keefe, John McNelis, 1978– author.
Title: Stranger citizens: migrant influence and national power in the early American republic / John McNelis O'Keefe.
Description: Ithaca [New York]: Cornell University Press, 2020. | Includes bibliographical references and index.
Identifiers: LCCN 2020037681 (print) | LCCN 2020037682 (ebook) | ISBN 9781501756092 (paperback) | ISBN 9781501756160 (pdf) | ISBN 9781501756535 (epub)
Subjects: LCSH: Citizenship—Social aspects—United States—History—18th century. | Citizenship—Social aspects—United States—History—19th century. | Immigrants—Social aspects—United States—History—18th century. | Immigrants—Social aspects—United States—History—19th century.
Classification: LCC JF801.O44 2020 (print) | LCC JF801 (ebook) | DDC 323.60973/09034—dc23
LC record available at https://lccn.loc.gov/2020037681
LC ebook record available at https://lccn.loc.gov/2020037682

Cover image: John Lewis Krimmel, *Nightlife in Philadelphia— an Oyster Barrow in front of the Chestnut Street Theater.* Courtesy of the Rogers Fund of the Metropolitan Museum of Art.

S | H The Sustainable History Monograph Pilot
M | P Opening up the Past, Publishing for the Future

This book is published as part of the Sustainable History
Monograph Pilot. With the generous support of the
Andrew W. Mellon Foundation, the Pilot uses cutting-edge
publishing technology to produce open access digital editions
of high-quality, peer-reviewed monographs from leading
university presses. Free digital editions can be downloaded
from: Books at JSTOR, EBSCO, Hathi Trust, Internet
Archive, OAPEN, Project MUSE, and many other open
repositories.

When you cite the book, please include the following
URL for its Digital Object Identifier (DOI):
https://doi.org/10.7298/c6p0-0g38

We are eager to learn more about how you discovered this
title and how you are using it. We hope you will spend a few
minutes answering a couple of questions at this url:
https://www.longleafservices.org/shmp-survey/

More information about the Sustainable History Monograph
Pilot can be found at https://www.longleafservices.org.

To those who have crossed borders

CONTENTS

ACKNOWLEDGMENTS

Thanks to everyone who took this project from idea to book and its many stages in between. This book began at the Department of American Studies at George Washington University. There, Terry Murphy spent many hours reviewing and discussing chapter drafts with me, and her willingness to take the time to read and comment with constructive criticism thoroughly enriched this book as we discussed how to think about citizenship and the people who made it. Additional thought and input from Tom Guglielmo and David Silverman also contributed to the strengths of the book, and they encouraged me to demonstrate what mattered about the information that I was finding in primary sources, while ensuring that my claims were backed with strong evidence. Chad Heap and Richard Stott also provided comments and guidance.

I have participated in several reading groups over the years, and they too have provided invaluable comments, insight, and exchange of ideas. In particular, I would like to thank Justin Pope, Mary McPartland, Sara Berndt, Andrea O'Brien, and Richard Boles. In additional to formal reading groups, formal and informal conversations at GW provided numerous insights from related and interdisciplinary fields of study. Kathleen Bartoloni-Tuazon has given me detailed advice on navigating the process from manuscript to publication, in addition to her careful reading of chapters. Lance Macon provided proofreading. Thanks as well to University of Nevada and Ohio University colleagues. Helpful reading and comments from Debra Nickles, Marguerite Hernandez, and Katherine Jellison helped to improve the manuscript, as did comments from the Ohio University history department's seminar, where many department members offered advice and insight.

Thanks are also due to scholars outside my home institutions who have taken time to provide comments on my work, including Iona Man-Cheong, Rosemarie Zagarri, Peter Hinks, Saskia Sassen, Ashli White, Dinah Mayo-Bobee, and Erin Aeran Chung.

I HAVE HAD a strong and supportive relationship with Cornell University Press while working on this book. Michael McGandy's editorial guidance through this whole process has been very much appreciated by this first-time author. Thanks also to Clare Jones as well as my anonymous readers, whose constructive criticism and advice have given this book additional scholarly insight. Additional thanks to Elsa Dixler, Ihsan Taylor, and Longleaf Services at UNC Press. A grant from the Andrew W. Mellon Foundation that has funded the Sustainable History Monograph Pilot has allowed this book to be published as a digital, open-access book available to all.

Thanks also to those institutions that have provided financial support for this research, and to the people at archival institutions who made their materials accessible. The Columbian College and American Studies Department at George Washington University provided generous financial support and stipends, as did the Smithsonian National Museum of American History. Ohio University provided conference funding to workshop draft materials, and the OU Regional Higher Education Faculty Development Committee as well as the OU Faculty Research Support Program provided additional funding to support the publication of this book. The Cosmos Club Foundation funded archival research travel to Belfast and Dublin. Thanks to the Public Record Office of Northern Ireland and the John Carter Brown Library for their assistance in locating difficult to find sources. Special thanks are due to the Cornwall Historical Society and Ann Schillinger, from whom I learned much about the Foreign Mission School and the students there.

A version of Chapter 3 of this book previously appeared as "Alien Enemies or Naturalized Citizens? Representations of British-born Residents in the United States during the War of 1812," in *Representation and Citizenship* (Detroit: Wayne State University Press, 2016). I thank Liette Gidlow, Richard Marback, Marc Kruman, and the anonymous reviewers for their comments.

FAMILY AND FRIENDS have also been a great help and support during this project. Especial thanks to my husband, Greg Brown, whose comments during proofreading helped this book be the best it can be, and who has been there throughout with love and support. Thanks also to Cynthia Owens, Laura Gosling, Ritija Gupta, and Gonzalo Gómez. Finally, thanks to my parents, John and Monica O'Keefe, as well as my sisters Laura and Meaghan, who have been loving and supportive family members throughout this whole process.

STRANGER CITIZENS

Introduction

A S MIGRANTS TO THE United States in the late eighteenth century, Adam Donaldson and Benjamin Maingault had much in common: both arrived in bondage. They both obtained freedom at the end of their indentures. Both of them attempted to exercise rights of citizenship, but found that either official or public hostility impeded their ability to do so: Maingault, a man of color, found his right to vote challenged in a Philadelphia election in 1807, while Donaldson, a British subject, was required to register as an "alien enemy" with the federal government during the War of 1812, and faced being ordered to move forty miles away from tidewater—an order that applied to all British subjects engaged in commerce. Both men were able to influence the application and recognition of their legal rights, as well as their treatment by the government. They differed, though, in how their rights were threatened. Donaldson, a white man, lost his status during a period of temporary national crisis. For those Americans who saw Maingault as a danger, however, the crisis was ongoing: they continually had to ensure white control of public participation in American politics, and exclude dangerous racial others from the polity.[1]

The experiences of Donaldson and Maingault illustrate the way migrants affected the development of citizenship in the early American republic. Although neither drafted legislation, they nonetheless engaged with the political process at a time when citizenship and its rights were acquiring definition in law and capturing the interest of the American public. Citizens began to acquire new rights, and foreign migrants new penalties, but the extent to which different citizens might be able to exercise rights was open to debate. Donaldson successfully lobbied for different treatment by mentioning his American-born wife, despite a legal tradition of coverture that made his wife a British subject. Maingault exercised the franchise and voted, a right increasingly associated with citizenship, despite white hostility. Maingault pushed for his rights even as white Americans sought to curtail them. Their actions, and those of other foreign migrants, demonstrate how the development of a national citizenship occurred during this early period, gaining form through definition against its legal opposite, the alien.

IN THIS TIME, geopolitical lines and concepts were not firmly set; early America was a vast, disparate place where identities and political relationships remained in flux, and citizenship was in its own process of acquiring shape and meaning.[2] What citizenship meant to Americans and in the broader Atlantic world was open to debate, and ideas and people from far-away places connected and worked to mold new forms of citizenship, both as a legal category and as an idea that circulated in public discourse. The relationship between citizens, their communities, and the state was still uncertain: people residing in the United States did not necessarily envision or seek the path to a nation-state where each citizen had a direct relationship to the central government. Individuals could be citizens of a town, a nation, or all the republics in the world. Additionally, citizenship itself competed with legal personhood as the category from which rights would derive from the state. Moreover, the development of citizenship was a participatory process that was affected by everyone who attempted to define or exercise citizenship and legal rights. Some people, such as President John Adams and Secretary of State Timothy Pickering, wielded considerable power in the formation of citizenship but others, such as Benjamin Maingault, were still able to affect the rights associated with citizenship. For those like Maingault, however, it was no easy task.

Although national citizenship would be fully forged in the crucible of Civil War and Reconstruction, it began to grow in importance in the decades immediately after US independence. This growth of national citizenship resulted in a shifting of rights away from legal personhood, a change that came at the expense of noncitizens with officially foreign allegiance residing in the US, be they foreign migrants, former Loyalists, or American-born women married to either: they all were legally designated as aliens. The extent to which a decentralized—but strong—state functioned in the years after US independence is an important historical question. Although local governments exerted considerable power over their inhabitants, one of the important ways a strong state emerged in these years was around the citizen/alien divide at the national level. That process included not only policing the nation's borders, both geographically and in the public sphere, but also the national government's exercise of its new powers, controlling and forcibly resettling noncitizen populations. Noncitizen migrants began to experience increasing penalties as citizenship during this period grew in meaning and power. Rather than accept their subordinate status, migrants pushed to secure what legal rights they could. In doing so, they gave shape to the rights that became a part of citizenship as well as those retained by legal personhood. From the initial drafting of laws to the enforcement of those laws in local communities, migrants pushed for their rights and interests.[3]

During this early formative period after independence, citizenship rights were forged from the creation of alien legal penalties such as compulsory registration, deportation, and forced internal removal—the term "alien" has a history as well. These new penalties resulted not only from the Federalist vision of a powerful national government and the need to safeguard it against foreign infiltration and corruption—Democratic-Republicans justified some of these penalties as necessary during a state of national emergency. Other penalties reflected the growing consensus among white Americans that people of other races should be excluded from citizenship.[4] Citizens retained privacy, freedom from banishment, and the right to stay in their places of residence, as well as a right to due process. Powers of deportation and internal removal may seem "natural" powers for an emerging modern state, but Federalists, concerned about the spread of revolutionary violence in the Atlantic world, also sought to link the right of free speech with citizen status as part of their desire to safeguard the public sphere from alien participation. These new and national alien penalties were among the first linkages that occurred between the nation-state and citizens. The strong citizen-alien divide that emerged during the early American republic provided a framework for the further development of citizenship as the font from which rights would spring, rather than legal personhood.

In addition, migrants themselves participated in the shaping of citizenship: in trying to develop a state that limited citizenship to men like themselves, American lawmakers, politicians, and judges ran into resistance. They had to contend with alternative understandings put forth by migrants, as well as more practical attempts to secure entry, residence, and life without government surveillance, regulation, and harassment. Migrants lobbied Congress, successfully defeating a proposed blanket ban on the entry of any French citizens to the United States. Migrants resisted deportation, argued against internal removal, and provided alternative definitions of who was a citizen and who was an alien. At times, especially when they were able to mobilize popular political ideologies in their favor, they succeeded in changing enforcement policies. They explored different conceptions of citizenship: white political radicals advocated a transatlantic revolutionary republicanism, and some people of color emphasized a possibility of a more racially egalitarian citizenship. Migrants' racial status upon entering the United States, however, also determined what claims they could successfully make and what strategies they chose to pursue in attempting to obtain citizenship rights. Migrants whom Americans were willing to accept as white could take

many of the benefits of citizenship for granted, while migrants whose racial reception placed them outside the category of white people needed to work hard to
obtain what rights of citizenship they could. This is in contrast to a view that as-
sumes that nativists successfully drafted, passed, adjudicated, and enforced their
laws without intervention, lobbying, influence, or resistance from the migrants
against whom these laws were directed. Such views miss the important role of migrants themselves in shaping the legal development of citizenship: change came
because of actions across a broad political, legal, and social spectrum, showing
that migrants' effects on citizenship were not confined to a narrow area of working as close allies of the leaders of political parties, or as key swing voters in events
such as the election of 1800. Rather, all sorts of independent forms of organizing
to push for reform as well as daily interactions with American society helped to
create and change citizenship in the early American republic.[5]

Furthermore, an examination of the role of foreign migrants in the building
and defining of citizenship in decades after US independence shows the rich va-
rieties and understandings of citizenship that were possible and contested in the
late eighteenth and early nineteenth centuries, in contrast to growing dominance
of a male democratic citizenship of the mid-nineteenth century. Some migrants
embraced a revolutionary citizenship that extended beyond national borders,
while others advocated for a citizenship that was closely tied to a more local elite
status. Still others used local citizenship in a longer early modern tradition of
crowd action, contrasting a citizenship of rights with a citizenship of practical
community mobilization and solidarity. Similarly, migrants' advocacy for citizenship was often, but not always, grounded in liberalism: for women in particular,
Scottish Enlightenment understandings of citizenship were more useful for white
binational couples where American women married foreign men. These ways
that migrants imagined, used, and deployed citizenship differed from the ways
that other ordinary people in the United States theorized and made citizenship.
In particular, as the historian Martha S. Jones has shown, native-born African
Americans engaged in both an intra-community practice as the nineteenth century unfolded and a broader antebellum push for citizenship. This push was part
of the continuous (and at times, radical) transformation of citizenship during
the middle of the nineteenth century, as the country shifted toward a democratic
citizenship more closely tied to the nation-state, and as political conflicts over
race led to the military conflict of the Civil War, followed by Reconstruction.[6]

In contrast to the continuous struggle for African American citizenship in
the nineteenth century, the construction of the citizen/alien divide was a discontinuous one: migrants grappled with policy makers during periodic crises

of ethnicity, particularly white ethnicity. The effect was similar to later crises that limited liberal citizenship and excluded suspect migrant populations. In the years after US independence, the Alien and Sedition Acts and the War of 1812 would result in attempts to temporarily strengthen the power of national citizenship and penalize suspect noncitizens. In addition to these temporary crises, migrants from outside of Europe had to navigate a society where race was seen as continually in crisis by many white Americans. Migrants fought to secure status through engagement not just with the courts, but with the federal executive branch as well. Their claims and assertions could blunt the force directed at them, redirecting and reshaping power and citizenship, even when they seemed to be in very marginalized positions.[7]

The discontinuous nature of the interplay between the nation-state, migration, and citizenship is in contrast to a view of migration and citizenship policies as a gradual American political development in the structure, functioning, and power relations of the state. This discontinuous exertion of federal power appeared despite a lack of executive bureaucratic capacity that forced officials to improvise. To accomplish their aims, these officials relied on partisan allies outside the government to engage in surveillance, secured the cooperation of merchants to assist in "voluntary" expulsion of refugees, and worked in cooperation with local officials such as county sheriffs to ensure enforcement of regulation of migrants. Outside entities in the form of formally organized pressure groups have played a significant role in the development of the state and its regulatory apparatus, but informal organizing and individual actions have contributed to the development of citizenship as well. Officials had to contend with crowds attempting to enforce different ideas about citizenship, or contend with individuals asserting rights and status in a one-on-one setting.[8]

Background: Theories and Practices of Citizenship

Although migrants had many different ways of conceptualizing and asserting citizenship, they had to confront ideologies that dominated popular and official understandings of political culture in the United States. The American Revolution had transformed British colonists into American citizens, both through a grueling, years-long war, and through a political reordering that emphasized citizens' rights to self-representation while also limiting access to full citizenship for outsiders and subordinated groups. In the American Revolution, individuals' own relationship to the sovereign state also changed: before the Revolution, all colonists were the king's subjects. During the Revolution, the inhabitants of the rebellious colonies were faced with a choice: did they remain loyal subjects, or choose to become citizens? Political status and membership itself became a mutable, changeable relationship. Citizenship also shifted away from a personal relationship akin to the lord-vassal bond of protection and loyalty to an idea of community membership in which the state granted rights to its citizens, and perhaps others within its borders. Naturalization also reflected this view: did people seeking to naturalize share the values of the community, and a commitment to republicanism? Citizenship could also be more exclusive than subjectship in other ways: enslaved people retained a political identity as subjects of the monarch, although from a hostile white perspective in the new republic they were (almost completely) socially dead and devoid of an official identity.[9]

Among the most dominant understandings of citizenship post-independence was republicanism. Differences in republican citizenship were related to questions of race, gender, and socio-economic status. Americans associated citizenship with the economic independence of the head of a household. Other household members received their citizenship status from the head of household, who was implicitly white and male. Americans often saw citizenship as part of the political public sphere in contrast to the private household sphere: the head of household represented himself and his dependents in the public sphere. Through his citizenship, he (ideally) both forged the laws that formed the social contract, and obeyed the sovereign state. Within his household, he was sovereign and held authority over his wife, children, other dependents, servants, and slaves. The members of his household had no independent political authority of their own: they were represented in the public sphere by the head of the household. This was the conception of citizenship that those facing exclusion had to engage with; they could argue that they fit the criteria for citizenship, or they could seek to change how citizenship functioned in the United States. This republican concept of citizenship was an ideal that encountered numerous practical difficulties, and the idea of fitness for citizenship itself was subject to change.[10]

Although republicanism emphasized patriarchal control over women and others in the household, and was seemingly validated by the law of coverture, marriages—and therefore women's citizenship—could be more complex in practice. Under coverture, a woman took her husband's citizenship status; if he was a citizen, so was she. If she married someone who was not an American, she took her foreign husband's citizen or subject status. Women held an independent legal status only if they headed a household on their own, which was usually the case only in widowhood, but during the War of 1812, British men emphasized that their wives were "American." Their seeming challenge to the tradition of coverture was possible because of a mix of understandings that allowed them to make claims for different treatment without destabilizing American gender-based hierarchies. Migrant men used this apparent contradiction to emphasize their American-ness in several ways: they included ideas about women's normative roles as transmitters of culture, (white) women's responsibility to counsel and instruct their husbands and sons on the duties of patriotic citizens, women's daily connections to their communities, and wives' roles as deputy husbands, standing in the husband's place when he was unable to do so.[11]

Whereas men used their wives to advocate for citizenship, women seeking to act as citizens on their own confronted growing postrevolutionary challenges to women's personal political activity. White women faced significant barriers to political participation, and women of color even more so. Women of color faced governments and publics much more hostile to their assertions of citizenship throughout the Americas, although the revolutions of the late 1700s would offer windows of possibility. The tenuousness of citizenship for women of color was consequently tied to their engagement with revolutionary governments and their quests for documentation of free and therefore citizen status. For white women, their citizenship was tied to the documents controlled and recorded by white men, and coverture therefore served as a check on white women's informal exercise of authority and independence in daily matters.[12]

Although citizenship held an inclusive promise for members of the nation, citizenship could also be exclusionary. As the relationship between citizen and nation grew, outsiders felt their exclusion more keenly. Revolutionary nation-states saw threats to their nascent government, and the emergence of the American nation-state meant that when noncitizens appeared to be the embodiments of those threats, they could be subject to social exclusion, surveillance, loss of political and economic rights, restrictions on freedom of movement, and violence. People who were citizens or subjects of another sovereign state were aliens, and possible agents of a foreign power. As such, they could be targets of xenophobia, and new nation-states attempted to put greater restrictions upon them, especially in time of war. Public panics and rumors could have still greater negative effects: arrest, detention, expulsion, and/or execution. What the state did not do could be accomplished by crowd action, which not only might receive tacit approval from elite men, but crowds would sometimes be led by them. Race, gender, and class status also served to divide the polity. In the United States, elite white men defined who deserved full citizenship and rights: themselves. Threats from below in the form of people of color, women, and the lowly seemed to be sources of corruption, effeminacy, and mob justice. Consequently, these people did not deserve equal political, economic, social, or legal status: to give them equality was the sign of impending downfall of the virtuous republic.[13]

IT IS IMPORTANT to keep in mind that not everyone arriving in the United States necessarily intended or wanted to become a citizen, either in a formal legal sense or in a broader informal sense of joining a culture and community. Many people traveled to the United States for economic reasons, while others were fleeing violence, and many of them planned to return to their places of origin instead of staying permanently in the United States. Among the people arriving, those encountering a hostile reception sometimes rejected citizenship, preferring their attachment to another polity or nation-state, while others who received a warmer welcome nonetheless viewed themselves in a state of exile, and hoped to return to their place of origin. Of course, those making these choices about becoming citizens also developed and engaged with their own conceptions and meanings of citizenship, even as they rejected a local, state, or national American citizenship. For these reasons, I mostly use the term "migrant" rather than immigrant, unless referring to a person who has clearly stated an intention to permanently settle in the United States.[14]

Background: Early Naturalization Laws

Although migrants influenced naturalization, citizenship, and the legal rights increasingly associated with citizenship, they nonetheless had to engage with the existing legal framework and laws directed at them. At the national level, the most important among these were the comity clause of the of the Articles of Confederation, which became formally effective in 1781, the Naturalization Acts of 1790 and 1795, and the 1798 package of legislation known as the Alien and Sedition Acts, which included the Naturalization Act of 1798, the Alien Act, and the Alien Enemies Act. At the national level, naturalization law varied in its provisions during the Confederation and early federal periods.

In the 1780s, after Great Britain formally recognized US independence, the status of citizenship during the Confederation period was relatively unclear, but was more clearly articulated at the state and local than at the national level. The Articles of Confederation contained a comity clause that required states to recognize one another's citizens. The patchwork of state naturalization laws and procedures varied considerably: some states required only one year's residence, while others required legislative acts. It was possible, under the comity clause, for one state to naturalize another state's aliens.[15]

The new US Constitution contained a provision to "establish an uniform rule of naturalization," which Congress passed in 1790, though it was not clear to what extent national and state citizenship might overlap or conflict. As originally drafted, the Naturalization Act of 1790 would have granted the rights of citizenship in stages, but concerns about conflict with state naturalization laws ultimately led simply to a grant of full citizenship rights after two years of residence in the United States. The most important change in the final version, however, was the new law's restriction of the right of naturalization to whites only. These new federal naturalization laws would continue to coexist with state laws for some time. This coexistence appeared in inconsistent court decisions: in 1817, the Supreme Court in *Chirac v. Chirac* ruled in favor of Congress's sole authority over naturalization, but the court partially reversed its decision in the 1830 case of *Spratt v. Spratt,* returning naturalization to the state of uneasy co-existence between state and federal government.[16]

Legislators viewed migrants through several different lenses. Their mercantilist views held that migrants would benefit the nation as either human capital who would invest in the economic future of the nation, or whose labor would support that growth. In keeping with this view, legislators also believed that European migrants would assist in the ongoing expropriation of Indian lands along the frontier, whose agricultural production would further support the American economy.[17]

Legislators wrestled, though, with a liberal view that citizenship was mutable and theoretically open to any independent white person who believed in republicanism. Legislators acted on a belief that a short residence in the United States would acculturate monarchists to the American political system, but when the French Revolution and the wars it generated resulted in the arrival of both republican radicals and ultra-monarchist aristocrats, legislators became concerned. In 1795, despite the emergence of the first party system, both Federalists and Republicans agreed that it was necessary to extend the residency requirement for naturalization to five years. Each party saw radicals from either the democratic left or the aristocratic right as a political danger from which republicanism needed to be shielded.[18]

In 1798 divisions over naturalization law became more partisan. Federalists noticed that recent migrants, particularly from Ireland, had been increasingly gravitating toward the Republican Party. When the diplomatic furor surrounding the XYZ affair resulted in widespread public alarm about radical migrants, Federalists swung into action and passed the series of laws known as the Alien and Sedition Acts. The Sedition Act targeted defamatory publications aimed at

Federalist leaders. The Naturalization Act of 1798 lengthened naturalization requirements to fourteen years of residence and instituted compulsory registration in federal courts for all white aliens. The Alien Act allowed the president to deport aliens he deemed dangerous, along with requiring incoming vessels to report alien arrivals. The Alien Enemies Act contained provisions allowing, in the event of a declared war, for the detention and "removal" of aliens over fourteen years of age either via the federal courts or by federal marshals.[19]

Following the election of 1800, immigrant activists hoped that the Republican Party would act swiftly to end the Naturalization Act's fourteen-year residency requirement and return to a shorter one. Neither Congress nor President Jefferson moved swiftly, and it was not until April 14, 1802, that a new naturalization act was passed. This act was a return not to the two-year requirement but to the stricter five-year requirement of the 1795 act, and stated that immigrants would first have to file a declaration of intent to naturalize, and then wait three years for naturalization itself. Migrants who did not file a declaration of intent in their first two years of residence would have to wait longer than five years. The 1802 act also retained the port data-gathering provisions of the 1798 act, and additionally required formal documentation, no longer relying on immigrant and witness testimony for arrival and declarations of intent. The 1802 act also meant that those immigrants who had experienced the barriers of the 1798 act would have to, in effect, wait an additional eight full years before being able to naturalize. Immigrants continued to lobby and send petitions but faced resistance, and Congress did not pass a law amending the 1802 act until March 26, 1804. Federal naturalization law experienced no further changes until the War of 1812; on July 30, 1813, Congress passed legislation allowing immigrants eligible for naturalization prior to the declaration of war to naturalize, as well as those who had declared their intent to naturalize.[20]

Demography of Migration during the Period of Atlantic Revolutions

Toward whom was naturalization law directed? Migrants came from many places, and those places varied over time as economic and political conditions pushed people to emigrate from their places of origin. In the years immediately preceding the American Revolution there was significant migration from Northern Europe to the United States. Britain's agricultural revolution and landlords' rising rents dislocated people in Scotland and Ireland who sought to resettle elsewhere. Many Irish immigrants were also Protestant dissenters: they were not members of the official, tax-supported Church of Ireland (equivalent to the Church of England) but were often Presbyterians, Quakers, or members of other Protestant sects. Similarly, German religious minorities sought to emigrate to the United States. Many migrants could not pay for their passage and relied on the system of indentured servitude, agreeing to serve a master who would select them upon arrival, with some room for negotiation. Indentured servants received no wages during their term of service, but contracts often stipulated a requirement for education for younger migrants, and usually came with "freedom dues," which in the late 1700s generally included clothing and tools to work in a trade.[21]

The American Revolution resulted in a temporary halt in economic and religious migrants, but replaced them with military ones: British and French regulars, as well as mercenaries hired from several German states, the Hessians. American leaders encouraged these soldiers to desert to the Patriot side, and when a number of Hessians remained after the conflict, it was a public relations coup for the American cause: the liberal, prosperous republic would make a better peacetime home than old, monarchical Europe.[22]

The period after the American Revolution saw a resumption of the previous patterns of migration, with some slight changes. Irish migrants still tended to be Protestant, but were often better off, with fewer arriving as indentured servants. German migrants would continue to arrive as indentured servants until after 1820, with slightly less than half of German migrants indenting themselves or their families from 1785 to 1804.[23]

Post-independence migration also resulted in conflicts between Britain and the United States over "desirable" and "undesirable" migrants. Part of the impetus for the Constitutional Convention was the export of convicts from Britain to its former colonies. However, the British government wished to retain other groups: officials had already been anxious about the migration of people from the British Isles to the colonies in the years immediately preceding the Revolution, as a general concern that depopulation of the United Kingdom would affect rent prices and have other negative economic effects. Independence rendered the United States sovereign over its own immigration laws, but did not impact existing restrictions on emigration from Britain and continental European states. Britain and Ireland especially restricted sailors and members of the armed forces from emigrating, but also had restrictions intended to preserve Britain's early monopoly on the industrial revolution; skilled factory workers were forbidden to emigrate. Immigrants from restricted categories did nevertheless sometimes manage to make their way out. Another industrial

group of emigrants, who did not face such restrictions, were the agents of manufacturers and shopkeepers who sold British industrial products in the United
States. This group would later face internal migratory pressure in the United
States as fears of Britain's economic strength combined with the revolutionary wars that embroiled the United States in the conflicts of the 1790s and
early 1800s.[24]

Another major group of migrants to arrive in the 1790s and the first de-
cade of the 1800s were the thousands of refugees from the French and Haitian
revolutions. Instability and violence caused many to flee France and its largest Caribbean colony, then known as Saint-Domingue, as the Atlantic world
plunged into revolution and warfare between the French and British empires.
The United States had remained neutral during most of this conflict, and so was
an attractive destination for people fleeing the French empire. Existing trade
connections, especially between the United States and Saint-Domingue, made
it a convenient and practical destination. This wave of refugees was a varied
group, politically and racially: royalists and republicans both came, and from
Saint-Domingue white colonists came, with enslaved people they forced to accompany them, as did significant numbers of free people of color. Aside from
the six thousand or so people who settled in New Orleans in 1809, whose arrival was carefully documented, numbers are difficult to estimate. Nonetheless, even a very conservative estimate would place the minimum number at ten
thousand refugees, most of them from Saint-Domingue rather than metropolitan France.[25]

A small number of migrants arrived from Asia and the Pacific. In the years
after American independence, the global dimensions of American trade grew,
and American traders voyaged to India, Southeast Asia, and the Far East.
During this period, the whaling industry also grew, and whaling ships plied
the world's oceans, stopping at various ports and remote islands. These ships
recruited local men and boys and returned to the United States after long voyages. These sailors sometimes remained in the US, often looking for work on
land. Their numbers are also difficult to estimate, but they remained a very small
group demographically. Because white American missionaries took an interest
in them, they created a wealth of biographical material about their lives while
focusing on narratives of religious conversion. Many of them were persuaded to
study at the Foreign Mission School in Cornwall, Connecticut. These boys and
men faced significant racism and economic marginalization, but they too made
subtle choices about citizenship and membership, as citizenship developed and
transformed in this early national period.[26]

AS DIFFERENT MIGRANT groups encountered and pushed for their understandings of citizenship and its enforcement on the ground, citizenship and legal rights took shape. Political leaders passed and attempted to enforce laws, but their choices were affected by immigrant lobbying, engagement, and resistance. This process of the emergence of citizenship, especially at the national level, would have important lasting effects: not least, the Alien Enemies Act remains part of the US legal code. Although they cannot serve as president, naturalized citizens today officially have all the other legal rights as non-naturalized citizens. Like their early US predecessors, though, they often found a gap between official legal rights and everyday experience. Early US legislators determined and enshrined in law who could legally be a citizen or alien, what rights citizens would have, and what rights aliens would not. Political leaders also determined from whence that authority would emanate, and gave greater power to the executive branch of government at the expense of the judiciary. But in so doing, those leaders encountered another check on state and legal power: the migrants whose actions and rights were subject to control and restriction. Because of the pushback from foreign migrants in the early US, rights such as free speech were not successfully tied to citizenship. And despite increasing attempts to restrict citizenship rights to whites only, some migrants of differing racial status from outside of Europe were able to secure a tenuous foothold of citizenship rights for themselves. The story begins in the next chapter, with a migrant who questioned the US government's authority to deport foreign residents without trial, and the experiences of other migrants like him from the French empire.[27]

CHAPTER I

Refugees Push Back

We did and do now reside . . . in Vine St. No. 167 [Philadelphia] and do intend to fix ourselves as long as by complying with the laws of the United States, we [should] find in this continent the safety peace and protection which has been heretofore granted us.

— Landing Reports of Aliens, No. 161, Marie Dominique Jacques D'Orlic and Marie Laurence Carrere D'Orlic, January 14, 1799

IN PHILADELPHIA IN THE summer of 1798, the French refugee Médéric-Louis-Élie Moreau de St. Méry recorded in his diary that President John Adams and Secretary of State Timothy Pickering had "made a list of French people to be deported" and, much to his surprise, Moreau de St. Méry himself was on that list. During his time in the United States, after fleeing France in 1794, Moreau de St. Méry had run a bookstore in Philadelphia and cultivated a small circle of French intellectual friends in exile. Perhaps he did associate with US Republicans, and wore a tricolor ribbon, but he was no French spy. Not without friends in high places, Moreau de St. Méry inquired through Senator John Langdon "to find out what I was charged with." In his diary, Moreau de St. Méry wrote down Adams's supposed reply: "Nothing in particular, but he's too French."[1]

The exchange between Adams and Moreau de St. Méry represents an important shift in the decline of alien legal rights that coincided with the rise of national citizenship in the 1790s. When Congress passed the Alien Act in 1798, the executive branch of the federal government gained the power to deport aliens— without a trial. But doing so also invited aliens like Moreau de St. Méry to issue a challenge to that law: was he not a person entitled to his legal rights? How could he be deported without having been charged with a crime? Adams's supposed reply also reveals a new way in which citizenship was being equated with nationality: Moreau de St. Méry hadn't done anything, but his birth within the French colonial empire and possession of whatever other qualities Adams deemed to be "too French" meant that he did not belong among the community of American citizens, and ought to be deported. Sensing a hostile climate, Moreau de St. Méry opted to join the many ostensibly voluntary migrants repatriating to the French empire, under pressure from Adams and Secretary of State Timothy Pickering.[2]

THE ALIEN AND Sedition Acts and related 1798 laws were an attempt to forge a national citizenship, but that national citizenship as it came to be was not necessarily one that fully reflected Federalist ideals. One of the key elements in the nationalization of citizenship occurred through the creation of specific rights of citizenship at the national level. These rights were carved out of alien penalties and responsibilities, even if it was not necessarily Federalists' intention to create national citizenship specifically in this way. The passage of the laws was part of the process of the formulation of national citizenship; it was driven by nativist fears, but altered in its legal form by the lawmaking process and political opposition. This linkage between legal rights and citizenship preceded the strong relationship between them that emerged from the conflicts of Civil War and Reconstruction.[3]

Migrants from the French empire were a part of this process of the creation and enforcement of the Alien and Sedition Acts and, with those laws, changes to citizenship and its associated rights. This chapter, in demonstrating the role of migrants in shaping the laws and their enforcement, critiques the approach of Rogers Smith, who has used a top-down model focused on actions of lawmakers and judges: Smith's work draws on national debates, laws passed by Congress, actions taken by federal appointees governing Western lands, and the influence of the courts. In contrast, this chapter, and this book more generally, emphasize the role of the migrants themselves in affecting the development of citizenship and its rights. It does not deny the power of political elites, and shows that they not only tried to shut foreign migrants and nonwhite people out of citizenship, but they placed further penalties on aliens by carving out rights of citizenship. Nonetheless, migrants were able to push back, most notably in preventing a blanket ban on the entry of French citizens. Migrants also worked to affect the law in their everyday engagement in public, and also with the government officials with whom they interacted. These engagements showed differing deployments of citizenship and rights-based claims: they included an assertion of cultural citizenship ("the right to be different") that included a liberal right to act in support of the French Republic as part of a broader right to be politically active. They also showed the deployment of a form of social contract wherein obedience to the law came with a reciprocal right of residence and asylum. Finally, French migrants also asserted a narrow citizenship that included legal rights for naturalized citizens, even though many of them rejected cultural integration.[4]

During the period of the early American republic, citizenship and nationality were not so intertwined as they are in the present. Citizenship was both a narrowly defined legal status indicating a subordinate relationship to a representative government, and also a marker of integration into the political sphere of the citizen's local American community. Nationality was an emerging cultural concept of membership in a broader community, the nation. Many elite Americans worried that significant differences among the inhabitants of the United States could jeopardize the nationalizing project. In the late 1790s, elite Americans agreed that "national characteristics" should define American-ness, but disagreed as to what criteria should qualify individuals for membership in the nation. Federalists chose to emphasize birth within the borders of the United States and white racial status. Republicans tended to emphasize a belief in republicanism and American political institutions, but agreed in equating whiteness with American-ness. Conflicts between liberals and nativists were inflamed by the Atlantic revolutions of the 1790s, and in 1798, Federalist lawmakers embarked on a legislative program that they hoped would strengthen national citizenship and exclude dangerous foreigners from the polity. Republicans worked to alter that program, and in the process also contributed to the creation of a national citizenship that accorded rights to citizens and assigned legal penalties to aliens.[5]

White migrants from the French empire were active participants in shaping the laws of citizenship that were formed in 1798. Moreau de St. Méry was part of a body of people who had migrated to the United States as a result of the Haitian and French revolutions, and who carried with them different ideas of citizenship and its relation to the nation. Through every step from conception, debate, passage, interpretation by the executive, and attempts at enforcement, the laws—and with them the processes of naturalization and the definition of citizenship—changed. Migrants from the French empire were among those who influenced those changes. Although these laws were driven by Federalist nativism and molded by the Republican opposition, French migrants actively lobbied and influenced the laws throughout the process. French migrants intervened to prevent the US government from forbidding them entry, countered hostile descriptions of themselves in the press, often refused to comply with compulsory alien registration, and attempted to influence the naturalization process.[6]

Citizenship, particularly during this period, was not necessarily national. Some migrants asserted liberal ideas of citizenship that were associated with political ideals more than national identification. Others asserted a kind of multicultural citizenship that incorporated national difference into the definition of citizenship. And some asserted the local citizenship preferred by native-born Republicans.[7] But the move toward national citizenship tended to eclipse these other options, even as they were asserted. In 1798, national citizenship began to supersede local citizenship while the two maintained an uneasy coexistence.

In 1798, concern over the possibility of war with France and the possible presence of foreign sympathizers and spies caused Federalists and other Americans to scrutinize the foreign migrant population in the United States for signs of disloyalty and danger. French migrants who openly expressed Republican sympathies found themselves the targets of both official and informal public hostility. Coupled with provisions in the Naturalization Act of 1798 that required all white aliens to register with the federal government, many French migrants would be compelled to respond and offer a defense of their beliefs and their presence in the United States.[8]

French National Characteristics: Cutthroats, Religious Danger, Licentiousness, the Tricolor, and Anti-Jacobinism

The naturalization laws that emerged in the 1790s, which ultimately began to create a US national citizenship, fed in part on fears of French national character. They were related to the emergence of a particular form of nativism—here defined as "the attitude, practice, or policy of protecting the interests of native-born or existing inhabitants against those of immigrants"—a form that saw French migrants as a particular threat to the nascent republic of the United States. Federalist nativism especially saw French migrants as a cultural and political threat to American people and the American political system. French migrants were repeatedly stereotyped in nativist press coverage of local encounters as lawlessly violent, irreligious, sexually licentious, and politically dangerous. Francophobic views in the 1790s were associated with members of the Federalist Party rather than Republicans, who tended to see the French Revolution in more positive terms.[9]

Francophobia in the 1790s United States drew on anti-Jacobin accounts of the French Revolution. In particular, Federalist newspapers chose to emphasize a supposed French thirst for lawless violence and bloodshed, adherence to non-Protestant beliefs, and sexual licentiousness. These alleged tendencies were symbolized by the tricolor cockade worn by not only (non-Royalist) French migrants, but also by adherents of the Republican Party in the US.

Conflicting views regarding French migrants in the United States borrowed from a number of traditions as well as American reactions to the events of the French and Haitian revolutions. Many Americans sympathized with white refugees from the Haitian Revolution, as well as those from the French Revolution. Yet many colonists had also long viewed France as a source of luxury, decadence, and atheism. A longstanding anti-Catholic tradition had centered on the role of France as the preeminent Catholic power in the eighteenth century. France was seen as the source of attempts to impose absolute monarchy and abolish traditional Anglo-American political liberties. The French Revolution upended these traditional views by disassociating France from Catholicism because of the Revolutionary government's disagreements with the Catholic Church and the Jacobin de-Christianization of France. While some Americans viewed the French Revolution as a source of political liberty, others saw it as a source of lawlessness and violence. If some Americans continued to admire France, an increasing number (even Republicans) began to suspect French migrants of harboring characteristics dangerous to the new republic.[10]

US criticism of the French Revolution began in earnest after the September Massacres in 1792, when Parisians seized and executed prisoners in an attempt to prevent counterrevolutionary activity during a period of military reverses and foreign invasion. Conservatives were alarmed by the revolution's mob violence and disregard for due process. In their eyes, France had ceased to be a civilized nation. The arrival in the US of European radicals, along with the public celebration of French revolutionary violence, including 1793 reenactments of the beheading of the French King Louis XVI and demonstrations of the guillotine in Philadelphia in 1794, caused conservatives to fear that revolution and mob violence could spread to the United States. These fears were further amplified by alarmist reports in the Federalist press. Although much alarm was directed at local Republicans and radicals from the British Isles, articles describing French Republicans attempted to describe a type of danger embodied by supposed French national qualities.[11]

First among these was a delight in lawlessness and violence. In one instance in June 1798, a concerned Philadelphian wrote to Fenno's *Gazette of the United States* reporting a truly shocking scene: a fire had broken out at the Philadelphia jail, and while the citizens of Philadelphia were attempting to put it out, they were obstructed by "some scoundrel Frenchmen" who displayed "the most open remarks of exultation at the alarming situation." The writer came to what was the most obvious conclusion for him: "They were doubtless of the infernal Jacobin brood." And really, what could "be expected of a Frenchman" who had "been received with open arms into a hospitable asylum" and yet wore a tricolor emblem, the "ensign of bloodshed, carnage, and malice?" Surely, such a man possessed "a soul ripe for murder, treasons, plots and dark conspiracies."[12]

Connecting the propensity for violence with the threat of importing revolutionary political change, the Philadelphia-based newspaper *Porcupine's Gazette* carried a story about a "Frenchman" who had been brought before a court for allegedly claiming that President John Adams's "head would be off in 6 months time" to be replaced by Thomas Jefferson, and that "If no one else could be found" that the Frenchman himself "would be the executioner."[13]

Similarly, the aforementioned Frenchmen who confounded the attempted extinguishing of the city jail fire shared a disregard for lawful institutions. Such activities might be viewed with greater suspicion when those same jails were used to imprison French privateers, who themselves also showed a flagrant disregard for American law and legal institutions. In one instance, an American sea captain who had just arrived in Baltimore encountered by chance the commander of a French privateer who had seized the American's ship. According to one newspaper account, the Frenchman, when confronted by the American captain, replied "*Heh*, that is nothing," and also "had the impudence to make him a low bow," prompting to the American sea captain to have him "immediately lodged in jail, to shew whether it was nothing or not." However, these jails did not always succeed in holding French privateers. Readers were warned of an escape made from the Lancaster, Pennsylvania, jail, where two French privateering sailors had escaped, along with a runaway slave on the same day.[14]

No news story involving French residents in the United States in 1798 captured the attention of readers more than a dramatic murder-suicide that took place in New York. Newspapers from Maine to South Carolina covered it, as well as non-English-language papers. Federalist readers encountered a very different version of story than the one that appeared in Republican papers, ascribing the violence of the event to the French national character rather than presenting it as a tragedy of domestic violence not unique to any ethnicity. Monsieur and Madame Gardie were refugees from Saint-Domingue; M. Gardie was "a young gentleman of considerable fortune" who was forced to flee the Haitian Revolution. Once in the United States, he and his wife "behaved with a coming deportment of people . . . who had seen better days." This deportment apparently included M. Gardie's teaching French and perhaps Mme Gardie's work as an actress, but their debts exceeded their income and M. Gardie was in danger of being sent to debtors' prison. Mme Gardie had received an offer of acting work in New Orleans, and she proposed that they separate and he return to France, out of economic necessity. M. Gardie appeared to agree, but nursed a grudge and jealous streak, purchased a knife from a French shopkeeper, and with it murdered his wife and then committed suicide. Coverage tended to be sympathetic to Mme Gardie, if also interested in the gory details of her death.[15]

Readers of Federalist publications learned where such violence came from. The anti-Republican *Porcupine's Gazette* covered the murder-suicide under the headline "French Philosophy." Another Federalist paper claimed that such behavior was typical of the French national character, noting that "every thinking man will be reminded of the country from which Gardie sprang," which was where "the seeds of his inhumanity were planted." While it made the murder no less unpalatable, his Frenchness could "sufficiently account for his barbarity," and the editor finally noted that "to abandon cruelty, a Frenchman must flee from himself!" Lest readers not be aware of the possible contamination of French traits, the article on the Gardie murder was immediately followed by a story headlined "MORE IMMORALITY!!!" recounting a Fredericksburg, Virginia, Republican feast at which "much wine was drank . . . on the SABBATH DAY" and was presided over by none other than the "professed deist" Thomas Jefferson.[16]

Also part of the French national character, according to Federalist newspapers, was a lack of Protestant faith. The opposition to French atheism (and "philosophy") was built on an earlier tradition of Anglo-American anti-Catholicism. By turning away from God, the French had gotten revolution and civil disorder as punishment for their sins. Americans should not be tempted to adopt French ideas and religious beliefs lest they suffer the same fate. In addition to Cobbett's headline of the Gardie murder as "French Philosophy," there were other newspaper stories. A New England newspaper reported a supposed interview between President John Adams and "a Frenchman" who "began to descant largely upon . . . the evils of [religion,]" arguing that the United States "had better do as we do in France, lay it all aside." When questioned, the "atheistical reformer" stated "I profess *No* religion," to which Adams replied "*there is the door*," ending the interview.[17]

For women from the French empire, there was the additional charge of sexual licentiousness. The case of Mme Gardie, for some readers, only served to confirm their attitudes. Mme Gardie was already engaged in acting, a questionable trade for women, and her offer of work in New Orleans, some articles implied, may have involved prostitution or courtesanship. William Cobbett also accused her of having cuckolded her husband, justifying his rage (according to Cobbett), even as such bloodthirstiness was part of his inherently depraved national character.

Cobbett's views also extended to the vogue for French fashions, in particular the French West Indies turban, and favored by "fiery frenchified dames." The word frenchified also meant suffering from venereal disease, meaning Cobbett was further attempting to present French fashions as vectors of decadence and disease.[18]

The chief symbol that seemed to exemplify the spread of French ideas and habits in the minds of Federalists was the French tricolor. This symbol was well explicated by a story regarding a Stockbridge, Massachusetts, gentleman farmer whose crops were being attacked "by a set of unprincipled, lawless Crows, who, like Frenchmen, regardless of the right of property, take it wherever they can find it." In response, the farmer made a scarecrow "dressed . . . in the Uniform of a French Soldier, with the National cockade in his hat." According to the news report, "The crows beheld this object of *Terror*, with surprise and horror" and formed a council of war, wherein they "determined that the Frog-eating Rascal, altho' he appeared in the Garb of a civilized being" was not so, and "had more of the Devil in his heart, than any *terrible* object they had ever seen." The crows decided that the time had come to leave, and "get out of the reach of the [French soldier's] *Fraternal embraces*." Here, the tricolor was combined with the French uniform, and referred not only to American actions toward the French and French depredations upon American shipping, but also French destruction or overthrow of fellow European republics.[19]

The tricolor was particularly alarming when it appeared on actual living Frenchmen, and in Philadelphia the tricolor was a part of the city's rough-and-tumble politics. The *Gazette of the United States* gleefully reported an attack on a French resident of Philadelphia who audaciously wore the tricolor, noting that "some spirited citizens very meritoriously struck the tri-*color* from his *chapeau*." Similarly, Moreau de St. Méry, residing in Philadelphia, wore the French tricolor. He noted the increasingly hostile climate and wrote in his diary, "Antagonism against the French increased daily." He further claimed in retrospect that he was "the only person in Philadelphia who continued to wear the French cockade." He met with Republicans who provided him "keys to two shelters in which I and my family could take refuge in case my house were attacked." Four days later, he booked passage back to France. It was at this time that Moreau de St. Méry wrote that he had appeared "on a list of French people to be deported" and issued his indirect challenge to the Alien Act.[20]

Collectively, the view that readers of Francophobic articles began to see was one that highlighted dangers to the republic: lawless violence associated with mob rule, an emphasis on the longstanding tradition of viewing France as a danger to traditional "English" liberties, further amplified by references to French destruction of the Venetian Republic. Many American readers subscribed to a belief that civic virtue was necessary for the survival of the nascent American republic, and that if the citizens of the republic lapsed into mob rule, decadence, and immorality, the republic would be destroyed, much like the ancient Roman Republic. The actions of French migrants were thus not only a danger to individuals, but a danger to the nation. As part of a national characteristic that was unchangeable, they could not be molded into new American citizens. The legal solution, then, would have to eliminate the migrants from political participation and the American public sphere, or send them outside the borders of the United States.

Federalists Legislate a National Alien Policy and Ascribe Rights to Citizenship

The above concerns about the French presence in the United States and belief in French national characteristics led nativists to seek a national, legal solution to the possible threat that they presented. They were greatly assisted in this task by the diplomatic crisis known as the XYZ affair, in which the French foreign minister Charles-Maurice de Talleyrand's intermediaries demanded a large payment before meeting with American diplomatic envoys, as well as making additional demands for loans to the French government. In the meantime, French seizures of American merchant ships continued, angering Americans engaged in commerce. When news of the scandal broke in the spring of 1798, war seemed imminent. And something would have to be done to counter the French threat from within.[21]

The ultimate legislative response was Congress's passage of the Alien and Sedition Acts, as well as the Naturalization Act of 1798. Legislators had designed these laws to exclude foreign migrants from the polity and prevent foreign espionage. The laws also allowed the federal government to surveil aliens, regulate their presence, and remove those deemed dangerous or whose residence in the United States was otherwise undesirable. But they were not simply a direct, unaltered implementation of the Federalists' intended legislative program. The laws instead took form as they moved from committee, to debate on the house floor, and faced amendments, changes, and obstruction by the Republican opposition. A key shift during this process was the exclusion of naturalized citizens from the provisions that otherwise penalized aliens. Although it was not necessarily the specific intention of legislators to do so, the debate and amendment process in Congress concerning national alien policy resulted in the ascription of rights to citizenship and legal penalties for aliens. Rights, in other words, drifted away from the complicated web of social status that gave rights to legal persons and citizenship began to be a source of rights in and of itself. The new laws privileged US citizens by exempting them from surveillance and deportation, while aliens felt the burdens of the national government's surveillance and harassment.[22]

THE FIRST STEP in this process of lawmaking was the intent to introduce bills to address the nativist concerns about foreign migrants and control their activities and movements. Nativists already had a vision of excluding dangerous migrants from the polity through increasingly high barriers to naturalization, allowing the federal government to regulate the presence of aliens within the nation's borders. To put this vision into law, it would first be necessary to draft a bill with these provisions. The change in public mood after Adams released the first of the documents relating to the XYZ affair on April 3, 1798, and the ensuing public uproar about the treatment of American envoys by the French government gave the Federalists the political momentum to draft and push their desired bills through Congress. After an initial flurry of war preparations, Congress acted to address the issue of aliens and citizenship. On April 17, the Federalist Joshua Coit of Connecticut moved for a committee to look into revision of the 1795 Naturalization Act.[23]

The resulting recommendations were an attempt to nationalize governmental authority over citizenship, secure control and knowledge about the movement and whereabouts of aliens in the United States, and prevent persons of foreign birth from naturalizing. On May 1, the committee issued a report that recommended longer terms of residence prior to naturalization, compulsory "report and registry" of all aliens, and a law that would allow for the "apprehending, securing, or removal" of male enemy aliens over fourteen years of age, as well as aliens who "shall threaten, attempt, or perpetrate any invasion or predatory incursions upon [US] territory," largely the provisions that would appear in the Naturalization Act of 1798, the Alien Act, and the Alien Enemies Act.[24]

The committee's recommendations contained several possible new penalties that, once passed as law, would not apply to citizens. The Alien Act would deny aliens the right to trial, and would also allow for the peacetime deportation of aliens. Both the Naturalization Act of 1798 and the Alien Act collectively contained provisions that would require compulsory registration of all aliens. Since these provisions were largely preserved during the debate and amendment process, they are discussed, along with the importance of their role in creating rights of citizens, in the following sections on those two pieces of legislation.[25]

The recommendations were then subjected to debate and amendments in the process of becoming law. During these debates, congressmen articulated their specific concerns about the foreign threat and what additional measures ought to be taken to address it. The debate and amendment process would also shape the laws so that rights and penalties adhered along an axis of citizenship/alienage.

The Federalists, in control of the federal government, had the power to draft the first version before it could be altered, reframed, or blocked by partisan opposition and immigrant lobbying. The Federalist project of national citizenship sharpened the divide between citizen and alien over two kinds of rights: right of residence, and a right to privacy. But other divides were on the table: nationality/ethnicity rather than citizenship per se, meaning that natives could have rights that naturalized citizens did not. Federalists also would consider laws that barred immigration over nationality/ethnicity. As the debates continued, opposition Republicans also influenced the shape of the laws, using constitutional objections and understandings of international law. As discussed in later sections of this chapter, French immigrants themselves would be active in further lobbying and resistance to enforcement, but in these earlier debates, Francophone influence was limited to the Swiss-born opposition leader Albert Gallatin.

In debating a federal bill to specifically exclude French passengers from entry to the United States, nativist legislators argued that French persons inherently possessed such dangerous characteristics that they should be excluded from the United States. When debating the laws that became the Alien and Sedition Acts, which targeted a broader swath of foreign migrants as well as the domestic opposition, legislators focused less on inherent national characteristics than on the extent to which French migrants in the US were acting as direct agents of the French government. Legislators asserted that these agents spied for France, or might issue privateering commissions for France à la Citizen Genet. They worked to "alienate the affection of the people," and printed French government propaganda.[26]

Some Federalists proposed more stringent regulations that would disallow naturalization entirely and restrict citizenship to those born in the United States. The Federalist congressman Harrison Gray Otis also recommended that citizens of foreign birth be excluded from holding office, as was the case for naturalized subjects in Great Britain. Republicans responded to both movements by successfully arguing that the Constitution did not grant the federal government the authority to restrict either ability, or create a second-class citizenship for naturalized citizens.[27]

The Republican opposition, led Albert Gallatin, centered on constitutional objections to Federalist measures. Republicans appealed to the Constitution as the document that checked, rather than enhanced, the reach of federal authority over national citizenship and alienage. The Republican opposition repeatedly argued that the Constitution did not grant the federal government the power to regulate alien migration and naturalization in the ways that nativists wished: either birthright citizenship only or new penalties for naturalized citizens that denied them the rights to political participation and officeholding. Their objections resulted in the creation of rights that adhered along an axis of citizenship/alienage, rather than an additional right of legal personhood attaching to birthright citizenship to the exclusion of naturalized citizens, as some nativists wished.[28]

Since constitutional objections halted the creation of a second-class citizenship, Federalists instead opted for an extremely long residency requirement that effectively barred alien residents from naturalizing. The amendment passed narrowly, 41–40. Albert Gallatin successfully included measures that allowed immigrants who had arrived before 1795 to naturalize under the terms of the 1795 Naturalization Act, which required five years of residence instead of fourteen. Republicans then further moved, unsuccessfully, to lower the residence requirement to seven years from fourteen.[29]

The Alien Act: Citizen Rights and Alien Penalties in Deportation and the Right to Trial

Although the Alien Act was devised chiefly as a way to expel foreigners whose presence Federalists thought endangered the United States, it nationalized regulation of migration by enabling the emerging nation-state to regulate the persons within its borders, and expel them if necessary. The act also created a new penalty for aliens: deportation in peacetime. Local attempts to regulate migration had centered on the exclusion of paupers and carriers of disease, but these paupers and disease vectors could be citizens or aliens; it was not their foreignness that subjected them to restriction of movement. The Act also allowed for deportation without charge of a crime. The law replaced the trial with an opportunity for the alien, once already served with a deportation order, to provide evidence to "such person or persons as the president shall direct" that "no injury or danger to the United States will arise from suffering such alien to reside within." In so doing, the act further contained the right to trial as a privilege of citizenship. Previously, aliens had held the right as legal persons to have a trial when faced with government prosecution.[30]

The Alien Act gave authority to the federal government to do what states and localities had done in the past—try to control migration within their borders. Local governments could "warn out" the undesirable wandering poor: individuals were informed by local officials of their ineligibility for poor relief and sent to their ostensible place of origin, often a nearby town. City ports could also institute quarantines and exclude paupers. State governments passed a flurry of largely ineffective laws barring the immigration of paupers in the 1780s and 1790s. South Carolina, concerned about refugees of color destabilizing Carolinian society, banned their entry in 1793. When panic about a rumored invasion from Saint-Domingue gripped Philadelphia in 1798, the Pennsylvania governor Thomas Mifflin "prohibit[ed] the landing of French negroes." The new federal power did not prevent local governments from continuing they had before—indeed, Mifflin saw the federal regulations as assisting Pennsylvania in enforcing its own exclusion more effectively.[31]

The move from aliens' rights stemming from their status as common law legal persons to a construction of rights around citizenship was spurred by fears of French spies. A number of French migrants had worked to gather intelligence on North American affairs for the French Directory. The most prominent of these was the French soldier Georges Henri Victor Collot. President Adams and Secretary Pickering also suspected that Johann Schweizer (sometimes spelled Sweitzer) and Pierre-Samuel Dupont de Nemours were engaged in similar activities. There had additionally been suspicions about the traveling French scientist Constantin-François Chasseboeuf, Comte de Volney. Adams and Pickering suspected that there were more French agents operating in the United States. Pickering also received warnings about European Jacobins and United Irishmen from other Federalist leaders. The "too French" intellectual Moreau de St. Méry's act of wearing a tricolor cockade, associating with Republicans, hosting a French intellectual salon, running a bookstore, and corresponding with prominent French officials, including Foreign Minister Talleyrand, must have earned his place on the list of deportees by his activities as well as his ethnicity.[32]

By simply beginning deportation proceedings against aliens, Adams and Pickering reinforced the strength of the federal government and reified its authority to police its borders and points of entry. More importantly, they made clear that there would not be a trial for the aliens they intended to deport. Pickering himself was to look over any proof of innocence that the aliens in question might provide, and in Collot's case, "permission to offer proof [could] be merely formal," because in Pickering's opinion, Collot had no "good reason for Staying here" and would be unable to provide "any fact" that he was not "a French intriguer & bitter enemy" of the United States.[33]

In practice, deportation was difficult to accomplish, because the executive lacked a large bureaucracy to adequately monitor candidates for deportation. Secretary Pickering, the law's chief enforcer, was overloaded with other duties, which caused delays in the process, "and the pursuit of . . . aliens was overlooked." Ultimately there were no deportations prior to the expiration of the Alien Act in 1800. The law, however, was most effective as a threat: Thomas Jefferson wrote that "the threatening appearances from the Alien Bills have so alarmed the French that they are going off" and that "a ship chartered for this purpose will sail within about a fortnight for France with as many as she can carry." At least two prominent French migrants chose to leave the United States while the Alien and Sedition Acts were being drafted. In addition to Moreau de St. Méry, there was the scientist Volney, whom Jefferson noted was "the principal object aimed by the law" and who received a passport from Timothy Pickering.[34]

Despite the broad powers of the act, it turned out that important, powerful, and dangerous migrants were more difficult to expel and deport than Federalists had originally expected. Secretary Pickering lamented that the law lacked the power to detain aliens prior to deportation, or "post sureties pending their departure." Adams and Pickering also differed over enforcement—Pickering wanted broad authority to expel as many migrants as he thought necessary, and wrote to Adams requesting blank warrants for deportation. Adams favored what he termed a "strict construction" of the law and wanted individual deportation cases to be cleared through him before he would sign any blank warrants. Of the small number of French aliens whom Adams and Pickering agreed were worthy candidates for enforcement of the law, each escaped expulsion for a variety of reasons. Volney left before the passage of the Alien Act, as did the newly arrived French Consul Victor Marie Dupont, whose diplomatic credentials Adams had refused to accept. For Victor Collot, Pickering concluded that the intelligence he had gathered would be more dangerous if he delivered it in France, so he halted deportation proceedings, despite having a signed order from President Adams. Instead, because Collot was a paroled British prisoner of war he persuaded the British minister to delay his exchange, preventing Collot from leaving with his information about weak American defenses along the border with Spanish Louisiana, a territory soon to be re-acquired by France. Pickering feared that Collot "had formed plans of attack upon the United States from that quarter" that would be carried out should he return to France. British Minister Robert Liston accordingly "prevented his departure" citing a halt in negotiations over prisoners of war. Collot would not be able to sail to France until after the expiration of the Alien Act in 1800.[35]

Ordinary migrants appear to have been more easily swept away by the hand of the national government. Pickering was aided in his organization of migrants' voluntary return passage by improved conditions in Saint-Domingue and metropolitan France. The Alien Act was not passed until June 25, 1798, but in early May, Thomas Jefferson wrote in the letter quoted above that a number of French residents had chartered ships for return passage to France and Saint-Domingue. Pickering viewed these activities with approval, and granted the ships documents for safe passage to France, a necessary step in the war-swept Atlantic of 1798, where ships were often stopped, boarded, and privateered. Pickering viewed these actions as a useful step toward removing undesirable French and other aliens from the United States, even if it was voluntary. Pickering recorded fifteen ships by August 23, 1798, and had taken care to work with customs officials to ensure that they were filled with passengers rather than goods: "If an American vessel is designed to deport French persons according to the [Alien Enemies Act], as many passengers will ordinarily be engaged as she can conveniently carry. . . ." Pickering wrote with the presumed expectation that the undeclared war would become a full-scale, officially declared war between the US and France. In the meantime, ships full of passengers would carry French citizens to various destinations in the French empire: Bordeaux, Cap-Français, Port-au-Prince, Guadeloupe, and Cayenne. [36]

In the view of Federalists, persons who did not possess what they deemed American "ancestry, manners, character, habits, language, and support of the government," were an obstacle to the unification of the citizenry. The removal of foreign persons, particularly those whose political views were at odds with the Federalist/nationalist vision, strengthened Federalists' belief in the possibility of realizing their vision.[37]

The Naturalization Act of 1798: Privacy for Citizens, Surveillance for Aliens

Deportation was not the only new power the federal government acquired in 1798. The federal government began to systematically gather information on aliens as well. The Naturalization Act of 1798 was a highly partisan measure through which Federalists hoped to exclude foreign migrants from the polity by lengthening terms of naturalization, and also a means to subject aliens to a "system of national surveillance." In requiring aliens to register through district courts, and in requiring local ports to collect and pass on registers of incoming aliens, the 1798 Naturalization Act envisioned the creation of a national citizenship by collecting information about aliens, partially in cooperation with local authorities. Moreover, by reserving the privilege of privacy for citizens and instituting compulsory registration for aliens, it added to the personal legal disabilities of aliens, in effect creating a right of citizens that applied at the *national* level. Similarly, the Alien Act gave the federal executive the power to deport aliens, while citizens could not be expelled under the terms of the act.[38]

Federalist fear of French (and other) migrants contributed strongly to the form that both acts took—in particular, the fear of infiltration by foreign spies such as Victor Collot, and the need to track their movements. To respond to this danger required a national, centralized gathering of information and data about aliens, among whom suspicious persons circulated and in whose communities they received assistance from witting or unwitting co-nationals. Federalists intended for the government to use this information to surveil, and hoped to seize and expel those foreign migrants deemed sufficiently dangerous to warrant expulsion—the two chief dangers in question were alleged spies, and editor-journalists of the opposition press. The second group is discussed in greater depth in Chapter 3.[39]

The Alien Enemies Act also worked to nationalize citizenship. It differed from the rest of the 1798 legislation in that it originated from the Republican opposition, who hoped to temper what they saw as arbitrary and excessive executive authority by demanding that the Federalist administration follow a legal process when arresting or expelling alien enemies in time of war. In other words, Republicans saw the measure as a necessary evil to prevent possible arbitrary actions by the Federalist-controlled national government. The act granted the authority to expel alien enemies to the federal executive (both to the president and federal marshals), as well as to state courts and federal courts. Like the Alien Act, the Alien Enemies Act broadened the authority of the federal executive to act where aliens were concerned, but also granted authority at the state level through state courts. Federal marshals, as appointees of the executive, were an extension of executive authority into local communities. But since the Alien Enemies Act did not come into force during the undeclared quasi-war with France from 1798 to 1800, its provisions and extensions of federal power would not be tested until the War of 1812, when it would be used by the Republican Party against subjects of the British Empire; its enforcement is further discussed in Chapter 4. Despite its lack of immediate effect, the Alien Enemies Act had the most lasting consequence of all the 1798 legislation, serving as the basis for the formation of alien policy for every declared war the United States has fought against a foreign nation, and remains in effect in 2012.[40]

A FINAL BILL, which never became law in part because of successful lobbying by French migrants, aimed specifically to exclude French passengers from entering the United States. Initially spurred by a panicky report suggesting collaboration between white Jacobins from Saint-Domingue and their Black counterparts, debates centered more generally on whether French migrants were so dangerous that the federal government, rather than local or state governments, should be responsible for excluding them.

The migrants arrived at the height of nativist fears surrounding the XYZ affair in 1798. The migrants, however, were not Jacobins but rather predominantly Royalist refugees who had sided with the British forces that had invaded revolutionary Saint-Domingue. Losing ground to Toussaint L'Ouverture's forces, British commanders negotiated a withdrawal from Saint-Domingue, and French collaborators in Port-au-Prince and in other British-held areas began to look for refuge elsewhere, and thought they had found it on ships bound for the United States.[41]

The migrants' arrival incited panic and demands that the federal government act to prevent their entry. Although the passengers were predominantly white and had brought with them some people in slavery, an inflammatory account by the French-born US general Louis Tousard claimed that the ships contained "between two hundred and fifty and three hundred negroes, well-armed, trained to war, and saying they will land." The Pennsylvania governor Thomas Mifflin wrote to John Adams, stating that he himself "had determined to prohibit the landing of any French negroes" but since he held jurisdiction only over Pennsylvania, federal action would be necessary, lest they land and come "through the Jerseys with all their owners to Philadelphia." He also suggested that the embargo be extended to "white men." Adams passed Mifflin's letter on to the Senate, and the Federalist senator William Bingham of Pennsylvania introduced a bill to exclude French passengers (including whites) from entry to the United States. Other 1798 legislation was written to target foreign migrants generally, but this bill, spurred by fears of "French negroes," was the only (potential) part of the legislative package that specifically targeted foreign migrants of a particular nationality.[42]

The bill quickly passed the Senate, while in the House debates on the bill led to a second debate over the nature of national characteristics and citizenship. American congressmen debated who was actually a Frenchman. This debate returned to the issue of the mutability of allegiance and the place of birthright or liberal citizenship. Could those Dominguans who had sided with British forces be regarded as Britons? Federalists argued indirectly for birthright citizenship and Republicans argued against it.[43]

The controversy was raised when the Republican Joseph Bradley Varnum of Massachusetts stated that many of the French passengers in question were British subjects, because they "had taken arms against the French Government, and . . . had of course alienate[d] themselves from it." Furthermore, Varnum stated, "the appellation of 'Frenchman' would [not] apply to persons born in the West Indies, though born of French parents." For Varnum, citizenship was a mutable characteristic that could change with political activities and was not necessarily tied to national origin.[44]

In contrast, Harrison Gray Otis stated, "A Frenchman is a Frenchman everywhere." Otis argued that nationality stemmed not from a changeable allegiance but rather from national character, elaborating that a Frenchman might "take his naturalization oath in this country, it does not alter his character; he is still called, and known to be a Frenchman." Otis argued that if the bill were to become law, nationality and citizenship would be treated separately by the federal government—the law applied to nationality rather than citizenship status—although he had previously argued for an immutable, birthright citizenship during the debates over the previous 1798 legislation.[45]

The French passengers bill ultimately did not pass, owing to timely intervention and successful lobbying by detained French passengers and the owners of detained vessels. Their lobbying efforts and effects on House debates are discussed later in this chapter. Congress passed no further laws directly relating to naturalization for the remainder of Adams's presidency. In the meantime, French migrants had to contend with the existing package of laws that were directed at foreign migrants and the emerging national citizenship that was strongly disadvantageous to them as aliens in an unfriendly nation.[46]

Migrant Response to the Federalist Program: Challenge or Leave?

French residents of the United States were compelled to respond to both the 1798 legislative program and the hostile public climate. The migrant response took several forms. Many migrants chose to leave the United States. Some migrants challenged the legitimacy of new alien legal disabilities. They asserted their perceived right to due process or refused to comply with compulsory registration. Some migrants did embrace violent resistance or preserved loyalties to

France or revolutionary Saint-Domingue. White migrants also challenged negative coverage of them in the press, presenting themselves as peaceful, law-abiding citizens deserving of the welcome and asylum given to white refugees in the early 1790s—a contrary form of self-representation. Also, in coordination with merchants trading in the French empire, they successfully lobbied to defeat a bill to exclude French people from entering the United States.

Some of these migrant responses successfully impeded the growth of US national citizenship, particularly the widespread refusal to comply with compulsory alien registration and the lobbying against the French Passengers Bill. But other forms of resistance that attempted to frustrate, impede, or challenge national citizenship inadvertently worked to strengthen it. Actions such as leaving the United States or attempting to assert local citizenship worked to justify the Federalist nationalizing program: nativists could justify it as an effective solution to the achieve their goals or prove the need for the laws passed in 1798. Thus, the impact of French resistance on the development of citizenship laws is more complex than previously recognized.[47]

THE MAIN FRENCH response, of which other foreign targets in 1798 generally did not avail themselves, was to leave. The reasons for leaving were not just the hostile US climate. As previously mentioned, conditions in the French empire had changed significantly. Both France and northern Saint-Domingue were returning to political stability. In France, the Terror had ended, and the Directory had curbed extralegal violence and seizure of property despite its shaky hold as a sovereign government. Directory officials also began to remove individuals from the list of émigrés who had been barred from entering France, while Toussaint L'Ouverture had consolidated his political hold in Northern Saint-Domingue and encouraged the return of the planter class to help revive the economy.[48]

The owners of the ships carrying migrants back to France and its colonies included British-Americans such as William Moodie and Thomas Caldwell and Franco-Americans such as "Lewis" Crousillat, Benjamin Nones, and Stephen Girard. Among the prominent French migrants in the United States who chose to leave at this time were Moreau de St. Méry and the scientist-historian Volney.[49]

By leaving, French migrants accomplished "voluntarily" what Federalist nativists hoped to accomplish by law: the removal of non-Anglo-Americans. With these foreign migrants gone, nativists hoped, Jacobinism and philosophy would disappear from America. Of course, if they stayed, their continued presence justified the continued legal deportation of aliens. Once they chose to remain, however, they had several options about how to engage with the federal government. A small number of migrants, overwhelmingly French, complied with the provisions of the 1798 Naturalization Act and registered themselves as aliens in federal district court. Most French migrants, however, did not, and they were joined in noncompliance by British and Irish migrants as well—in effect, completely frustrating federal compulsory registration of aliens.[50]

Moreau de St. Méry's response to his appearance on President Adams's list of deportees also exemplifies part of the French migrant challenge to Federalist alien policy, and with it, the adherence of rights and citizenship. Targeted as a suspicious person, he inquired through intermediaries "to find out what crime [he] was charged with," an indirect challenge to the law's removal of the right of trial or defense for alien deportations. In other words, Moreau de St. Méry was arguing that under common law, he had rights as a legal person and a free white man despite his status as an alien. Never formally deported but subjected to xenophobic street harassment and official political pressure, and sensing an improved climate in France, Moreau de St. Méry departed, but not before he attempted to change and influence alien policy. This view of alien legal rights, however, would not prevail.[51]

MANY MIGRANTS ALSO refused to comply with compulsory registration that was part of the national system of alien surveillance instituted under the Naturalization Act of 1798 and the Alien Act. The full extent of noncompliance is difficult to determine, but migrants were able to frustrate the enforcement and the federal government was unable to punish those who refused to register. This noncompliance was practiced primarily by aliens already resident in the United States as opposed to new arrivals, who were already subject to local port information-gathering, which the 1798 legislation decreed would now be forwarded to the federal government. In Federalist-controlled areas such as New England and Petersburg, Virginia, at least, returns were forwarded. The widespread noncompliance in 1798 was not repeated during the War of 1812, when British subjects registered as alien enemies with the federal government in large numbers, as detailed in Chapter 4.[52]

Noncompliance can be determined by the relative absence of extant alien returns, although records are incomplete. Nonetheless, the federal court district for Pennsylvania registered only 172 heads of household during this period, when a much larger number of foreign migrants resided in Philadelphia and nearby areas. The act required aliens to register in a federal court, and this was the only one available to them without crossing state lines.[53]

Some French migrants did embrace violent resistance or announced public sympathy with such resistance, although there is only secondhand evidence recorded in alarmist accounts in the Federalist press. The violent resistance included the previously mentioned incident involving the alleged French migrant who claimed he would be willing to behead President John Adams and was prosecuted for uttering "seditious words." Taken at face value, his activities show several different strands of political activity. First, by supporting Jefferson, he was taking an active part in American politics. Second, by mapping the execution of Louis XVI onto John Adams, he was, like many Americans, placing the politics of the United States in the broader context of a pan-Atlantic republican struggle. He also spoke about national figures and the presidency rather than about local partisan concerns, and it was his discussion of the presidency that spurred his prosecution. Last, he intended to fully integrate himself into the polity by naturalizing the day after his arrest. This "seditious Frenchman" simultaneously sought to resist the Federalist program while also bringing about coverage of his actions that the Federalist press presented as justifying the exclusionary and punitive measures taken against foreign migrants: this Frenchman should not be allowed to naturalize, and was, in the eyes of the *Porcupine's Gazette*, deserving of his prosecution for his seditious utterances.[54]

In Newark, New Jersey, another French migrant was prosecuted for the same crime. Lespenard Colie (also Lespinard, and possibly L'Espagnard) was prosecuted along with Luther Baldwin and Brown Clark for remarks concerning the cannonade greeting President Adams as he rode through Newark. Baldwin allegedly remarked that John Adams "was a damned rascal and ought to have his a[rse] kicked, and one of the cannon shot through it." Clark and Colie, associates of Baldwin, were also charged with "seditious words." According to one account, Colie also stated that "if the French came he would joint them & fight for a shilling a day, & deliver up any that were inimical to them." These remarks were seditious not only for being defamatory toward the presidency, but were indicative of the threat of violent resistance to the US government.[55]

Colie had initially pled not guilty, but then changed his plea on the same day, and paid a fine of $40, "being very poor," while his friends were brought to trial one year after the incident. Colie and his friends found the Adams welcome ceremony rather pompous and, in keeping with Republican concerns about political ceremonies and the presidency, perhaps veering uncomfortably toward monarchy. The inhabitants of Newark, including the dram-keeper who had supplied them with alcohol that morning, felt that their remarks had become seditious, and rather than actually dangerous, were an affront to the display of community

harmony and order. According to the Newark *Centinel of Freedom*, the inhabitants of the town were disappointed that Adams did not stop when he passed
through, and in consequence "bent their malice on poor Luther [Baldwin] and
the cry was, that he must be punished."[56]

FRENCH MIGRANTS ALSO engaged in a frequent public defense against the
depictions of them in the nativist press. They countered the view of French migrants as lawlessly violent Jacobins by presenting themselves as predominantly
white, peaceable, unarmed, wealthy, and strictly obedient to local and national
American laws and regulations. Additionally, they, like other foreign migrants,
emphasized the American national vision as a place of asylum from the war-torn
Atlantic. They did so not only in public forums such as newspapers, but also in
their encounters with the American government. This defense was intended to
sway public opinion, and to bring about more favorable treatment in personal
encounters with federal officials and other enforcers of migration laws. Engagement could strengthen federal authority by acknowledging the legitimacy of
that authority, while at the same time migrants forced officials to explain why
harsh measures were being taken against migrants who presented themselves as
peaceable and nondangerous.

Among those aliens who did register with the federal government, a number
departed from the simple data that they were required to provide and explained
more about the circumstances that caused them to come to and remain in the
United States. They chose to emphasize their status as refugees and the asylum
they received in the United States. Elite women asserted their legal status in
these documents alongside their husbands. Those who did take steps toward
becoming citizens seem to have been motivated by their dislocations as a result
of the Haitian Revolution. [57]

Among those who emphasized their status as refugees were those who had fled
from the 1793 battle and subsequent fire that engulfed the city of Cap-Français
(now Cap-Haïtien) on the north coast of Saint-Domingue. Jacques Julien Robert Malenfant, a "sugar refiner and overseer of sugar plantation" working as a
clerk for Peter Stephen Duponceau at the time of his registration, stated that he
was "a Fugitive from the Conflagrat[ion] of Cape François in the Island of St.
Domingo" and that "he left that town [on June 24, 1793] when it was actually
in Flames." Francis (or François) Mery, a "Watch-maker" also stated that he had
fled from Le Cap "where he resided at the Time of the Conflagration." Migrants
could also more clearly emphasize the importance of racial solidarity that they
felt white Americans owed them. Charles Collet, "following the profession of

ice cream maker" in Philadelphia, stated that he was "a fugitive from the persecutions of black men in the Cape Français where he had arrived one year before from france."[58]

Other registrants emphasized their peaceful nature and willingness to live quiet, law-abiding lives while in the United States. Joseph Marie Thomas, a clerk and "teacher of the French language," his wife, Jeanne Felicité, who was "about 44 years having no trade" as well as her adult sons from a previous marriage collectively stated that that they settled in Philadelphia "after the Conflagration of Cape Français," where they "intended to fix their residence" until they could return "with safety" to Le Cap. In the meantime, "bound by Gratitude" for "the Hospitality they have received in this Country" they stated that they all would continue to "behave in a Manner as suitable with the Government of the United States as it become honest people that Misfortune has struck but not debased." Lewis Francis (Louis-François) Morin Duval, a "chemist" and paroled prisoner of war who arrived from Jamaica, stated that although he was "bound to an Oath of Allegiance to the French Republic" he registered himself as an alien "to shew himself submissive to the Laws of Government in which he resides" conditionally stating "the two Countries as yet being at peace with one another." Jean Lefeve, "by trade a glass cutter," and living in Philadelphia "from six months ago" resided with his uncle "opposite city tavern exercising my trade," which Lefeve hoped "to pursue in the United States in the most peaceful manner and with honesty." Also "pursuing their trade in the most peaceable manner and with honesty" were the coopers Etienne Paris, Pierre Nauze, and Louis Neau, who reported themselves as a single household.[59]

Similarly, the D'Orlic family attempted to emphasize the peaceful nature of their stay in the United States. Marie Domin[i]que Jacques D'Orlic and his wife, Marie Laurence Carrere D'Orlic, both signed their alien report. Mme D'Orlic was not unusual in cosigning the landing report: many elite-status French women did the same. Their report noted that M. D'Orlic was "late employed in King's household" although the couple had in fact arrived in the US from the French West Indies in 1793. Unsurprisingly, they described themselves as subjects of the king of France rather than citizens of the French Republic. They lived in reduced circumstances, living "upon the means we brought with us" at "Vine Street No. 167." The D'Orlics hoped that "by complying with the laws of the United States, we [should] find in this continent the safety peace and protection which has been heretofore granted us." The D'Orlics were clearly emphasizing that prior to 1798, they had been relatively unmolested and indeed found safety, peace, and protection in the United States, but that recently that had seemed less the case, despite their impeccable Royalist credentials. While not condoning the law, they hoped that their compliance with it demonstrated that they were not in the class of dangerous aliens who needed to be expelled or could be subjected to informal violence or harassment. The D'Orlics hoped to succeed in obtaining favorable treatment from the US government while also maintaining a French identity and legal status.[60]

In short, families like the D'Orlics and those who chose to present themselves similarly sought to change and influence the enforcement of the laws on the ground—they complied with the law but made clear that they saw a different picture of the United States and their particular place within it. They were peaceful people, refugees, seeking asylum. They felt that presenting themselves in that way to officials of federal courts was a beneficial strategy. Like Moreau de St. Méry, they viewed their rights as legal persons as entitling them to dignified treatment by their host country. This strategy had its limits, in that it did not prevent federal officials from enforcing compulsory registration and using the threat of deportation against those French migrants whom they wished to expel from the United States.

Some migrants displayed a different challenge to national citizenship by refusing to associate citizenship with nationality, either by showing their integration into the Philadelphia community, or by explicitly claiming to be citizens of foreign localities rather than the French Directory. Royalists explained that they had fought with coalition forces and argued that they were no longer legally French, regardless of how nativists like Harrison Gray Otis chose to view them. A few men, already required to list their alien dependents, mentioned their American-born wives, while others displayed their investment in their communities as taxpayers. Louis Duvivier, who "practice[d] phisick and kept an apothecary shop," stated, "I am maryed to an American and living in South Front Street Number 375." Similarly, Joseph Aubaye, a "merchant taylor" stated that after arriving in Philadelphia from Saint-Domingue in 1794, he "married an American lady." Petter Joubert, a goldsmith who "emigrated from Cape Phrensy" stated that he "has paid tax since his arrivle in . . . 1793" Lewis (Louis) Deseuret, not only "paid tax" but also "married a native of this country" [the US] from which union he had "one child born a daughter." Deseuret intended "to be and remain a true citizen as long as I remain in [Philadelphia.]" Despite these provisions, federal officials in the 1790s made no move to treat binational couples differently, although they would in the War of 1812. Similarly, the presence of taxpayers, who qualified as Pennsylvania voters, indicated that national citizenship overruled local standing—the penalties of being a national alien overruled local status.[61]

Other migrants chose to unlink citizenship from nationality by disassociating the terms from one another in alien registrations, much as Deseuret attached himself to Philadelphia rather than the US. Francis (François) Rosset displayed just such a disassociation by stating that he was "a citizen of Grenoble subject of the Government of France." Jean Baptiste Lamdry, a tailor, reported himself as "a citizen of Abbeville in the French Republic." Andrew Vanderherchen, who arrived in the US from Cap-Français in 1793, stated that he was "a native of Namur" which he described as being in "Germany," or what was then the Holy Roman Empire and what is presently Belgium. Similarly, Jean Baptiste Thiry, "a native of the province of Luxembourg," stated that he was "a subject of the Emperor" but also that he was an "Officer in the army of his Britannic Majesty at St. Domingo." Henry Roberjot was born in Bordeaux but stated that he was "a citizen of Hamburg since the 10th may 1784."[62]

Still others noted that their aid to British forces that had invaded Saint-Domingue or as aristocratic émigrés in Europe had caused them to cease to be legally French. Charles Colbert stated that he was "lately from England where he was Captain in the British Service." Thomas Badaraque stated that he was a "subject of his Britannic Majesty by letters of Naturalization Granted to me by Lord Balcares Governor of the Island of Jamaica." The aforementioned Louis Duvivier was "a native of Paris" but a "subject of the King of England."[63]

Looking at the overall self-presentation of the migrants appearing in the landing reports, their attitudes toward naturalization itself show that citizenship was most important for those fleeing from revolution and sensing that return was not feasible. The sense that naturalization was a valuable protection competed with other possible understandings of their status: exile from their true homeland and a cultural premium on things French, especially for those employed in occupations such as dancing instructors, French teachers, and artists. More broadly, migrants were especially likely to have taken steps toward naturalization if they were middle-aged, well-off, highly skilled artisans. For people who held high positions in government, or hoped to revive plantation slavery on Saint-Domingue, naturalization held less appeal.

What these documents also show is a community of foreign migrants who were well-informed about American public events and had a working knowledge of the American legal system. These migrants worked with their lawyers and cultivated a relationship with the federal district court in Philadelphia for their naturalization and other legal needs. Thus, the accounts of suffering in Saint-Domingue, and expectations of asylum, safety, and peace in the United States make clear that they believed that their accounts of themselves would elicit favorable treatment from federal authorities and allow them to avoid deportation in the event of a declared war. In order to effect changes in alien policy, it was necessary to engage with federal officials and work with the machinery of the state. That engagement would have to be on terms with which decision-makers were familiar. Thus, refugees from the Haitian Revolution emphasized their status as asylum seekers and depiction of the United States as a neutral refuge from the wars of the Atlantic revolutions, and indirectly attempted to validate their presence based on an American self-conception of the United States as an "asylum for mankind."[64]

ONE OF THE most effective attempts to influence national policy relating to citizenship and migration was the successful halting of the passage of the bill that would have prevented French citizens from entering the United States. The Senate had already passed the French Passengers Bill and it was being debated in the House, while panicky rumors of a combined invasion of French "Jacobins" and Black Dominguans swirled around Philadelphia. The passengers of the ship *Melpomene*, predominantly French Royalists who had aided British forces in Port-au-Prince, were detained and forbidden entry into Philadelphia. Together with the merchants who owned the *Melpomene* and other ships arriving from Saint-Domingue, they launched a public campaign to halt the bill and allay fears stemming from the misinformed rumors gripping Philadelphians.[65]

On June 29, as the House debated their exclusion, the passengers and crew on board the *Melpomene*, along with its owner, signed a memorial that they forwarded to Congress and to local newspapers. The memorial was a public reply to published rumors of the supposed invasion that had appeared the previous day, which the memorial stated were "false, groundless, and calumnious." The passengers emphasized their white racial status and control of people of African descent on board, their peaceableness, their lack of arms, their wealth, and their strict obedience to local and national American laws and regulations.[66]

Countering accusations of low economic status, they stated that "we are not vagabonds and 'without any funds,'" but rather possessed "sums [of money] on board more than sufficient to convince the government" of the contrary. Rather than overwhelmingly Black, the passengers were evenly split between white (fifty-six passengers) and "negroes" (fifty-five). The memorial stated that rather than rebellious, "All of the slaves have followed their owners from choice . . . nor is there one of them that ever bore arms." The crew was predominantly white as well.[67]

The passengers strongly emphasized their obedience to the law. They stated that "we have submitted ourselves to the laws of the country, and so strictly have we done this" that they had prevented "two Americans" from carrying a sailor off the ship in violation of quarantine, and that all communications with other vessels had been done in good order and obedience to quarantine. The effectiveness of the memorial can be seen in the sudden change in the terms of the debate of the bill in Congress. Shortly after Otis had argued that "a Frenchman is a Frenchman everywhere," Congressman Samuel Smith of Maryland and Albert Gallatin began to argue along the lines of the memorial that Congress was about to formally receive—that the passengers had been compelled to board the ships in Saint-Domingue, and that the merchants who owned the ships were at risk for financial hardship over a controversy in which they had no choice but to accept the passengers. Reflecting the memorial of the passengers, Smith also argued that the enslaved people aboard accompanied their masters by choice, and were "determined to abide by their masters," and it would be "cruelty" to "separat[e] these faithful slaves from their masters, who had preferred this state with them, to freedom without them." It would be even worse, according to Smith, to require the ships' owners to deport the passengers at the merchants' expense, which would be "cruelty never before heard of." The House did not pass the bill.[68]

In this instance, French migrants were able to mobilize a public response and effective lobbying campaign in coordination with Philadelphia-based merchants, defeating an attempt to achieve further national governmental power to regulate immigration. The merchants do not appear in the congressional record by name, but they are probably the same merchants involved in trade with revolutionary Saint-Domingue—including the Franco-Americans Stephen Girard, Benjamin Nones, and the Bousquet brothers. But responses by French migrants were not always effective in stemming the growth of a nationally regulated citizenship.[69]

THE PRESENCE OF French migrants, refugees from the Haitian and French revolutions, spurred nativist fears about foreign intrigue, which in turn led the passage of the Alien and Sedition Acts. The acts were part of a Federalist attempt to create a national citizenship. The acts linked rights to citizenship by denying rights to privacy and freedom from deportation to aliens in peacetime, which explains how citizenship and rights became linked in the process of the nationalization of citizenship. More practically, the Federalist program gave the federal government powers it had previously lacked. The Alien Enemies Act, in particular, would come very much into force during the War of 1812, as described in Chapter 3.

Alien resistance to the Federalist program and nationalization of citizenship, however, could also work to strengthen national citizenship. Migrants who threatened violent resistance gave nativists a chance to enforce the new laws against them, as Colie's prosecution indicates. The presence of actual French spies such as Victor Collot provided an excuse to place the entire foreign population in the United States under surveillance. Even when migrants sought to influence the on-the-ground enforcement of national citizenship, they were forced to acknowledge federal authority and allow the laws the power of enforcement. Nonetheless, migrant lobbying also won important victories that limited federal power, most notably in defeating the blanket ban on the entry of French citizens into the United States.

French migrants employed a number of strategies, but differed from British and Irish migrants from the 1790s in their engagement with the American public sphere. While French migrants carefully lobbied against laws specifically directed at them, and engaged with federal officials enforcing compulsory registration, British and Irish migrants engaged in a boisterous public campaign against the Federalist program, and worked closely with the Republican opposition and press to challenge the Federalists. These activities are discussed in the following chapter.

CHAPTER 2

Virtual Citizens

Strangers . . . should be admited to all the Priveleges of Citisens.

— Letter of John Shaw to Robert Tennant, December 10, 1801

I N 1796, JOHN DALY BURK, a new arrival in Boston from Ireland and editor of the *Polar Star*, made an audacious claim to his readers: "I too am a
citizen," he stated, and not just of Boston, but of "those [United] States."
He further claimed that his failure to naturalize was irrelevant to his citizenship
status. "From the moment the stranger puts his foot on the soil of *America*," Burk
argued, ". . . he becomes a FREEMAN; and though the civil regulations may refuse
him the immediate exercise of his rights, he is *virtually* a Citizen." Burk presented
himself to his readers as a "fellow-citizen," not because he had naturalized, but
because he, like them, was participating in the open political deliberation and discussion that occurred in the United States and was increasingly being mediated
and influenced by journalists like himself. Burk claimed that such participation
made him not a formal, legal, citizen, but instead a virtual citizen.[1]

But Burk found that there were limits to the kind of citizenship he proposed.
When Burk wrote inflammatory articles against the Federalist government in
1798, Secretary of State Timothy Pickering was so incensed that he had trouble
deciding whether he should deport Burk or try him first for sedition.[2] Federalists like Pickering rejected, or perhaps did not even consider, Burk's concept of
virtual citizenship. Instead, they responded to the public politicking of Burk and
other radical migrant journalists with an attempt to legislate a form of tiered
rights in the public sphere, restricting free speech rights as well as granting the
federal government the power to deport undesirable foreign residents without
trial. Ordinary citizens, they felt, did not have a right to dissent so audaciously
from official policies in the public sphere, and if they did dissent, they should be
punished. Aliens certainly did not have this right. Rather than merely prosecute
them for seditious libel as citizens were, seditious aliens were to be deported,
where presumably they would not meddle in American affairs.

Burk, like many British migrants, approached issues of citizenship in ways that differed markedly from most French migrants residing in the United States. Both French and British migrants faced nativist hostility and, in particular, suspicions that they were dangerous radicals. As discussed in the previous chapter, French migrants countered by asserting their legal rights, particularly as they faced the XYZ affair and 1798 passage of the Alien and Sedition Acts. Migrants from the British Isles had a different response. Overall, they appear to have been far less interested in legal citizenship and instead advanced an idea of citizenship defined by participation in an imagined public sphere coterminous with the boundaries of the nation. They also put these ideas into practice in their everyday lives, along with their interactions with (or avoidance of) the American legal system that regulated naturalization and migrant behaviors.

Burk's advocacy for virtual citizenship was part of the lead-up to a conflict over what rights were inherent in citizenship, a conflict that exploded during the passage of the Alien and Sedition Acts through the election of 1800. The conflict was not only about local versus national visions of citizenship and rights but also about what rights citizens had that aliens did not. During this conflict, migrant journalists from the British Isles were among the clearest advocates and practitioners of virtual citizenship, and their public actions ran directly into Federalist opposition. That opposition varied, as some Federalists demanded that only persons born in the United States should be considered as citizens, while more moderate Federalists also accepted immigrants who had gone through the formal process of naturalization.

One way of understanding the motivations behind the passage of the Sedition Act and the conflict between local and national conceptions of citizenship during the 1798 crisis and its aftermath is to see the period as a failed attempt by the national government to take control of the meaning and rights of citizenship from local governments. Similarly, the Sedition Act was a struggle over freedom of the press, the First Amendment, and the power of the federal government, as well as a partisan attempt to silence political dissent. Federalists saw the Sedition Act as a means to end radical printers' influence over an electorate that those printers had made unruly, silencing the printers and restoring the electorate to a quiet deference. The Sedition Act and its enforcement was more than all this: it not only regulated free speech but its enforcers sought to associate free speech with citizenship by treating alien violators of the Sedition Act differently from citizen violators. Free speech became a right of legal personhood. This process of nationalization occurred through migrant activism and everyday resistance, but also as a result of choices made by key actors in the executive, particularly

John Adams and Timothy Pickering, rather than by the courts and Congress. Additionally, rather than disappearing until the Civil War era, national citizenship persisted, and would be revived to enforce the citizen-alien divide at the national, rather than local level; the Republican Party allowed this national citizenship to persist after the 1800 election.[3]

Radical migrants saw their political agency as an inherent right that entitled them to a form of citizenship, while members of the Federalist Party saw their writings not only as a vector of revolutionary fervor but also as a direct attack on the Federalist conception of citizenship. Federalists sought to remedy the situation by physically removing dangerous aliens from the nation via the Alien Act, reinforcing the relationship between the imagined community mediated through print discourse and the regulated geographical boundaries of the emerging modern nation-state. Naturalized citizens obtained a respite from such a measure: despite calls for birthright citizenship by some Federalists, Federalist enforcers of the Sedition Act rejected the distinction between naturalized and non-naturalized citizens when enforcing the law. But they did reinforce the official divide that accorded naturalized citizens freedom from federal deportation.

During this period migrants had low rates of naturalization, and the idea of virtual citizenship helps to clarify migrants' reticence. Virtual citizenship was an appealing alternative to male migrants from the British Isles because it offered most of the same benefits as legal citizenship. It was more than residence: virtual citizenship included active exertion of the rights and privileges of citizens. In Burk's vision, it also included participation in the mediated public sphere, and through that, membership in the imagined community of the nation. Because Americans accepted migrants from the British Isles as white, and because those migrants overwhelmingly spoke and often wrote English, they were able to participate publicly in American politics through newspapers. Furthermore, migrants' decisions not to naturalize were further compounded by a reluctance among native-born Americans (and even other migrants) to see them as culturally American, regardless of their legal status. Virtual citizenship appealed to migrants when they could avoid the penalties of their alien status, but also when they found the remaining benefits of citizenship proved elusive.[4]

Foreign migrants from the British Isles had at their disposal several ideologies or understandings through which to frame their citizenship as a relationship to government and society. Citizenship could be (classically) liberal, giving them rights, political and economic, that the government could not violate, allowing citizens to exercise free choice in their lives. It could be a revolutionary transatlantic republican vision, united in support for the overthrow of monarchy and tyranny, often based on artisanal radicalism. It could be a status debated through legal discourse, where identity and the self were reflected through official documentation, or it could be an imagined relationship to the nation-state and fellow citizens. There were many different ways for migrants to be citizens. Of these ideologies, virtual citizenship drew primarily on liberalism, and for some radicals, the revolutionary transatlantic vision, while migrants' engagement with legal discourse reflected opposition and resistance to enforcers of the law.[5]

In addition to the ideologies of citizenship, migrants also needed to address the practicalities of citizenship. There were different ways not just to think of their status but different ways to act as citizens. Where did they find it useful, and how did they apply and deploy their status? For many of them, virtual citizenship was not necessarily a passive identity, but built into their public activities and encounters with government power and regulation. Sometimes a limited de facto status proved useful, and gave migrants the benefits of citizenship (absent a national emergency.) For men especially, this could coincide with a republican understanding of citizenship: they still represented the public face of their household. Even those activities supposedly reserved to "true" citizens, such as property ownership and holding public office, could be within reach as well. As such, their citizenship was active in a liberal sense, largely free from government control, regulation, or intervention.

THIS CHAPTER ALSO draws on the records of alien registrations made by foreign migrants in 1798 and the period shortly thereafter to argue for a difference in deployments in citizenship between migrants from the French empire on the one hand, and everyday migrants from the British Isles on the other. French migrants showed a willingness to naturalize, while rejecting an American national identity. In contrast, migrants from Britain and Ireland saw the virtual citizenship proposed and theorized by migrants like John Daly Burk as also being useful in their daily lives. This analysis is based on 173 registrations of migrant heads of household with the federal court in Philadelphia, and an examination all 761 extant registrations from the War of 1812 for the state of Pennsylvania.[6]

When the concept of virtual citizenship collided with Federalist ideas of citizenship, radical journalists put up a compelling fight. Their resistance paid off. Ultimately, the right to participate in public political debate was deemed to belong to all free men rather than just citizens: aliens obtained a right to free speech in the press along with citizens. Of course, those who were illiterate, people of color, or women were effectively excluded from this right, either formally or informally. Nonetheless, important boundaries had been established around the idea of citizenship as a result of the debates and conflicts surrounding the Sedition Act.

The Expulsion of Radicals from the British Empire

The politically active migrants discussed in this chapter shared the experience of government attempts to silence them while they engaged in public, political debate in Great Britain and Ireland, at a time when the British government feared pro-French agitators. Their stories, and decisions to leave for America, began in the British Isles.

In his later years, John Daly Burk was recalled as "high and lofty in his carriage, haughty in his manners, and imperious and impulsive in his disposition." Despite this haughtiness, he "exerted great influence over the young men of his day, literally leading them captive at his will." Another described him as "a fine-looking man, of medium stature; well built, of imposing presence." It would be his mediated presence in the public sphere, however, that brought him the greatest controversy and public attention. [7]

Other than his birth in Ireland around 1772, relatively little is known about Burk's early life. Raised a Protestant, he was admitted to Trinity College in Dublin in 1792. Trinity College was a key institution in Ireland's eighteenth-century Protestant Ascendancy, and its graduates made up much of Ireland's political and cultural elite. Despite the economic benefits that Ireland's Protestants reaped, they grew increasingly restive and resentful of British control, and Dublin and Trinity College were sites of venting of discontent and "criticism of established authority." The students of Trinity College also were sympathetic to parliamentary reforms such as reducing or eliminating property requirements for voting, and to Catholic emancipation. The French Revolution greatly inspired Irish reformers, and pushed them toward radicalism, leading to the founding of the United Irishmen.[8]

It was in this milieu that Burk began to express political views, perhaps first in the *Dublin Evening Post*, which sympathized with the French Revolution. According to Burk, his affiliation with the paper and the articles published there came to the attention of the government, which pressured Trinity to expel Burk; he was tried for heresy and blasphemy, convicted, and expelled. Thereafter Burk became involved in a secret society, part of a network of societies that would become the United Irishmen movement, which in turn would organize the 1798 rebellion against British rule. The government was already prosecuting members, and Burk, who was under suspicion, decided to leave for the United States in 1796.

The journalist James Thomson Callender was another radical who would be expelled from Britain in the 1790s. Like Burke, little is known of his early life. Most likely he was born in 1758 in Scotland, his father was a tobacconist, and he may have been orphaned at a fairly early age. He may or may not have been the nephew of Scottish poet James Thomson. He was raised as a Presbyterian, probably of the more strict, evangelical, and strongly Calvinist variety. After receiving a decent elementary schooling, though probably not attending university, Callender obtained a government job at the Sasine Office, copying real estate documents indicating changes in ownership. He probably married in the late 1780s, and had children soon after.[9]

The Sasine office charged fees for searching for, recording, and copying documents. Built into the British patronage system, these fees benefited officials with sinecures, and although subclerks like Callender were also paid through these fees, they benefited far less. A new chief clerk, Thomas Steele, manipulated the fee system to his own benefit at the expense of the poorly paid subclerks. Since the right to vote was tied to qualifications for property, the office was also involved in the creation of fraudulent voters, once again tied to the patronage system. Callender's experiences there informed his later political views, especially when he went over Steele's head to expose the corruption in the office, only to find that Steele had cut his government career short in retaliation.[10]

Pushed out of government employment, Callender turned to writing to make a living. He had already, in 1782, begun a bold entry into the printed public sphere with a pamphlet excoriating Samuel Johnson. In 1790, his poetry, which had been published in local newspapers, attracted the attention of a local patron of the arts, Francis Garden, Lord Gardenstone. Callender produced more poetry, some of which criticized British expansion in India, and attacked the patronage system. Callender then published a pamphlet on brewers' excise taxes, exposing corruption in the taxation system, and portraying it part of a system of English economic domination over Scotland. In 1792, he followed that pamphlet with another, *The Political Progress of Britain*, which had originally appeared as a series of letters in a Scottish newspaper. In his pamphlet, Callender criticized British imperial policy, the ideology of mercantilism, the manipulation of elections in Scotland to serve English interests, and advocated for Scottish independence.[11]

What followed was a brief surge in nationalist sentiment in Scotland, in part colored by the events of the French Revolution. Callender may have produced leaflets calling for demonstrations in Edinburgh in 1792, and participated in

the Associated Friends of the People, a political society whose members encompassed a range of views from reformist to radical revolutionary, with Callender
among the latter. Callender's participation greatly influenced popular views,
both through his dissemination of radical writings and through his personal
influence with other members of the Friends of the People in Edinburgh.[12]

By this time, Robert Dundas, Lord Advocate of Scotland, became sufficiently
concerned about political activities of nationalists and radicals to crack down on
their activities. Callender's *Political Progress of Britain* continued to sell swiftly,
but it had been published anonymously. Dundas determined to find the author
and prosecute him into public silence. Facing arrest, Callender fled Scotland,
and his former patron denounced him. At the same time as Callender came
under pressure in Scotland, another radical writer from the north of England
would also come under public attack, the polymath Thomas Cooper.[13]

In contrast to Callender's struggling origins, Thomas Cooper was born to a
relatively prosperous family in England. His father pushed him toward a career
in medicine or law, but Cooper's talent for chemistry led him to join a Manchester calico-printing firm, at a time when chemical applications were gaining
importance and value in the industry; the firm also possessed a dye-works that
Cooper seems to have supervised. Cooper was a man of diverse interests, presenting a medical history essay to the Manchester Literary and Philosophical Society
in 1783, while branching out into political and religious philosophy over the
next few years. Cooper later published his early writings in a collection, *Tracts,
Ethical, Theological and Political*, after his comfortable establishment as a Pennsylvania Supreme Court justice.[14]

Most notable among his early writings is an advocacy of the Lockean the right
of revolution, and his arguments against the slave trade were apparently the first
to be published in Manchester. Cooper organized an antislavery petition and
donated to antislavery causes during his Manchester years. He was also, briefly, a
leader among the Manchester Dissenting Protestants during a period of controversy over religious policy. Cooper's own beliefs, leaning toward Unitarianism,
would bring him into contact with another radical: the theologian-scientist-phi-
losopher Joseph Priestley.[15]

As the French Revolution expanded possibilities for change, Cooper became involved with secular political radicalism in the 1790s. Cooper traveled to
France in 1792 to watch the progress of the Revolution. There he attended events
of the Jacobin Club in Paris, where he and other members of the Manchester
Constitutional Society were introduced by the Jacobin leader Maximilien Robespierre. This introduction took place before the radicalization of Robespierre,

the Jacobins, and the Reign of Terror. Cooper left Paris before the September Massacres, the first event that turned away many early moderate supporters of the revolution.[16]

Upon his return from France in May 1792, Thomas Cooper discovered that he had become the target of denunciations by the conservative parliamentarian Edmund Burke. Cooper responded with an eighty-page pamphlet of his own, a *Reply to Burke's Invective*, wherein he defended his trip to France and association with the Jacobins. The *Reply* also contained criticism of Britain's privileged classes and a forceful advocacy for political reform in Britain, at a time when government leaders increasingly saw the reform movement as a step toward revolutionary overthrow of government. On May 21, the government issued a proclamation against sedition, which the British government used to silence political radicals and, casting a wide net, reformers as well.[17]

Cooper's enthusiasm for the French Revolution dimmed with the start of war between Great Britain and France in 1793, and the beginnings of the Terror. Cooper had begun to consider emigration to the United States, and conducted a preliminary trip there. In the meantime, the government brought greater pressure against Manchester radicals and reformers. The government arrested another radical, Thomas Walker, and put him on trial. Upon returning to England, Cooper took up his cause, contributing to a conviction of one of the witnesses for perjury.[18]

After his initial trip, accompanied by two of Joseph Priestley's sons, Thomas Cooper decided to emigrate to the United States, arriving in 1794. He chose to settle in Northumberland, Pennsylvania, partly out of a desire to reside in a free state. Joseph Priestley joined him there, as there were plans to establish a community for English emigrants nearby. Like many immigrants, Cooper arrived looking for work. Both he and Priestley, who had been friendly with John Adams in England, wrote to Adams requesting a government appointment, a request Adams chose not to answer rather than decline, as was his general policy with office seekers. Cooper and Priestley's request would later become a source of political embarrassment and controversy. They both managed fairly well economically. Cooper saw medical patients but did not charge them fees, and instead supported himself through legal work. Although his friend Joseph Priestley remained active in the public sphere, Cooper kept a relatively low profile for the next several years. In the meantime, Federalists became increasingly concerned about radical migrants in the United States; by 1798 they had begun to debate whether such migrants' rights should be restricted regardless of citizen status.[19]

Federalists, the Movement for Birthright Citizenship, and Its Rejection by the Executive

Although Republicans claimed to favor a liberal citizenship that allowed all white aliens to naturalize, many Federalists believed that citizenship was a fixed status tied to the place of one's birth. Federalist advocates for birthright citizenship, headed by Congressmen Harrison Gray Otis and Robert Goodloe Harper, did not successfully pass any legislation establishing birth in the United States as the sole criterion for determining citizenship. Federalists in the executive branch, John Adams and Timothy Pickering, continued to view naturalized citizens as legally different from non-naturalized migrants, and equal in rights to citizenship as birthright citizens.

Federalist nativism reflected in part the proportion of foreign-born constituents in the areas that Federalist legislators represented. The leading proponents of birthright citizenship were Otis of Massachusetts and Harper of South Carolina. These states had comparatively low numbers of white foreign-born residents. Federalists from states with larger numbers of foreign-born residents (and voters) sometimes argued against birthright citizenship, or sought exemptions for earlier migrants: although the Maryland Federalist William Craik was willing to prevent any post-1798 arrivals from naturalizing, he advocated allowing migrants who arrived prior to 1795 to naturalize, stating that many of them were "Germans, and . . . whose neglect to become citizens was probably owing to their ignorance of our language and laws." John Williams, representing New York State, explained that "he knew a number of men who had taken advantage of the naturalization law, who perhaps were as good men as any in the United States," and argued that "foreigners who come here to reside, and behave well" should not "be prevented from becoming citizens."[20]

Leading Federalists also saw the full rights of citizenship as adhering only to elites, or themselves. In particular, although voting citizens had the right to remove unfavored candidates from office during elections, Federalists believed that they did not otherwise possess the right to dissent by publicly arguing against government policies, especially during times of political emergency. Moreover, as representatives of the will of the people, elected officials needed to preserve their public reputations and dignity. Calumnious, false attacks upon them therefore needed to be prosecuted. The public sphere was to be polite and deferential, at least to Federalists.[21]

These views would come into conflict when newspapermen from the British Isles brought a new journalistic style to the United States. Rather than abstract discussions of policy, and anonymous attacks on unpopular policies and leaders, the new journalism gave newspapermen an independent, personal voice of their own, and they used it to personally and publicly attack the reputations of political leaders and other persons in the public sphere with whom they disagreed.[22] The new journalism was mean, both in the sense of being vulgar and in being unkind to its targets. Rather than elevate political leaders through public praise, the new journalism tore them down to the same level as the general public. Federalists feared that without the means to protect their public reputations, they would be so leveled. Worse yet, they feared that these journalists, many of whom were sympathetic to the French Revolution, would bring the Terror to American shores, and that Federalist heads would roll in the streets. Federalists feared for their own reputation, for their own safety, and for the future of the nation. While Federalists worried and determined how to respond, the British and Irish radicals participated actively in American by churning out political writings in newspapers, pamphlets, and other works.[23]

British Radical Migrants' Advocacy for and Practice of Virtual Citizenship

The migrants who entered directly into the public sphere as journalists and newspaper editors were a subset of the migrants coming from the British Isles to the United States for economic reasons. This subset sought employment in the growing American publishing industry. The politically active radicals dove into the American newspaper wars and aligned themselves predominantly with the Republican Party. Like many of their fellow migrants, they often did not bother with the process of formal naturalization. Although they possessed strong political beliefs, the radicals' entry into American politics was eased by their status as journalists; many of them found jobs in the United States as printers, writers, and newspaper editors. These migrants began to act as the virtual citizens that John Daly Burk believed they were: they were politically active in domestic American politics, regardless of formal legal status.[24]

Radical printers theorized and attempted to explain the workings of the public sphere; they postulated a citizenship defined by participation in the public sphere, which was egalitarian yet restricted other persons from participation. The eighteenth century was a crucial period for the development of the public sphere, its relationship to the state, and its functioning as a vehicle for social and political change. Although the public sphere appeared to create a level playing field for all participants, it subtly excluded subaltern groups and certain modes of expression. Nonetheless, public political participation and coverage of those events in newspapers served to create a national political culture, and to give national meaning to local political activities—in part making local citizenship more national. Printers such as Burk understood their role as active, political participants in the public sphere, but Federalists such as John Allen also theorized a public sphere even as they acted in it. In other words, contemporary scholarship has theorized the public sphere, but eighteenth-century Americans both theorized and attempted to shape the public sphere in thought and deed.[25]

Virtual citizenship reflected the emerging *persuasive* power that editors began to wield in the public sphere through their influence on their readers and on political debate, while the reaction was an attempt to reinforce a system of social hierarchy that was coming under increasing pressure from public *dissent,* using *force* to silence that dissent, actions noted by other scholars studying the public sphere. This section, and this chapter, rely especially on an understanding of the eighteenth-century public sphere elaborated by John L. Brooke—his key theoretical terms are italicized within this paragraph. Brooke distinguishes between the formal, legal aspects of the public sphere that are bounded within the term *deliberation*; not just the top-down functioning of the state but also parliamentary debate, jury deliberation, and elections, though these aspects of participation are restricted to government officials and full citizens. Immediately outside deliberation is the field of *persuasion,* wherein all persons interact—though some have a greater ability to do so, because they can more easily disseminate their views through emerging print capitalism. Through their public actions, those people in the public sphere can either act *hegemonically*: they can wield cultural power to reinforce the state and social norms, and work against social change; or they can *dissent*; and the hegemonic reaction to dissent can increasingly drift from dissuasion to *force*.[26]

Migrant journalists examined and understood the eighteenth-century public sphere, which led them to articulate a citizenship defined not by deliberative rights, but by participation in persuasion mediated through the emerging newspaper culture. By attacking Federalist officials during a time of political emergency, they also revealed that Federalists understood the distinction between the deliberative political sphere and the broader persuasive portion of the public sphere that constituted civil society. The Federalists saw migrant journalists as exercising undue political and even deliberative power, and their solution to that threat was legal policing of political participation: Federalists saw full citizenship as closely bounded by the strictly deliberative role given to full citizens, while journalists imagined a wider public sphere, still bounded by the nation, but incorporating free (and implicitly white) men in a wider, informal debate over the deliberative process.

LIKE OTHER MIGRANTS from the British Isles, many of the migrant journalists did not bother with naturalization prior to 1798. James Thomson Callender of Scotland had not naturalized, and neither had John Daly Burk. William Duane claimed that his alleged birth in Vermont in 1760 gave him US citizenship, even though he had moved to Ireland prior to the Revolution. All these men would come under pressure for their writings in the 1798 crisis, and Callender would hastily naturalize to avoid deportation. Burk chose to go into hiding rather than return to the British Isles, and Duane was denaturalized in an 1801 court case, though he reobtained citizenship in 1802.[27]

Without legal citizenship, radical migrants at times felt a need to explain their presence in the public sphere. Burk had fled Dublin and begun to edit a newspaper in Boston, the *Polar Star,* in 1796. It was in this paper that he published the address discussed in the beginning of this chapter. In it Burk claimed that though he was not a legal citizen, he was a virtual one. Burk argued that he and other migrants upon their arrival in a nation under republican government experienced a transformation from irrational, uninformed, prejudiced monarchical subjects into rational, informed, thoughtful, and enlightened men. Changed, they rejected their old-world prejudices and participated in public debate and politics with their new neighbors, in the process becoming viable republican citizens.[28]

Burk's address rejected a legal definition of citizenship. Excluded from the formal category of legal citizenship, Burk instead equated citizenship with participation in the public sphere, specifically the persuasive portion that served as a counterbalance to official governmental power and actions. Doing so gained him powerful currency among eighteenth-century readers who viewed the public sphere and its participants as reasoned, disinterested persons collectively seeking to further the public good. Burk also placed himself safely on the proper side of two important boundaries of the public sphere as his readers viewed it: first within the bounds of the nation ("those states"), and second as a journalist contributing to the public good and public order rather than someone irrational and dangerous. Burk had thought conscientiously about the norms and boundaries of the public sphere, as well as the political meanings of participation in it, and wrote a careful placement of himself that legitimized his political activities.

Burk further defended himself and other migrants by arguing that republican government was naturally appealing to migrants and molded them into citizens.

He tied his belief in virtual citizenship to a theory of republican government that suggested legal relationships were not really necessary. Republican governments, Burk argued, created an atmosphere that new migrants wanted to join and participate in, "a moral, intrepid, and enlightened community." Indeed, new migrants could not resist participation because of their "natural sympathy" to such a community, and the migrant "finds his affections irresistibly attracted" to the community. This attraction itself transformed the migrant into a proper citizen, thus causing the melting down of prejudices in Burk's metaphorical crucible. This magnetic pull and transformation affected not just a few, but it was "the way in which all strangers are affected when they enter those [United] states." For Burk, virtual citizenship was coterminous with the borders of the American republic.[29]

Under Burk's editorship, the *Polar Star* also incorporated advocacy for a local version of citizenship within the face-to-face community of the town. This form of citizenship was defined by the respectful treatment of other members of the community, as well as a hope for the further refinement of Boston. A letter writer complained that it was difficult to pass pedestrians on the city's narrow sidewalks. The people of Boston had heretofore not observed the "right every person has to the civilities of his fellow citizens in his town." The article envisioned a community where people would not endanger and harass one another, where each public stroller would be accorded respect and space on the streets of the city, and where members would accord the proper respect due to their fellow citizens. The author, in particular, hoped that the new proposed rules of public conduct would "be particularly observed by coachmen, truckmen, cartmen &c. that strangers may admire the politeness of all classes of citizens."[30]

Federalists dismissed Burk as a rebel Irishman who was simply looking for a place to escape punishment from his true country. In 1797, a Connecticut author, in a satirical poem entitled "The Muse; Or Guillotina," had accused Burk of fleeing Ireland "to save his Bacon." Burk responded that his ties to his nation of birth and to those of his adopted nation were not in conflict with each other. Burk stated that he was "an Irishman well known in his country as a patriot and a rebel." But Burk was also "a lover of the federal constitution" and "attached to the people of America." Thus, in Burk's mind, it was possible to be loyal to the United States and Ireland simultaneously, by linking Irish nationalism as a struggle against British imperialism (and for republicanism) akin to the American Revolution. Burk's defense was later employed by other Irish migrants, who linked the Irish and American struggles to petition against the Alien Act.[31]

Finally, Burk expressed his virtual citizenship by one other important excursion into the public sphere: the production of a patriotic play, which he had written on his voyage to the United States. Using his new home, Boston, as a backdrop, he wrote what proved to be a popular depiction of the Battle of Bunker Hill. *Bunker-Hill; or The Death of General Warren: an Historical Tragedy in Five Acts* debuted to Boston audiences at the Haymarket in 1797. Although thinly veiled Republican propaganda, it succeeded in winning over audiences in Federalist Boston because it was the first play that depicted local events in the American Revolution. That it made use of constructed scenery for stirring battle scenes also helped. Aware of the new and vulgar journalistic style imported from the British Isles, the manager of the rival Federal Street Theater claimed that the play was "a tragedy, of the most execrable Grub-street kind" but he could not help noting that "to the utter disgrace of Boston theatricals, [*Bunker Hill*] has brought . . . *full houses.*" As a success, the play began to be performed elsewhere, and when Burk moved to New York, a production there was attended by President John Adams. At about the same time, Burk's second, less commercially successful play, *Female Patriotism, or The Death of Jean d'Arc,* opened at the Park Theatre in New York—it was before the age of Broadway plays, but technically off Broadway across from soon-to-be-built City Hall. At a time of war between revolutionary republican France and monarchical Britain, and its reverberations in domestic American politics, the play recast Joan of Arc as a (secular) revolutionary heroine. The play suffered from bad acting and a hostile reception, appearing at the same time as news of the XYZ affair and French demands for American bribes became public knowledge in New York. The audience laughed at dramatic moments and hissed at the stage; it was a flop despite later praise from critics. Burk would find that anti-revolutionary feeling in the US would result in personal and professional difficulty for him as he forged ahead in the crucible of American political journalism. As did Burk, James Thomson Callender would soon find that the backlash against revolutionary movements would affect him on both sides of the Atlantic. [32]

THE STATE OF war and internal crackdowns on dissent meant that the United States served as a beacon of asylum for many refugees, as it was still neutral in the French revolutionary wars and as yet relatively unaffected by hostility to radicals. Callender had initially fled to Dublin, but sensing that he was not safe from arrest there, he sailed for the United States, arriving in the spring of 1793. Callender needed work, and thanks to letters of introduction from Dublin friends, he obtained it from the Irish-born Philadelphia printer Mathew Carey. In addition to editing sections of a geography book, Callender published his first political writing in the United States, arguing for US neutrality in the European conflict on the grounds of preserving its prosperous shipping trade. Callender was quite willing to participate vocally in American politics, but his political views on arrival were not necessarily in lockstep with either emerging party.[33]

Callender then obtained a front-row seat to American politics when he was hired to cover Congressional debates for the *Federal Gazette*. This was no easy task, as congressmen's speeches were frequently drowned out by loud conversation. Despite the shorthand skills that landed him the position, he found the speeches too fast to be fully and accurately recorded.[34]

Transparency and public access to Congressional debate was not uniformly embraced in the early 1790s. Many politicians and members of Congress instead viewed the final product of laws and acts passed as the will of the nation—to expose the deliberative process was to invite factional dissent and chip away at national unity.

The reticence to expose Congressional debate to public scrutiny combined with controversies over accurate transcription to embroil Callender in the growing conflicts between the Federalists and the Democratic-Republicans. Callender later noted that in particular, he had "especially irritated" several prominent Federalists: Theodore Sedgwick and Samuel Dexter of Massachusetts, and Robert Goodloe Harper and William Smith of South Carolina. Of these "Dr. Smith was far more rancorous than the other gentlemen collectively." Callender recorded that during a 1794 debate on British trade policy, "Mr. Abraham Clark of New Jersey said, [while] *looking at Mr. William Smith*, that a stranger in the gallery might suppose there was a British agent in the house." The charge stuck and became Smith's nickname, and he was "burnt in effigy in Charleston."[35]

In the meantime, House debates became more rancorous. Callender's transcriptions became a source of ire not only for the Federalists but even for some Republicans who denounced his work, with William Giles claiming that it had "not only misrepresentations, but falsehoods, and contradictions," while John Nicholas alleged that supposed speeches he had made had in fact been fabrications, albeit "written in a handsome stile—better than he [Nicholas] was master of." Some members of Congress began to push for an official stenographer. In the meantime, relations deteriorated with Callender's employer, who took the opportunity to fire him after discovering that Callender had been moonlighting and writing freelance for another paper, the *Aurora*, an increasingly prominent opposition paper. Callender believed the firing was at the behest of the thin-skinned and vindictive William Giles.[36]

At the *Aurora*, Callender became more closely allied with the emerging Republican Party, and wrote in support of its positions on major national issues in the mid-1790s. He defended the newly formed Democratic-Republican societies, criticized the harsh response to the Whiskey Rebellion, and opposed the Jay Treaty, including condemning President George Washington for approving it. In short, despite his foreign birth, Callender had become a vigorous and strongly partisan participant in American public debate.[37]

ALTHOUGH CALLENDER DID not articulate a concept of citizenship grounded by participation in a republican public sphere so clearly, he implied it when discussing political matters and rights. When championing free speech, Callender wrote that Americans possessed the right "of discussing and expressing an opinion on public men or measures—of influencing by argument—by words as many of our *fellow-citizens*, whether rulers or ruled, over to our opinions." More explicitly linking free speech to citizenship, Callender further opined: "This is the right of every *citizen* in his individual or aggregate capacity." In other words, a citizen possessed a right to free speech as an individual and also the collective right to peaceably assemble, to organize politically, and to discuss political opinions and issues. Callender was extending what Federalists saw as exclusively parliamentary privilege, and applying it broadly to participants in the public sphere, either as actual embodied citizens or as virtual citizens in printed discourse. Callender practiced Burk's conception of citizenship by addressing his "fellow-citizens" on political matters. Callender showed no great interest in naturalizing until he was threatened with deportation in 1798. Callender not only equated public participation in the press with citizenship but he also saw free speech as egalitarian and believed that both governmental officials and public citizens should be free to speak their minds.[38]

Federalist Rejection of Virtual Citizenship: Tiered Citizenship and Enforcement of Naturalization as the Citizen/Alien Divide

Federalists ignored Burk's and Callender's model of citizenship in favor of tiered rights for citizens, with leading citizens exercising full rights. The attempts to deport foreign-born migrants and prosecute them for sedition also solidified naturalization and citizen status as the attribute that determined whether a person could be expelled from the boundaries of the United States. This occurred because the enforcers of the Alien Act, John Adams and Timothy Pickering, rejected native birth as the litmus test of protection against

deportation, and instead chose to deport only legal aliens like Burk: they allowed naturalized citizens to remain even if those migrants engaged in seditious activities.

Federalist prosecutors went after John Daly Burk in 1798, shortly after passage
of the Alien Act and the Sedition Acts. By that time, he had begun editing the
New York *Time-Piece*, a paper that was more radical than his previous journal.[39] Federalist prosecutors demonstrated not only a belief that rights of free
speech belonged to citizens alone but that citizenship was tiered. Elite citizens,
Federalists believed, had rights that common citizens did not. They possessed
these rights because of their supposed lack of economic dependence on other
men, and also because they believed themselves to be genuinely not subject to
private interests. Federalists did not view artisans as independent because they
depended on the wealthy as a customer base.[40] When lower status (and artisan)
alien printers like Burk threatened the Federalists' concept of citizenship and
sought to bring political leaders down the level of ordinary voters, Federalists
called for aliens like Burk to be literally expelled from the boundaries of the
American public sphere.

Federalists believed that Burk possessed no right to publicly denounce official government policies. He and other foreign migrants were not, in the view
of Federalists, party to the social contract that bound American citizens to the
Constitution, so their dissent was egregious and dangerous in a manner different
from American-born writers who uttered seditious remarks: unlike wayward
lower status citizens who had exceeded their station, they were likely to be carriers of foreign ideas that endangered the nascent American republic, or perhaps
even foreign agents bent on its destruction.

Even if they disagreed on the validity of virtual citizenship, all participants
in American politics agreed on a conception of the public sphere bounded by or
coterminous with the nation. They recognized that public political remarks resonated beyond their local communities in the wider nation and would be heard
by its national government.[41] Thus, when migrant journalists made intolerable
pronouncements, they had to be placed beyond the bounds of that public sphere
through deportation.[42]

Federalists responded so vehemently because they believed that their public
reputations were necessary for ensuring public acquiescence to their status as
political officeholders, and saw the Sedition Act as a tool for preserving those
reputations from attacks in newspapers. The new kind of journalism that began
to appear in the 1790s included personal and public attacks upon prominent
Federalists. Public reputations were the clothing that shielded Federalists from

being evaluated on the basis of their private lives and actions. The Sedition Act protected their vision of how citizenship should operate in the United States: tiered, deferential, and limited. Citizens outside of the federal government should have only very limited rights to dissent from government views.[43]

The Connecticut representative John Allen articulated these views on the floor of Congress. When Republicans attempted to vote down a second reading of the Sedition Bill, Allen accused them of supporting a dangerous press, stating that the French Jacobins had used the press to sway the "poor, the ignorant, the passionate, and the vicious" to support the Revolution's excesses, and that the "Jacobins of our country" also hoped to "preserve in their hands, the same weapon [the press]; it is our [Federalists'] business to wrest it from them."[44] Nor was Allen alone during path from bill to law. Federalists like Harrison Gray Otis, John Kittera, and Robert Goodloe Harper had already spoken about the need to silence domestic critics during debates over the Alien Act. Overall, the Sedition Act passed the Senate easily, 18-6, along straight party lines, while passing the House more narrowly, 44-41. The law "received the enthusiastic support of Federalists both in Congress and out," including Alexander Hamilton and Fisher Ames, and in fact every Federalist who wrote on the issue in 1798, with the exception of John Marshall, who thought the Sedition Act constitutional but who presciently saw the law as politically unwise. John Adams publicly defended the law, stating that "licentiousness" and "the profligate spirit of falsehood and malignity . . . are serious evils, and bear a threatening aspect upon the Union of the States, their Constitution of Government, and the moral character of the Nation." More moderate Federalists supported the bill, sensing that even if a malicious and foreign-influenced press might not bring revolution, it nonetheless could destroy political leaders' reputations, mislead the voting public, and thus turn Federalists out of office, removing gentlemen from their proper role steering the ship of state.[45]

Similarly, Allen defended the Sedition Act as necessary to maintain public reputations by preserving the public/private divide. Allen painted a bleak picture of the dissolution of the public-private divide if the Sedition Act was not passed. "The country will swarm with informers, spies, delators [accusers and denouncers], and all that odious reptile that breed in the sunshine of despotic power," he warned, telling his audience of a gothic, almost vampiric, danger: they would "suck the blood of the unfortunate, and creep into the bosom of sleeping innocence, only to wake it with a burning wound." This danger would dissolve the barrier between private and public, exposing the intimate private sphere to the cruelties of the public:

The hours of the most unsuspecting confidence, the intimacies of friend-
ship, or the recesses of domestic requirement, afford no security. The com-
panion whom you trust, the friend in whom you must confide, the domestic who waits in your chamber, all are tempted to betray your imprudence
or guardless follies, to misrepresent your words, to convey them, distorted
by calumny, to the secret tribunal where jealousy presides.[46]

The picture Allen drew was one in which private utterances were suddenly
thrust into the public, not only by equals (friends) but also by servants and slaves,
undermining men's abilities to present themselves and be received in a gentle-
manly or respectable manner. And much as Louis XVI and Marie Antoinette
went from figures of public awe, majesty, and respect to figures of public calumny, abuse, and hatred, so a similar fate might pass to the American governing
class if the Sedition Act were not passed to protect government officials from
such attacks.

Allen's descriptions of the threats upon public reputations bear a remarkable
resemblance to a fable that appeared in an eighteenth-century British publication, the *Spectator*. A letter to the editor of questionable authenticity described
the activities of a "Club of She-Romps." At their meetings, the She-Romps sus-
pended the rules of public decorum that respectable women were expected to
obey, and threw "off all that Modesty and Reservedness," which resulted in a
room "filled with broken Fans, torn Petticoats" and other assorted accoutrements
the club referred to as "*dead Men*." The club's high point, however, was "once a
month [when] we *Demolish a Prude*," during which "some queer, formal creature"
was brought to the meeting at which the members would "unrig her in an in-
stant." The male editor of the *Spectator* was invited to just such a meeting, which
he declined, for he "should apprehend being *Demolished* as much as the *Prude*"
by his presence and witness of the scene. Rather than welcome strangers, like a
public should, the She-Romps attacked and demolished them, removing the materials with which they presented themselves as respectable persons. So it was in
John Allen's descriptions. Intimacy was ripped open before everyone to see, and
reputations would be destroyed. To preserve their public presentability, the press
must be carefully regulated, lest it cease to function as a public properly should.

More practically, Federalists believed that printers had acquired political power beyond their station, and in a manner that endangered their ideal
of the public sphere in which disinterested gentlemen governed impartially to
promote the general good. Newspapermen acquired the power to influence the
general public, which would become misinformed and insubordinate. It was

troublesome enough when the newspapermen were native-born but when they were foreigners importing revolutionary views from Europe they were much more dangerous. Through their distribution of opposition and revolutionary opinions, the radical migrants had accrued power and influence that was not only above their station, but also put a power that should be reserved for officials in the hands of foreigners who would use it for their own disloyal ends. Federalists hoped to restore public order by clamping down on such printers.[47]

DESPITE THEIR DISTASTE for some naturalized radicals, President Adams and Secretary of State Pickering upheld naturalization as conferring the rights of citizenship. As leaders of the executive branch, Adams and Pickering were responsible for enforcing the Alien and Sedition Acts, which Congress had successfully passed in June and July of 1798.[48] Pickering sought to target the most dangerous members of the opposition, citizen and alien, to prevent the spread of seditious ideas among native-born and migrant alike. In the process, he and Adams rejected the idea of birthright citizenship that had been championed by men such as Otis and Harper. Although Adams and Pickering were outraged when foreign migrants they had targeted for deportation managed to naturalize, they refused to deport anyone who had become a legal citizen. Thus they gave naturalization greater significance.

For example, they did not target the English radical Thomas Cooper, who settled in Northumberland, Pennsylvania, and had naturalized. Pickering saw Cooper's political writings and activities as threatening, and hoped to deport him, but made an unfortunate discovery: "Cooper has taken care to get himself admitted to citizenship," Pickering wrote to Adams. "I am sorry for it," he continued, "for those who are desirous of maintaining our internal tranquility must wish them both [Thomas Cooper and Joseph Priestley] removed from the United States." Pickering once again expressed the Federalist view that once outside the United States, political radicals would cease to affect US politics— deportation was, theoretically, a successful remedy for aliens who endangered the nationally bounded public sphere. Although deportation was not an option for Cooper, Pickering was no doubt gratified when Cooper's political writings proved grounds for a prosecution under the Sedition Act.[49]

Cooper's foray into print and politics began when he filled in for the editor of the local Northumberland newspaper, who may have been feeling the heat of an increasingly partisan public sphere. Cooper wrote political essays for the paper, which were collected into a printed volume and sold. As they addressed US national politics, including opposition to the Sedition Act, and were strongly against Federalist policies, they drew the attention of the wider public and the scrutiny of Federalists on the lookout for possibly seditious writings.[50]

Up to this point, however, Cooper had written in the tone of a political thinker to some degree above the partisan fray. But he soon chose to engage in more partisan attacks, beginning in June 1799. In the *Northumberland Gazette*, Cooper attacked Federalist policies and argued that taken collectively, they were tantamount to an attempt to establish a monarchy in the United States. Cooper became directly involved in the 1799 Pennsylvania elections, supporting the Republican candidate for governor, Thomas McKean.[51]

A different incident would ultimately lead to Cooper's prosecution for seditious libel. Cooper served as counsel for William Duane, whom the US Senate had charged with defamation. A constitutional question arose: did the Senate have jurisdiction to prosecute? Duane and Cooper worked with the white Jamaican immigrant Alexander Dallas and Thomas Jefferson, then the vice president, to coordinate a strategy. Both Dallas and Cooper declined to serve as counsel in published letters, illustrating the unjustness of a possible trial where the Senate had already determined guilt. Instead, they urged Duane to decline to appear before the Senate. Cooper's vigorous public defense and rabble-rousing language, along with his now-close ties to the Republican leadership, made him a target of the Federalists. Cooper was charged with seditious libel under the Sedition Act on April 9, 1800, but the charge was based on his previous statements in the *Northumberland Gazette* about the establishment of a monarchy in the United States.[52]

Despite Cooper's attempts to delay the trial in order to acquire better evidence for his defense, judge Samuel Chase proceeded with relative swiftness. Chase allowed Cooper the use of newspaper excerpts rather than official copies of Adams's speeches, which were the cornerstone of Cooper's defense. Since there was no doubt about the fact that Cooper had published his writing, his defense rested on proving the truth of the claims that he made and further emphasizing the right to criticize the political decisions of those in power. Since the trial itself was presided over by a Federalist judge appointed by Adams, and an acquittal was unlikely, Cooper expected his defense to reverberate in the public sphere. Chase pronounced Cooper guilty and provided the maximum fine allowable under the law and a sentence of six months. Nonetheless, of the prosecutions intended to silence the opposition press, Cooper's trial was one in which Chase proceeded with relative fairness.

Cooper served his sentence, while friends and associates unsuccessfully lobbied Adams for clemency, although Cooper's fine may have been paid by

Republican benefactors. Cooper, after a short time, resumed political advocacy in Northumberland, and he would become involved in the controversies over Alexander Hamilton's alleged attempts to manipulate the electoral college in favor of Aaron Burr rather than Thomas Jefferson.[53]

Pickering also refrained from deporting James Thomson Callender, who naturalized specifically to avoid the Alien Act. Callender hastily naturalized in Philadelphia in 1798, and then fled to Virginia to avoid prosecution for the Sedition Act. Through Republican connections he obtained the editorship of the Richmond *Examiner*, and continued to produce criticism of the Federalist government.[54]

Pickering may not have tried to deport Callender and naturalized radicals like him, but he and other Federalists wanted to make clear that the federal government could exert force in areas where Republican opposition was strong. Callender and his Richmond newspaper, in the heart of Republican Virginia, were ideal targets. Pickering gave instructions that Callender's Virginia newspaper and other writings were to be carefully monitored and examined for seditious writings, and duly prosecuted. Callender soon published a pamphlet, the *Prospect before Us*, which contained no less than twenty passages deserving of prosecution for seditious libel. Callender was tried, convicted, and imprisoned. Importantly, however, despite his hatred of Callender, Pickering respected the legality of his naturalization, even though it was undertaken only to avoid deportation. Callender, no matter his foreign birth and suspiciously timed naturalization, was still a citizen.[55]

ALTHOUGH JAMES THOMSON CALLENDER and Thomas Cooper had naturalized and could not be deported under the Alien Act, others under threat had remained aliens. Cooper's friend, the chemist and theologian Joseph Priestley, another radical exile from the British Isles, was concerned about deportation but did not naturalize. He was saved from deportation by Adams's refusal to sign a warrant for him despite Pickering's wishes. "I do not think it wise to execute the alien law against poor Priestley at present," wrote Adams, "... his influence is not an atom in the world." John Daly Burk, on the other hand, was targeted for deportation by Pickering, and in his case, Adams made no intervention.[56]

Burk's targeting for deportation started out when he shifted back to newspaper editing (and away from playwriting) in the spring of 1798. Partnering with the elderly Dr. James Smith, and probably receiving support from Aaron Burr, Burk became the primary editor of *The Time Piece*. Burk's editorship coincided with the controversies of the XYZ affair and the passage of the Alien and Sedition Acts, as well as the 1798 rebellion in Ireland. Unsurprisingly, considering his support for transatlantic republicanism and involvement with Irish resistance, Burk began to closely ally himself with the Republican Party. Burk argued fiercely against Federalist actions, especially the Sedition Act.

Burk, already part of a vociferous newspaper war with pro-Federalist editors, came under suspicion of the government. Burk "claimed that . . . the seals of his letters [were] damaged, and his mail examined." Rumors had begun to circulate about Burk, and the New York *Commercial Advertiser* printed a story about him.[57]

But the real danger began when John Allen quoted the *Time Piece* on the floor of the House of Representatives, drawing attention to articles that "implied that the President had tampered with" diplomatic dispatches in order to provoke war, and that Secretary of State Timothy Pickering had some role in the mysterious death of an Irish refugee.[58]

Tensions then spilled out into the streets of New York, where, as in Philadelphia, men wore black or tricolor cockades to publicly demonstrate their political standing, and young rowdies gathered before the residences of the politically prominent. Burk, gaining the support of the New York Irish community, "stationed a guard of seventy men to protect the office of the *Time Piece*." With such threats, and expecting an indictment for sedition while in financial straits, Burk ceased printing his newspaper, with the last edition on August 30, 1798.[59]

From there, things took an ugly turn with his business partner, Dr. James Smith. The two disagreed about matters relating to the dissolution of the business, and to whom remaining subscriptions fees were owed. Burk took out newspaper advertisements urging his former readers not to pay their balances to an unnamed "person or persons," and holding out hope that the paper would be revived to once again launch its salvos against the Federalist Party. Smith replied with a number of claims that put Burk in a bad light: that the original contract did not allow for the printing of seditious material, and that Smith had done the heavy financial lifting in getting the paper started and Burk still owed him money, and that Smith was collecting moneys due because he had also "assumed the debts of the partnership."[60]

With the Adams administration targeting politically active foreign migrants in general, and Burk in particular, the government persuaded him to self-deport. Burk planned to board a ship bound for Bordeaux in France, but later claimed that there was "an actual attempt to seize me" despite his willingness to leave voluntarily. He was also "watched by the spies of the British minister" and "induced by the advice of some of the best men in America to postpone my departure."

Burk informed Pickering that he planned to travel instead to New Orleans, then under Spanish rule. Pickering was suspicious of these claims, warned the governor of the Mississippi territory, and indicated a willingness to prosecute Burk. Pickering was right to be suspicious: Burk chose to go into hiding in Virginia, with the assistance of his Republican friends.[61]

Despite acquiring the power to deport during the 1798 crisis, the federal government did not directly exercise this power. Rather, the power to deport served as a tool in the coercive arsenal that Pickering and other Federalists deployed against foreign migrants. The Department of State was overwhelmed with a large number of duties for its tiny staff. Consequently, direct proceedings, even when working in concert with the judiciary and federal prosecutors, could prove unwieldy. Instead, Pickering opted for a strategy of encouraging "voluntary" departure and self-deportation. This strategy was discussed in the previous chapter, as the largest group to voluntarily leave were migrants from the French empire. What matters more specifically here is the role of naturalization: naturalized citizens were not brought under the same pressure, only foreign migrants. It was the threat of deportation, rather than deportation itself, that Pickering deployed, and he used it only against aliens and never against citizens. Inversely, he did not choose to prosecute aliens under the Sedition Act, only citizens.[62]

Federalists did score a legal victory when they successfully denaturalized William Duane and more closely associated citizenship with the territoriality of the United States rather than a liberal incorporation of those migrants who had supported the Patriot cause elsewhere. In the eyes of Federalists, the newspaper editor Duane was not, despite his claims, an American. Duane claimed to have been born in Vermont in 1760, but his Irish-born mother moved her family back to Ireland in the early 1770s, before the Revolution. Duane subsequently lived in India and England, coming to the United States in the 1790s. In 1801, a libel suit against Duane, stemming from a statement published in January 1800, came to trial in the suit *Hollingsworth v. Duane*. The court ruled that all persons born in the British dominions but not present in the United States at the time of the Revolution were not citizens of the United States, which set a legal precedent that continued to be enforced through the nineteenth century. The decision came too late for Pickering to target Duane for deportation. The court restricted citizenship to the borders of the United States as established in 1783: it was not possible to choose republicanism elsewhere in the British Empire and be eligible for US citizenship. Regardless of whatever support British subjects elsewhere in the British dominions gave to the rebellious colonists, they were not eligible for citizenship. In Federalist eyes, a discrete community (comprising the colonies) had severed its governing ties and established a republic (the United States). Those not present at this time of separation had not been in the position to choose a Patriot or Loyalist side, and would have to be slowly incorporated into the community through naturalization. In this particular instance, the broader, liberal possibilities of citizenship were curbed to conform somewhat more closely with national border delineation.[63]

The end result of the enforcement of the Alien and Sedition Acts and the election of 1800 that installed Thomas Jefferson in the presidency was a victory for virtual citizenship, but also the disassociation of the right to free speech with citizenship and its subsequent attachment to legal personhood. Despite Federalist attempts to treat citizens and aliens differently, that right did not ultimately adhere to citizenship. This transition was aided by Republican electoral victory in 1800, which ended federal attempts at deportation.[64]

AS FOR THE radicals specific to this chapter, their transitions represent a political-cultural Americanization that continued post-naturalization. Of those who lived a significant time past Jefferson's election, many shifted toward a regional, white American identity, particularly John Daly Burk, James Thomson Callender, and Thomas Cooper, who all acculturated to Southern surroundings. In contrast, William Duane remained in Philadelphia and continued to be a leader in the Irish-American community.

John Daly Burk had decided, at the last minute, against his own self-deportation and had gone to Virginia to live under Republican protection. Burk did not initially prosper; the Virginia Republican elite, while hostile to the Federalist-controlled national government, were not fully disposed to give him work. Burk languished and accumulated debts, and, he would later claim, "notified Pickering of his whereabouts and readiness to stand trial." The Virginians came through shortly after the 1800 election with a position as a trustee of the newly established Jefferson College. With the Alien Act expired and Federalists defeated, Burk could once again come out into the open.[65]

But it was not to last. Burk, who "had a way with the women," was rumored to have had an affair with a local married woman, which led to an attempt on Burk's life. Although the husband later "publicly admitted his wife's innocence," Burk decided it best to leave. He moved to nearby Petersburg, established himself as a lawyer, and became a naturalized US citizen in 1802. Burk settled into Petersburg society, married, had a son, was widowed, was accused of fathering a child in a bastardy case, and wrote several more plays. He also wrote a three-volume history of Virginia, a well-received work with numerous excerpts from primary sources that continued to be used among historians into the early twentieth century.[66]

John Daly Burk, advocate of virtual citizenship, lost his life owing to continued nationalist conflict in the Atlantic world, in an incident where international war played out into local, interpersonal hostility. Powell's Tavern had become the place where Petersburg's local elite wined, dined, and talked politics. The French government began to "sequester" US ships as part of the development of Napoleon's Continental System, despite President Jefferson's embargo against Great Britain. Dining at Powell's Tavern on the evening of April 9, 1808, Burk took part in the political talk and began to express anger at French actions at a time when the US was attempting to extricate itself from the British trade bloc. Burk went "so far as to call the entire French people 'a pack of rascals.'" At this discussion, a Frenchman, Felix Coquebert, was present and took personal offense, and wrote to Burk demanding an apology. Burk declined to give one and a duel ensued. Coquebert shot Burk through the heart and he died at the scene. Dueling was then legal, but owing in part to this incident, the Virginia legislature banned it in 1810.[67]

Like Burk, Thomas Cooper adopted Southern ways, and even became a leader of South Carolina's nullification movement. Prior to his move south, while still a Pennsylvania resident, Cooper became involved with settling land claims between Pennsylvania and Connecticut while he angled for a federal judgeship, which he received in 1804. He retained a politically independent streak despite a warm relationship with Jefferson in the period immediately after the 1800 election. Cooper nonetheless began to drift in a more politically conservative direction, brought shortly to the fore in the political split between radicals and moderates among Pennsylvania Republicans in 1805. Cooper disassociated himself from both state factions, and lost his judgeship in 1811. He then shifted toward science, becoming an instructor of chemistry at Carlisle College, now Dickinson College, and subsequently at the University of Pennsylvania and then at South Carolina College in Columbia, where he served as president of the college.

In his final years, Cooper became a strong advocate for South Carolinian ultraconservatism, grounded in white supremacy and vigilant protection of South Carolina's slave society. He was one of the leaders of South Carolina's nullification movement, and would remain politically active until shortly before his death in 1839. He favored the legal denization of African Americans, denying citizenship to them, supported prohibitions against interracial marriage, and viewed slavery not as a Jeffersonian necessary evil but rather as a positive good for slaveholder and enslaved. Cooper's shift from his early antislavery advocacy in England is in many ways similar to the experience of many European immi-grants to the US, especially those who came to reside in the South, as was also the case with James Thomson Callender.[68]

When Callender came to reside in the South, he stayed closer to his working-class roots while adopting strongly racist views. The year 1801 started off well for Callender. Not only was he released from prison but he was literally the toast of Virginia: Virginian leaders raised their glasses to his name at public celebrations. It seemed that Virginians and the Republican Party had recognized the sacrifices he had made for Jefferson and other leaders, and surely they would reward him for his efforts. Jefferson, now president, could dispense patronage and federal positions to his allies. Callender felt that, considering his service to the cause and aid to Jefferson, the postmastership of Richmond was not an unreasonable request.[69]

Jefferson did not come through with the job. He chose to favor moderates over radicals, and when Callender visited Washington to seek work from the ad-ministration, his lack of success, despite a meeting with Secretary of State James Madison, turned to rage. Callender destroyed his relationships with the party leaders, and they were even less interested in offering him employment after the visit. Furthermore, Callender had quarreled with nearly all the printers in Rich-mond and nearby Petersburg, making his regular work difficult to obtain.[70]

Nonetheless, Callender's situation improved slightly. His fines from the ear-lier prosecution were finally paid off by his Republican allies, and Callender held back from his vicious, attacking style in print. He began to write for the Richmond *Recorder*, a paper established by a new printer, Henry Pace. Their relationship soon turned into a business partnership. Pace leaned Federalist, but Callender, no longer expecting anything from the Republican Party, provided independent political coverage. In particular, Callender declared war on the Virginia gentry, regardless of party, and sought to expose what he saw as their hypocrisy.[71]

The chief hypocrisy, in Callender's mind, was miscegenation. Elite Virginia men began relationships with enslaved women, often laboring as prostitutes. Despite what had arguably been antiracist views while in Scotland, Callender shifted toward a proslavery stance after spending some time in the United States. Unsurprisingly, in his reporting, he was not especially sympathetic to the actions and limited choices that enslaved women faced. Sex work may well have been one of the few avenues for women of color to accumulate property and money with which to free family members. Nor did Callender seem to have viewed any of what transpired as rape or even tenuous consent between two very unequal parties. What Callender disapproved of was the sexual excess of Virginian men, and what he saw as Virginian men's preference for relationships with women of African descent over relationships with their own (white) wives. Callender further disapproved of white men's willingness to be seen in public with such companions, and their willingness to spend time in Black society. In short, he disapproved of women whom he believed to be sexually disreputable rising above their station, a view reinforced by racist views about women of African descent. Specifically, the widowed Callender was not especially troubled by unmarried men engaging in these activities, so long as women of color did not occupy a permanent station that should, in Callender's view, be reserved for a white woman.[72]

Americans had a taste for gossip and Callender was starting to deliver it, sometimes backed with substantial evidence. Readers soon learned about fellow printer Meriwether Jones's killing another white man during a duel started by a dispute over sexual access to a woman of color. Stories like this, coupled with Republican press counterattacks upon Callender, broadened his audience outside Virginia.[73]

The attacks also resulted in the publication of Callender's most notorious exposé: he made public Thomas Jefferson's relationship with Sally Hemings. Callender chose to do so in response the claims from Republican newspaperman William Duane that Callender's wife had died of a sexually transmitted disease, while Callender spent his money on drink and left his children starving. Callender broke the news with the following item in his newspaper:[74]

The President *Again*.

It is well known that the man, *whom it delighteth the people to honor*, keeps, and for many years past has kept, as his concubine, one of his own slaves. Her name is SALLY. The name of her eldest son is TOM. His features are said to bear a striking although sable resemblance to those of the president himself. The boy is ten or twelve years of age. His mother went to France in the same vessel with Mr. Jefferson and his two daughters. The delicacy of this arrangement must strike every person of common sensibility. What a sublime pattern for an American ambassador to place before the eyes of two young ladies![75]

He continued with updates on the story as he obtained more information, and other newspaper editors looked to confirm details. The exact sources for Callender's story are not entirely clear: he may have received a visit from Federalist (and chief justice) John Marshall. Jefferson had received many visitors at Monticello, and the story had circulated for some time among the Virginia gentry. The appearance of biracial children in planter households was a frequent topic of gossip among white slave owners, along with speculation about their parentage. Less common, however, was the acknowledgment that these relationships were part of the system of exploitation by white men of women and people of African descent. Strangely, one of the few acknowledgments came from Callender's newspaper rival, Meriwether Lewis, who attempted to explain away Jefferson's children as the product of some other interracial relationship:[76]

> In gentlemen's houses everywhere, we know that the virtue of unfortunate slaves is assailed with impunity. . . . Is it strange, therefore, that a servant of Mr. Jefferson's, at home where so many strangers resort . . . should have a mulatto child? Certainly not.[77]

Callender's discussion of the relationship showed a disconnect between his stated views and his disclosure of Sally Hemings's relationship with Jefferson. Jefferson, a widower, was in a similar position to Callender himself. Although the relationship was the subject of talk among white Virginians, it had, up to that point, existed in the private sphere. As the historian Annette Gordon-Reed has shown, Callender's decision to expose was motivated by racism, or more specifically, several kinds of racism that women of African descent have long experienced: first, a view that Black women's feelings, desires, and wishes did not matter—what Hemings might feel about her exposure to the mediated public sphere almost certainly did not come into his thinking; second, the view that women of African descent were sexually disreputable and could be picked up and discarded by white men, but were never to occupy a social place reserved for white women. To deny or obscure white men's overwhelming power in these relationships, the idea of the Jezebel, a sexual temptress who manipulated men's desire to extract what she wished, further legitimized Black women's exploitation. Callender probably viewed the Jefferson-Hemings relationship in this light, and saw it as preventing Jefferson from allowing a white woman to occupy the place of wife and mistress of Monticello, and producer of legitimate white offspring.[78]

Callender did not confine himself to Jefferson, but continued to expose the embarrassing details of the lives of Virginia's rich and powerful. To attack Callender, or challenge his claims, would only result in more embarrassing public revelations. Ultimately, Callender would be silenced by his former lawyer, George Hay, and as the historian Michael Durey has noted with irony, Hay was also the "author of the extreme libertarian *Essay on the Liberty of the Press* (1799.)" While Callender was out one day, seeking the translation of a work, Hay approached him from behind, and began to deliver a brutal caning, an incident that Callender described as follows:[79]

> I felt a violent stroke on my forehead. An immediate effusion of blood was so violent, that, for some moments, it was impossible for me to distinguish who my adversary was. . . . I had hitherto considered that high crowned hats were a mere species of foppery. But it was this kind of hat which saved my life.[80]

Callender chose to take the incident to court, and Hay countered with a legal maneuver: in Henrico County Court, he sought "a recognizance of Callender, preventing him from publishing anything detrimental to Hay's, or any other Virginian's character." Hay's legal team argued that Virginia's interpretation of common law "permit[ed] persons of ill fame to be bound over on account of their bad reputations" with no need even for a prior libel conviction. Callender refused to offer recognizance, "and was committed to Richmond jail." His stay was brief, for three weeks after the caning incident "a new bench of magistrates in Henrico County . . . rejected Hay's arguments" and ordered his release.[81]

BUT THINGS WENT downhill for Callender after that. The Richmond *Recorder*, which had at its peak a then-impressive thousand subscribers, began to taper off in popularity. Callender had already printed all his juiciest stories, causing readers to lose interest once he ran out of the most salacious items. Relations with his copublisher Henry Pace deteriorated and they began to fight over money. The tables turned when it came to shocking gossip: ugly details about the two began to come to light, and Pace accused Callender of expressing sexual interest in Pace's brother, while Callender claimed that Pace had acted as his pimp. Callender began to drink heavily, wandering the streets of Richmond drunk, and not long after, his dead body was found in the James River. He was forty-five years old.[82]

Ordinary Migrants and the Utility of Virtual Citizenship

Ordinary migrants from the British Isles also sought their own conception of citizenship, and it was often the virtual citizenship described by John Daly Burk. Virtual citizenship, and its emphasis on participation in the public sphere, especially as mediated through printed newspapers, was not just a theoretical construct of a few radical migrants but rather the everyday way in which many, if not most, migrants from the British Isles saw their public and political lives as operating in the United States. They were able to apply Burk's conception of virtual citizenship by making use of the privilege they had as white persons and, for many, as English speakers. Moreover, they could participate as fully in the printed public sphere as their native-born neighbors. Belief in virtual citizenship proved popular with migrants from the British Isles, but it was by no means universal.

One migrant who personally rejected virtual citizenship nonetheless described its popularity. The former United Irishman John Caldwell wrote disapprovingly to his associate Robert Tennant in Belfast about Irish emigrant politicking:

> . . . I wish I could say so much of our Country men—the Labourer, the farmer, the weaver, on coming here, all incline to live in large Towns, this may arise from the known character of the Irish—we are to use a trite saying, so warm hearted, we wish to live together & to be in the way of hearing often from our friends, but this disposition is often attended with ruin to Individuals and dishonour to our National character—I have often seen the Man, who with his family might have made a figure a 100 Miles from Town & there been respectable as a Citizen & a man—lose his little property in the dram shop he kept—lose his time by attending to Political controversy & matters that as an Alien did not concern him or at all events which his interference could not better, & lose the respectability of himself & his family by the consequences which must generally arise from such a line of conduct. . . .[83]

Although they were not citizens, if Caldwell is correct in his claims, these Irishmen were actively engaged in politics and the public sphere, and operated as virtual citizens. The men in question were investing themselves deeply in the emerging political cultures of American cities. Men who operated "dram shops" or grocery stores became a nexus of a male-dominated social world that enabled them to network, court potential voters, manage ward politics, and provide spaces for both public and private political meetings. Such politicking was useful, and provided political and economic opportunities beyond the dram shop's immediate success. Such political activity also created and fostered ethnic constituencies, although they were not necessarily as organized as they would become in the mid-to-late-nineteenth century. Just as Burk described a form of citizenship that was implicitly male, this urban politicking incorporated artisanal and laboring free men at the expense of people of color, women, and unfree men.[84]

Another migrant, the Irish-born John Shaw, found that his personal connections in New York allowed him to enjoy the benefits of citizenship without having to naturalize. Nor was he shy about voicing his views on American politics back home. "The Pressedents Spech is now on the deske before me," he wrote to Robert Tennant in Belfast, referring to Jefferson's 1801 speech prodding Congress to repeal the Naturalization Act of 1798, and Shaw wrote hopefully of the new president:[85] "[Jefferson] recomends Strongly that all Restrichons Should be taken off Strangers that they should be admited to all the Priveleges of Citisens and except the privelege of being officers which he alows they may be eligible to in a Short times residence they should be taken in to Confidence"[86] In other words, what pleased Shaw was not so much the repeal of the fourteen-year restriction on naturalization, but rather the penalties applying to alien status. Similarly, Shaw found that New York State's restrictions on alien land ownership made it difficult to buy the farm he wished to own, but he was able to exercise personal political leverage to get what he wanted:

> Br[other] W[illia]m recomended to me to Comence farming... but when I made enquiry & could not own property and dispose of it as being an alien I have over the notion of purchasing, but an old veteran General Clinton who is my Neighbour and a real Republican advised me to petition our State Legeslature for this privelage and he is one of our Representativs so that I and 12 others got that prevelage....[87]

Once again, Shaw was concerned less with his alien status than with integrating himself into the Republican establishment. He was able to obtain the same treatment as a citizen, and successfully obtained the right to own real estate. Shaw viewed his experience so favorably that he thought that the distinction between citizen and alien would cease to matter: "The very name of Alien will not be known among us," he wrote back to his friend in Ireland.

Naturalization Patterns in the 1790s: Naturalized but Still French vs. Virtually American Britons

Ordinary migrants from the British Isles often opted for virtual citizenship, just as many printers did, or contented themselves with it when full citizenship was unavailable. This contrasted with a common pattern among migrants from the French empire, who more often pragmatically entered into the naturalization process. This may have occurred because British migrants were able to obtain many of the advantages of citizenship without naturalization, including participation in the English-speaking public sphere, while migrants from the French empire found their language to be more of a barrier.

Documents from the 1798 crisis reveal the different ways citizenship was deployed among British and French migrants. Under the terms of the Naturalization Act of 1798, all white aliens were required to register with the federal government. Not only did this requirement apply to aliens entering the country, whose information was to be recorded and passed on by local port authorities, it also applied to alien residents who had arrived prior to 1798. Information about recent migrants was easier to record and gather, but there are few extant records of alien registrations of foreign residents who entered prior to 1798, all of them from the federal judicial district that comprised Philadelphia and nearby areas.[88]

Despite the large presence in Philadelphia of many unnaturalized migrants from the British Isles, none of them registered. They ignored the law, and do not appear to have suffered any consequences. In contrast, 173 heads of household from the French empire did register. Many came not from metropolitan France but from the colony of Saint-Domingue, the future Haiti. When registering, they were required to state their reasons for remaining in the United States, and whether they had begun the naturalization process. Whether citizens of the French Republic or subjects of the king of France, they often displayed similar attitudes toward naturalization: they pragmatically moved to gain legal citizenship at the same time as they continued to emphasize their French cultural identity. Indeed, many of these migrants expressed a clear desire to return to their country of birth.[89]

An earlier migrant is a good example of this combination. Charles-Maurice de Talleyrand-Périgord, Marquis de Talleyrand, described in his memoirs his decision to leave France for England in 1793, fearing for the future of the monarchy and his own personal safety. Increasing anxiety about French refugees led the British foreign secretary William Grenville to seek and secure Parliament's passage of the 1793 Alien Bill, whose provisions served as a model for the American Alien acts. Talleyrand claimed that he was one of the chief targets of the act, and that his letters of intercession to cabinet leaders "Mr. Dundas, Mr. Pitt, and to the king himself" were unsuccessful. Thus in 1794 he found himself on a ship bound for Philadelphia. Talleyrand seems to have viewed his status in the United States as an exile, but he maintained a pragmatic attitude toward legal-political citizenship. He took the oath of allegiance in 1794, a time when the political future of exiles from France seemed especially uncertain. Even so, he wrote to the politically active intellectual *salonnière* Mme. de Staël about his strong desire to return: "If I stay here another year, I shall die." Talleyrand's fortunes, however, revived: de Staël secured permission for his reentry. Talleyrand returned to France in the spring of 1796, where he used his political skill and connections to secure the post of minister of foreign affairs under the government of the Directory.[90]

Also exemplary of French attitudes and naturalization patterns, if not so well known, was Jean Simon Chaudron, perhaps the same Chaudron who was the legal guardian to Benjamin Maingault, who was discussed in the introduction. Chaudron also took steps toward naturalization after the end of the Haitian Revolution, commencing legal action in United States District Court in Philadelphia on June 21, 1805. Chaudron was a watchmaker, and elite artisans (goldsmiths, watchmakers, and jewelers) were more likely than lower-status artisans to take steps toward naturalizing. Out of the eleven elite artisans who appear in the 1798 alien registrations, six took steps toward naturalization, while only five of fourteen nonelite artisans did so. Elite artisans had a higher rate of taking steps toward naturalization than other elites such as planters, lawyers, doctors, and highly ranked French government and military officials, where only thirty out of sixty-four did so. Chaudron left Saint-Domingue in July 1793, "on board the American Schooner Charming Betzi [Betsey] Cap[tain]: Hart [Art]." Although he does not explicitly say so in his landing report, Chaudron was probably a refugee from the 1793 battle and conflagration of Cap-Français, when that city's inhabitants sought escape from fighting and fire in the French ships docked in the harbor, depositing thousands of predominantly white refugees in the United States. Those who identified themselves as refugees from that battle were more likely to take steps toward naturalization than migrants from Saint-Domingue who did not. Among the alien registrations, there is a very slight trend toward naturalization among migrant heads of household who indicated refugee status: only thirty-five out of eighty-eight (or 39.8 percent) of nonrefugees took clear or possible steps toward naturalization, while forty-two out of eighty-nine (or 47.2 percent) of refugees did. Fourteen out of the twenty-five refugees from the conflagration (or 56 percent) took steps toward naturalization. The disruption of white Dominguan society and reordering of the economy left many migrants sensing the instability of their condition, and for someone like Chaudron, these conditions still held in the 1790s. Although many former planters sensed that Toussaint L'Ouverture's revival of the plantation economy would allow them to resume their former status in Saint-Domingue, the elite artisans who had supplied them with luxury goods before the revolution do not seem to have been as optimistic, and were more likely to take steps toward naturalization than planters.[91]

Many other French migrants provided evidence of the cultivation of an exile or refugee status when registering as aliens. In the landing reports, registrants were required to state why they had chosen to stay in Philadelphia. Most responded with a boilerplate response: "until his business shall carry him elsewhere." Among those who offered other reasons, the most common, given in six forms, were those who remarked on the lack of safety in their previous places of residence (e.g., "until the peace should be restored in his native country"). In contrast, only two respondents indicated a firm intention to remain in Philadelphia permanently. Many migrants from the French empire saw naturalization as useful, but ultimately did not intend to stay in the United States.

British migrants, by contrast, do not appear to have registered. There are no extant returns for migrants from the British Isles among the alien registrations in Philadelphia. They ignored the law, with few consequences. Despite the threats of the Alien Act and the organization of passage back to France and Saint-Domingue in 1798, no similar actions were taken against migrants from the British Isles. Pickering and the enforcers of the 1798 laws chose to focus their energies on a few prominent troublemakers rather than on the British and Irish migrant populations as a whole.

Why did French and British migrants approach citizenship differently? Language was certainly one factor, but there may have been other reasons as well. Migrants from the French empire worried about their political and economic well-being in ways that the British migrants did not. The migrants from the French empire in the United States comprised refugees from two revolutions: those who had fled the French Revolution in Europe, and those who had fled the Haitian Revolution (some even fled both.) These upheavals meant that refugees had experienced great changes in legal, social, and economic status: political leaders became enemies of the state, bishops became laymen, subjects became citizens, slaves became freewomen, planters became umbrella makers. Uncertain of whether they might be allowed to remain in the United States during a period of hostility to aliens and fearful of reprisals in their homelands, many opted for naturalization. Still others saw the economic conditions in their places of flight as insufficient to carve out a living, while others hoped to use US citizenship as hedge even as they worked on regaining their lost properties and status in France or Saint-Domingue.[92]

French migrants found that retaining a French identity was useful in the United States, regardless of whether they became legal citizens. French migrants carved out an economic niche in marketing gentility in a culture that placed a premium on things French. Americans felt that music was best taught and played by Frenchmen, French artists drew better drawings and painted more pleasing paintings, and so on with glassmakers, dressmakers, milliners, and naturally French teachers all finding a commercial advantage in emphasizing their ties to France. Persons seeking to charge better prices and bring in more clients found it necessary to emphasize their Frenchness and consequently retain a French cultural identity.[93] An identity and presentation as exiles also helped in regaining property, status, and rights of entry to France and Saint-Domingue, which in the late 1790s seemed more amenable to the resettling of émigrés.

In contrast, migrants from the British Isles did not need to cultivate a foreign identity. Instead of having to find new occupations and livelihoods on their arrival, migrants from the British Isles of both high and low economic status often had a job waiting for them on their arrival. British manufacturers sent their sons or other male relatives to sell wares in the United States, while the weavers and other industrial workers they employed in Britain emigrated with the expectation of finding employment through their social networks.

Naturalization was a long process that offered few benefits, and many migrants saw no need to bother with it.[94] This was particularly the case with migrants from the British Isles. Alien status was one of many legal disabilities, and a mild one when migrants from the British Isles could legally assert their rights and privileges as white persons in a legal system of common law with which they were already familiar. Consequently, migrants from the British Isles, in particular laboring male migrants, opted for Burk's vision of citizenship because it fit their everyday needs as public actors.

ALTHOUGH IT WAS possible to avoid alien legal disabilities, virtual citizenship also appealed to migrants because the full cultural benefits of citizenship did not always accompany naturalization. Sometimes the benefits of naturalization were illusory—migrants might legally be American, yet still be perceived as foreign. Some migrants wrote glowingly of the post-1800 changes, but others remained frustrated by the ongoing disconnect between the liberal promise of volitional allegiance and the ascriptive American identity that prevented naturalized Americans from being perceived as truly "American." Republicans and Federalists both engaged in such behavior. For instance, when the members of the French Masonic lodge (including Jean Simon Chaudron, who was discussed earlier in this chapter), offered a eulogy to the recently deceased George Washington, Thomas Jefferson wrote to Auguste Belin, a member of the lodge, characterizing the activity not as one of informal citizens honoring their deceased leader but rather of "foreigners" offering Americans a "fraternal homage."[95]

There is also an 1809 document that demonstrates migrant frustrations with nativist unwillingness to view naturalized migrants as fully American, although the circumstances of its generation means it should not be taken at face value. Despite those circumstances, it offers clear evidence that such attitudes resonated with the foreign migrant community. The "adopted Republican Citizens of the City of New York . . . unanimously adopted, and ordered to be published" an announcement decrying a nativist unwillingness to accept naturalized citizens on equal terms with the native-born, stating that:[96]

> We complain not of the constitutions and the laws: they are liberal in principle and benign in operation. They enjoin an abjuration of former allegiance: have we not with alacrity complied with the injunction? They require an oath of fidelity to the union and to the states: devoted in spirit and in truth to both, we have eagerly taken it.[97]

In other words, the naturalized Americans had agreed to renounce their allegiance to the sovereign of their birth. But despite this compliance, even though "the law places upon the same undistinguishable level, the citizen of native and the citizen of foreign birth," full equality and acceptance had proven elusive:[98]

> . . . we have complied with the injunctions of the constitutions and the laws, and we will support them, upon equal terms, with our lives and our fortunes. *But how are we treated? What has been our reception? Has good faith been observed? Have the promises been performed? Are not we, who are citizens by all the solemnities and obligations of law, treated as aliens—stigmatized as foreigners?*[99]

In short, the full statement argues that despite a belief in republicanism, and the United States' supposed status as an "asylum for the oppressed of all nations," there remained a resistance to accepting naturalized Americans on the same terms as the native-born. The liberal promise of full acceptance of volitional allegiance had proved elusive—no matter how American they acted and how American they thought, there was an unwillingness to accept these legal citizens as cultural citizens of the United States.[100]

The story behind this document is a bit more complicated—the "adopted Republican citizens" there gathered were not a hodgepodge of all ethnicities, but specifically a gathering of Irish Americans. Shifting factions in New York politics meant that the Irish vote had been split between those supporting De-Witt Clinton, and endorsed by such former United Irishmen as Thomas Addis Emmet, and others, the authors of the statement, led by James Cheetham, who had split off from the Republican Party. Cheetham failed to end Republican control of the city assembly, but made a dent in the Republican majority. And thereafter Clinton and other Republican leaders in New York no longer took the Irish vote for granted, taking care to accede to Irish demands for inclusion in the party.[101]

So this document was in part an attempt by Cheetham to capitalize on Irish resentments to further his own political career—which causes the historian to wonder to what extent this mobilization came from the grassroots or was the 1809 version of political astroturf. But its very existence indicates that these resentments at the failure of liberal promise could be capitalized upon, and carried weight and meaning in the Irish community. This feeling was probably even stronger in the atmosphere after the anti-Catholic rioting in New York in Christmas of 1806. Still, the open-ended language of Cheetham's appeal, which did not specify Irish ethnicity, must have been intended to appeal to all New York voters of foreign birth. Ten years later, an English visitor, Henry Bradshaw Fearon, quoted the appeal in an account of his journey, while also noting that despite Emmet's successful legal career, "native Americans speak of him with great jealousy" because he "was guilty of two unpardonable crimes," being "*a foreigner*" and the "second and greatest of all, in being an *Irish rebel!*" Fearon noted the existing widespread distinctions between "*citizens of native and foreign birth*" and attended a debate where the audience cheered a speaker who advocated the exclusion of the foreign-born from all political offices.[102]

But for many migrants, the experience of Thomas Holmes was probably more typical. Holmes arrived in the United States in 1803, after much of the controversy over citizenship had died down. Shortly after his arrival, he declared his intent to naturalize, the first step in the process. But he never followed through with a petition to naturalize, which would have made him an American citizen. Holmes lived with his wife and four children and made a living as a copper-plate printer. For the next nine years no experience as an alien was sufficient to prompt his naturalization—there were few consequences for not doing so.[103]

WHETHER ORDINARY MIGRANT or radical journalist, many British and Irish migrants found that virtual citizenship met their individual needs, or was useful substitute for the fuller citizenship that native-born Americans were not always willing to give them. Such citizenship particularly appealed to migrants from the British Isles, while migrants from the French empire found naturalization more pragmatic and useful, even if they often rejected a culturally American identity.

When radical journalists attempted to exercise their virtual citizenship in more direct ways, such as criticizing Federalist political leaders and their policies, they came into conflict with the Federalist conception of tiered citizenship that did not accord artisans such as printers full citizenship—and many Federalists also refused to view them as American because they insisted on birthright citizenship. The conflict between proponents of virtual citizenship and the Federalist attempt to suppress their views and political activities showed that both groups theorized and attempted to explain the functioning of the public sphere. John Daly Burk and other radical migrants equated citizenship with political participation in the public sphere and saw such activities as a right and a useful check on state power. In contrast, Federalists, especially Timothy Pickering, viewed such men as exercising power inappropriate to their station, and as dangerous accumulators of political power. In treating aliens and naturalized citizens differently, much as it pained him to do so, Pickering gave the legal status of citizenship greater weight and power. Ultimately, federal power to regulate free speech failed to attach to citizenship despite Pickering's attempts to deport seditious aliens and prosecute seditious citizens.

Alien rights were subjected to greater testing when the United States declared war on Great Britain in 1812. British subjects who had thought themselves secure as virtual citizens suddenly found that the Republican government revived the Alien Enemies Act and directed its provisions at them. The growth of the federal government's power, and the alien reaction and resistance, is described in the next chapter.

CHAPTER 3

Married to an Alien Enemy

[Adam Donaldson] was ignorant that he was violating the law and really thought himself a citizen in consequence of his marriage with a native.

— James Mercer to John Minor, March 31, 1813

D URING THE WAR OF 1812, John Smith, the US Marshal for the district of Pennsylvania, was a busy man. He had already been responsible for enforcing court orders, serving subpoenas, and other related duties when, at the outbreak of the war, the Department of State suddenly tasked Smith with collecting data about every British household within the Commonwealth of Pennsylvania. The State Department's orders required him to gather considerable information: name, age, time in the US, place of residence, occupation, and whether the British subject had previously initiated the naturalization process. A large amount of information began to flow through Smith's hands, provided to him by the aliens who came to report themselves at his Philadelphia office.[1]

Smith soon discovered that some aliens attempted to persuade him that they were less alien than others. William Nottingham, a Philadelphia merchant, informed Smith that although he was a British subject, his wife was "a Lady a native of New Jersey Daughter of a Revolutionary Officer." Surely, the influence of a woman who grew up in a Patriot household had some sort of moderating effect on Nottingham's sympathies.[2]

And some aliens thought that they were not aliens at all. William Young had arrived in the United States as a child, served "9 years apprenticeship" and had since become a "Carver & Gilder." Most important, he had grown up in an American household. Until the war, Young thought he had been "entitle[d], to the privileges of a Citizen," because he grew up in a household headed by an American citizen and had since finished his apprenticeship.[3]

Was William Young an American citizen? Should William Nottingham be treated differently than other British subjects? Smith, acting in his executive capacity, would make these decisions, rather than refer such cases to a judge. Indeed, as the war progressed, officials like Smith gained increasing power and authority over the lives of British subjects in the United States. He was ordered by the Department of State to ensure that alien enemies did not travel within the United States without express written permission. Another directive demanded that new arrivals not to be allowed to settle in coastal areas. And then, in February 1813, the State Department ordered all British subjects engaged in commerce to remove themselves at least forty miles from tidewater. The city of Philadelphia was within this forbidden region, and also home to a large number of alien enemy merchants, which meant that Smith became increasingly powerful and busy as the war progressed.[4]

JOHN SMITH'S GROWING power over foreign migrants demonstrates how control over citizenship and alien status became increasingly nationalized during the War of 1812. Moreover, that control was increasingly exercised by the executive rather than the judicial branch of the federal government. In the face of increasing penalties for failing to obey regulations, many British civilian residents relinquished the virtual citizenship discussed in the previous chapter. The stories of men such as Nottingham and Young, however, show how migrants from the British dominions resisted some of these rules in new ways. They pushed for cultural inclusion in (white) American society, advancing claims centered on their acceptance in their communities and place in American or Americanized households. The arguments that these alien enemies made during the War of 1812 for citizenship or differing treatment had a cultural rather than legal basis: they asserted that American households altered the alien status of foreign subjects. Those claims had no standing under common law, yet British migrants were at times successful in their claims, especially when they emphasized the presence of American women in their households.

Important legal changes occurred in citizenship and the legal rights and abilities of aliens in the War of 1812. Although we know more historically about claims to citizenship by military personnel and claims of subjectship and political agency by people escaping enslavement during this period, we know less about the actions and treatment of free British civilians residing in the United States and their effect on citizenship law and the rights associated with citizenship. Alien responses to their treatment, coupled with initial government actions that targeted British-headed households, led to a debate about the extent to which each household was represented in the public sphere by its head. Dependent claims to citizenship during the war weakened this relationship. This debate gave the concept of Republican Motherhood practical utility in allowing binational households to avoid forced removal.[5]

Long-standing immigration policies and systems are governed by path dependency—once in place, policies tend to stay in place because important actors in policy formation and enforcement have an interest in maintaining the status quo. The War of 1812 was a crucial point in the formation of alien policy and the creation of that path dependency. Issues such as the legal definition of aliens, their legal rights, and who had the authority to distinguish between citizen and alien were all in flux, but trending against alien rights and toward increased power for the executive branch of the federal government. The federal government enforced the Alien Enemies Act with vigor, exercised for the first time the power to control the movements of aliens within its borders, and established a precedent for the treatment of aliens in future foreign wars. The path upon which policy began to travel was discrete and periodic rather than continuous and slowly changing; when the United States went to war in the future, policymakers could dust off the Alien Enemies Act, interpret it, and try to enforce those parts of it they found useful or necessary. The War of 1812 was the first and formative instance from which future policymakers would determine how to deal with alien enemies within the nation's borders. In particular, the shift away from the courts and toward the executive, and the use of emergency power to impose severe controls on suspects began during the War of 1812.[6]

During the Civil War and Reconstruction periods, citizenship and the nation-state became more closely integrated and less obstructed by local/state citizenship and private slaveowning. But the War of 1812 was part of the precedent-setting period during the early American republic when political actors were trying to come to an agreement on the rights of citizens and the legal penalties for aliens at the national level of government. Could alien enemies have legal agency? Should authority over them continue to rest with the courts, or should the federal executive branch have the authority to enforce the citizen/alien divide and exert control over the alien population? Their decisions would have a permanent mark both on the US legal code, where the Alien Enemies Act remains in effect, and on legal precedent, where people who fall into the category of alien enemies continue to suffer severe legal disabilities.[7]

But this process was not completely top-down. Much as in 1798, migrant resistance limited the government's ability to surveil the alien population and exert control over alien movements. Migrants' resistance was most successful when they exploited differing ideas about how citizenship related to the household, especially in the case of the government attempt to forcibly move British subjects from areas of strategic concern. Carefully deploying the idea of Republican Motherhood, they argued, at times successfully, that the American presences in their binational or multinational households had successfully Americanized them. Other British subjects successfully lobbied for the legalization of wartime naturalizations, deploying classical liberal arguments and gradualist understandings of citizenship. Moreover, resistance to orders from the national government came not only from migrants, but from the supposed enforcers of the laws. Lower-level government officials chose to selectively determine citizen/alien status, decide which aliens to remove, and interpret orders from the central government as they saw fit for their localities. Alien policy was shaped by the concerns of high-level officials but also by the cooperation of or obstruction by lower-level officials, and by the people and communities who were affected by federal policy. The end of the war left executive emergency power strengthened while alien enemies' right to legal agency and due process remained unresolved.

Origins of the War of 1812, Fear of British Economic Domination, and Federal Surveillance of Alien Enemies

A Jeffersonian economic worldview, influenced by the transatlantic struggles between Great Britain and France, determined the Madison administration's treatment of aliens and allowed for increased executive authority over citizenship. These views differed sharply from the Federalist view that merchants contributed to the wealth of the country, which led them to continue trade ties with Great Britain. Jeffersonians reversed the fear of foreign powers and their citizens/subjects: in 1798, many members of the Federalist Party feared France and "Jacobinism," while adherents of the Republican Party (sometimes called the Democratic-Republican Party) feared Great Britain, monarchical rule, and economic strangulation by Britain's ever-increasing commercial and manufacturing clout. In contrast to the Federalists, Republican leaders viewed merchants as a drain on "productive" members of society. Consequently, in the light of increasing British-American political tension, they saw British merchants as vectors of British economic power, and Madison administration officials thought they needed to implement a system of surveillance over British residents and control over their movements once the United States and Britain went to war.

The system of trading blocs that emerged during the Napoleonic Wars would influence Republican views. In 1806, Napoleon Bonaparte decided to pursue his goals through economics rather than military force. The result was the Berlin Decree, issued on November 21, 1806, which forbade all trade between Great

Britain and areas under French control. In response, the British government issued the Orders in Council on November 11, 1807, which forbade trade between
neutral countries and territories under French control. The British Navy was
able to effectively enforce its blockade. Napoleon countered with the Milan decree, issued on December 17, 1807, which also forbade neutral shipping to trade
in ports under the control of Great Britain and its allies. Both powers pushed
merchant traders from neutral countries to trade only in territories controlled
by one power or the other.[8]

The resulting system of competing trading blocs put the President Jefferson in
a tenuous position: he sought to avoid becoming completely aligned with Britain
or France, and to keep the US neutral. Both British and French forces wanted
access to American grain, and attempted to coerce American traders into their
respective trading blocs. Additionally, the British Navy, short on manpower
after twenty years of almost continual warfare, sought available men wherever
it could, and searched American merchant vessels for British subjects to man its
ships. Citing rampant fraud, British officials often refused to recognize naturalized American citizens' claims that they had ceased to be British subjects. British
impressment often left American merchant vessels short-staffed, and searches of
vessels close to the American coast exacerbated US-British tensions. Meanwhile,
French officials occasionally seized American merchant vessels in retaliation for
trading within the British bloc.[9]

Jefferson and his successor James Madison responded to British actions with
a series of embargo measures of decreasing effectiveness. Both Jefferson and
Madison realized that in practice, the United States was effectively drifting into
the British trade system. Their economic and political philosophies cast this relationship as a shameful dependence on Great Britain. In response, Madison
worked with the Republican-controlled Congress to pass legislation by which
the United States offered to participate in either the British or French trading
blocs in exchange for a halt on the seizure of American merchant vessels. Shortly
afterward, several diplomatic disputes with Britain, coupled with a French acceptance of the American offer, pushed the United States further toward war
with Britain. Madison obtained a declaration of war from Congress, which he
signed on June 18, 1812.[10]

Because Republican leaders worried about British economic power, they believed it necessary to monitor and control the movements of British subjects residing in the United States during the war. The Republicans valued some British
subjects not only as a source of potential Republican voters but also as a source of
white settlers who would carry out Jefferson's vision of a nation of (supposedly)

economically independent yeoman farmers. But others they feared: Republicans had long expressed qualms about British economic warfare, and they saw British merchants, as well as the newly arrived representatives of British manufacturers, as potential infiltrators that would allow Britain to economically strangle the nascent United States. Federalists, on the other hand, believed that any disadvantages caused by the presence of British merchants in the US were outweighed by the benefits of the British Empire's value as a market for American goods and shipping, while British immigrant merchants contributed to building the economic strength of the nation.

Republicans, however, continued to view events from their own political-economic perspective. Building on a long-standing fear that consumption of British manufactures would reduce Americans to state of shameful dependence, government officials and much of the population at large were alarmed at a new migration trend: in the years leading up to the war, British businesses had begun to send young male family members to American seaboard towns to manage exports. These men began to threaten local businesses by selling cheaper British goods. Once the war started, there would need to be a system to monitor the activities of these possibly dangerous alien enemies.[11]

FOLLOWING THE DECLARATION of war, the Madison administration attempted to impose a surveillance system on the British subjects residing in the United States, which was focused especially on merchants as a vector of espionage, infiltration, and economic danger. Its initial measures did not directly target merchants but rather sought to erect a surveillance system. Government officials had a model to draw from, which Federalists had attempted to import in the 1790s: the British Alien Laws. The first feature to be implemented was compulsory registration of all alien enemies in the United States, in July 1812. Suspicious of Federalist judges, they chose instead to pursue surveillance and enforcement primarily through the executive branch of government.[12]

A body of laws that Congress had passed granted the Madison administration authority to engage in monitoring and controlling British subjects residing in the United States who, following the declaration of war, fell into the legal category of alien enemies. This legislation, particularly the Alien Enemies Act of 1798, allowed the executive branch of the federal government to operate with considerable authority over alien enemies during the War of 1812. The Naturalization Act of 1798 had been replaced by the Naturalization Act of 1802. The 1802 Act had restored the five-year residency requirement of the 1795 Naturalization Act; but under the 1802 act "alien enemies were still barred from naturalization." The

1802 act also retained the 1798 provisions requiring information to be gathered on migrants coming through ports of entry. The Alien Act expired in 1800, two years after its enactment in 1798, while the Sedition Act, also passed in 1798, expired at the end of the Adams's term of office on March 3, 1801. The remaining piece of legislation in the Alien and Sedition Acts, the Alien Enemies Act, remained in force. Because the quasi-war with France that was fought between 1798 and 1800 remained undeclared, the provisions of the Alien Enemies Act never came into force in the 1790s.

Although the Republican-controlled Congress did not repeal the act, they had not forgotten about it, and passed a supplementary act on July 6, 1812, less than a month after the start of the War of 1812. The act stated that "nothing in the . . . [Alien Enemies Act] shall be extended or construed to extend to any treaty, or to any article of any treaty, which shall have expired, or which shall not be in force, at the time when the Proclamation of the President shall issue," abrogating unpopular provisions of the 1794 Jay Treaty with Great Britain that allowed Canadian fur traders to trade in the United States. This legislation presumably would allow the Madison administration a free hand regarding alien enemies. Moreover, newspapers such as the New York *Columbian* noted the acts were still in force, and opined on the status of alien enemies and pending legislation regarding them.[13]

Authority over aliens was maintained through the executive branch, and although it would shift between offices, policies continued to reflect the Republican views outlined above. With the declaration of war, the treatment of aliens initially fell to the Department of State, which issued orders reflecting the administration's concern about the activities of British subjects residing in the United States. The presence of foreign migrants was a worry, but the department was small, much as it had been in the 1790s, and its employees were overloaded with duties during a time of international crisis. Eventually, authority would be transferred to the Office of the Commissary General of Prisoners, militarizing what had been under civilian control. The policies that the Department of State developed continued to reflect the Jeffersonian fear of merchants, as well as the belief that other migrants were economic assets, less capable of independent political action on their own, and consequently less of a possible threat.[14]

The government's initial measures were intended to gather information about the British population in the United States. Madison administration officials were uncertain just how many British merchants were in the United States, and estimates ran wild; some newspapers claimed that as many as "fifteen or twenty thousand English merchants, runners, collectors, etc., not naturalized" resided in the United States.[15] So on July 7, one day after Congress passed a supplementary act to the Alien Enemies Act, the administration issued the following directive:

All British subjects within the United States are required forthwith to re-port to the marshals (or to the persons appointed by them) of the respec-tive states or territories within which they may reside, their names, their age, the time they have been in the United States, the persons composing their families, the places of their residence, and their occupational pursuits, and whether, at what time, they have made the application to the courts required by law, as preparatory to their naturalization; and the marshals, respectively, are to make to the Department of State returns of all such British subjects, with the above circumstances attached to their names.[16]

The order not only was an ambitious attempt to begin the imposition of the surveillance system directed at alien enemies; it also revealed how the Madison administration viewed citizen/alien status as attaching to the head of household: each alien was to report "the persons composing their families." (This intrusion of the official public into the private domestic sphere would prove too much. Except for Massachusetts, returns of aliens only recorded family, boarders, and servants/enslaved people by number, rather than supplying details about the persons over whom the head of household held his authority.) The interest in declarations of intent to naturalize also suggests that lawmakers still accepted a view that citizenship could involve a gradual incorporation into the community.

The inclusion of occupational pursuits among the data also indicates the orig-inal purpose of the order: to find out just how many British merchants there were in the United States. In this matter, public estimations were greatly exag-gerated. Out of the 7,500 alien heads of household who appear in the returns, there were only about 800 who might qualify as "merchants, their clerks and bookkeepers," compared to 1,000 heads of household employed in the textile industry, and 1,600 "farmers, planters, [and] gardeners."[17]

Through the order, the executive branch of the federal government also gained the power to determine citizen or alien status. They were free to reject migrants' (and de-naturalized natives') claims to citizenship. They could also accord citizenship to other migrants whose legal claims courts may have been less willing to accept.

The order also revealed that the surveillance system was to be centralized and controlled by the national government. But the federal government could not do so alone: the gathering of information about the tens of thousands of British aliens in the United States would be done not only through the regional (and centrally appointed) federal marshals but with the further cooperation of county sheriffs and local and state law enforcement. Marshals published notices listing local persons to whom aliens could report themselves if they did not reside near a US Marshal.[18]

The order was largely effective and sufficient for the administration's needs in the early stages of the war. Madison's administration had designed a program of surveillance by which information collected would be passed on and processed in the new capital, where policymakers would continue to issue new requirements regarding enemy aliens. These measures seem to have been mainly precautionary: during the first six months of the war, the United States attempted to invade Lower Canada, and also experienced losses in the Great Lakes region at the hands of the British and their Indian allies. Meanwhile, the British Navy was not yet successful at defeating the American Navy and establishing naval supremacy; the invasions and raids into the United States did not occur until the later parts of the war.

The order's relative success greatly strengthened the government's reach and authority over citizenship. As previously discussed, Federalists in Congress had unsuccessfully attempted to impose compulsory registration on all white aliens in the United States through the Naturalization Act of 1798, but few migrants complied and neither the Adams administration nor the federal courts seem to have taken action against them. In 1812, however, the federal government was able to extend its information-gathering reach into interior regions and areas of strong partisan resistance. After the order was promulgated, aliens began to report themselves, marshals sent in their returns, and returns arrived even from areas of strong opposition to the war, such as Connecticut and Massachusetts. As the executive branch of the federal government exerted its emergency powers, it began to determine who was a citizen and who was an alien, a process that would have important consequences for citizenship and the people categorized as one or the other.[19]

Compulsory Registration, Loyalists, and the Shift of Authority over Aliens from the Judicial Branch of the US Government to the Executive Branch

The compulsory registration of aliens gave the executive branch of the federal government the ability to recategorize citizens into aliens and vice versa, eroding the power of courts over citizen/alien status. When enforcers of compulsory registration chose to reject claims they thought invalid, they did so without resorting to the court system. This change caused former Loyalists and their children, in particular, potential loss of citizenship. Government officials evaluated the claims of former Loyalists on the basis of their political affiliations. Association with the Federalist Party, in particular, could justify citizens' recategorization into aliens.

Compulsory registration during the war differed from the previous Federalist attempt at compulsory registration in one important respect: a greater reliance on the executive branch of the federal government. The Naturalization Act of 1798 envisioned a surveillance system that relied primarily on the federal courts for the issuing of documents to aliens, their examination, and any punitive measures taken against alien violators. In both the 1790s under Timothy Pickering and in the War of 1812 under James Monroe, actions against violators and execution of policy issued from the Department of State. Pickering had relied heavily on local prosecutors and the courts, where Federalist allies were numerous and the federal government retained national reach. The retention of Federalist judges after they lost power in other branches of the federal government made the courts a less reliable ally in controlling alien enemies during the War of 1812. Consequently, the Department of State relied more on US marshals, who were appointed by the president, and later shifted responsibility to the military under the Office of the Commissary General of Prisoners, headed by Gen. John Mason.[20]

Many Loyalists successfully made the transition into US citizens, but the emergency conditions of the war pushed some of them into alien status, sometimes owing to their neighbors' suspicions that they continued to sympathize with Great Britain. Most Loyalists who remained in the United States acquiesced to citizenship despite their opposition to US independence, and although some might have slowly come to accept it, others still quietly mourned for colonial days. Elizabeth Drinker, the wife of an elite Quaker of Loyalist sympathies, noted a loud and raucous Fourth of July in Philadelphia in 1801, which included "guns firing, Drums beating from day break, rejoycing for Independence." She confided in her diary that "the most sensible part of the Community, have more reason to lament than rejoice—in my opinion." Drinker, who was born in 1734, died in 1807, before the outbreak of the War of 1812. But a few Loyalists were either unwilling to acquiesce to citizenship and reject their allegiance to Britain, or their Patriot neighbors were unwilling to admit them to citizenship. One of these longstanding Loyalists was Frederick Smyth, a "Gentleman" who listed his length of residence in 1813 as "50 years" and his age as eighty. Frederick Smyth had, prior to the Revolution, been chief justice of the Supreme Court of New Jersey, in which position he carefully, but unsuccessfully, worked to prevent colonial independence. During that time, Smyth's lower public profile and cautious diplomacy allowed him to avoid the radical anger that was largely directed at Royal Governor William Franklin. After independence, Smyth split his time between his 77 Union Street address in Philadelphia and the nearby town of Roxborough. Smyth was the only extant permanent Loyalist resident who registered himself as an alien in Pennsylvania during the War of 1812. He registered much later than other migrants, at the time of the 1813 removal order, a choice that indicates that he probably thought it more prudent to acknowledge alien status and remain in Philadelphia than be seen as someone eluding surveillance and subjected to imprisonment or forced removal into the interior. The public political presentation of Loyalists like Smyth, whether they claimed to be either citizens or aliens, would be subject to evaluation by government officials.[21]

As gatherers of returns, US Marshals and local sheriffs exercised especial executive power when they decided whether to categorize former Loyalists as citizens or aliens. Officials evaluated Loyalists' claims to citizenship on the basis of local reputation and political activities. If a Loyalist had a reputation of active participation in Federalist politics, the gatherer of returns might choose to categorize the Loyalist as an alien, a status that applied to all members of the household. Gatherers of returns might do so even if a Loyalist had naturalized or otherwise possessed valid qualifications for citizenship. US Marshals and sheriffs were particularly likely to do so in areas of political opposition to the war, or in areas in danger of invasion or raiding by British forces.

In areas of concern about disloyalty, Republican compilers of the marshals' returns were especially vigilant about former Loyalists in their communities. Connecticut was one of these regions; Robert Fairchild, US Marshal for Connecticut, recorded that Peter B. Rindle of Norwalk was "A pilot to the enemy in the last war," but also a "British pensioner & bad inhabitant." Reports from Connecticut, along with reports from upstate New York, where much of the War of 1812 was fought, were especially likely to list which aliens expressed Federalist sympathies: Sheriff Barnabas Smith reported that Timothy Reddy, a tailor in Scipio, New York, was "opposed to the administration." Sheriff Smith also noted that a farmer, William McMillan, was a stranger, but tempered his remarks: "however I believe him to be an inoffensive man." In Danbury, Connecticut, Fairchild's report stated that the coincidentally named Irish migrant Joseph Moneypenny was "said to have been convicted of passing counterfeit money." Fairchild's report also noted that James Richards of Litchfield was an "Englishman & Laborer a State Pauper." Richards, like potentially threatening merchants or spies, was also a foreign drain on community resources in the form of public relief.[22]

Gatherers of returns not only reported those aliens of suspect loyalty, but also in at least one instance recategorized a citizen as an alien, on the basis of anti-administration political activity. John C. Gray was born in Halifax to Loyalist parents originally from Massachusetts. They resettled in Boston in 1790, and Gray established himself as a printer in Danbury, Connecticut, where he published the *Connecticut Intelligencer*. Gray's Federalist partisanship made the gatherer of returns suspicious about Gray's true motives and citizenship status. Gray "claim[ed] to be a citizen of the US" and thus a legal citizen rather than a virtual one, and "sa[id] he had bee[n] admitted to the right of suffrage in Mass and Connect for 10 years past," but the collector of returns for Danbury thought it necessary to group him with the alien enemies. The collector further noted that "Since he came into this State (about 5 years ago) [Gray] has been a tool of the federal party, to print a newspaper full of abuse & falsehood agt the govt of U.S." Gray's activities were simply too public and active to allow them to be brushed aside, and he was, like a true Tory, too disloyal and opposed to the national government to truly be a citizen. The collector of returns was also attempting to silence a long-standing and vocal Federalist opposition in the region. Connecticut in particular had been a place of particularly vocal Federalist editorializing, such that Thomas Jefferson considered prosecuting several Connecticut journalists for seditious libel in 1807. Ultimately, despite Gray's claims of citizen status, the gatherer of returns, acting for the executive branch of the federal government, rejected Gray's claims to citizenship, viewing Gray's challenges to the federal government through his newspaper as an attempt to undermine its authority.[23]

Overall, the success of Loyalists' claims to citizenship depended on how officials viewed their political actions after the Revolutionary War. Former Loyalists and their children who associated with the Federalist Party, who received pensions or had half-pay retired status from British armed forces, or who were remembered in their communities as prominent Tories, could all find that gatherers of returns considered them to be aliens. In contrast, former Loyalists who kept a low profile or demonstrated their newfound patriotism could have their US citizenship status affirmed.[24]

The Executive, Control of Aliens, and Internal Removal of British Subjects

With alien registration continuing, the State Department began to issue increasingly strict orders that attempted to exert greater control over the movements and residences of British subjects in the United States and further strengthen the surveillance system. It did so first by subjecting aliens to an internal passport system. This effort culminated in orders ordering British merchants away from coastal and tidewater regions, reflecting a shift away from exerting control over US borders to exerting control over internal areas of the United States. US regulations had negative consequences for those British subject residing in the United States who had not felt the need to naturalize.

The increasing control began in the fall of 1812. On October 13, 1812, the Department of State provided further instructions to marshals, announcing that alien enemies who had recently arrived within a marshal's jurisdiction were to be ordered to travel to "particular places of residence, at least thirty miles distant from tidewater, to the limits of which designation they are to be confined." The department further followed that order with a proclamation issued on February 6 of the following year. That order required recent arrivals to report to the marshals. It also prohibited alien enemies from traveling without first obtaining a passport from either a US Marshal or a collector of customs. Moreover, the State Department forbade marshals to issue passports unless they were "acquainted with the nature of the [applicants'] pursuits, know them to have a reputation for probity, and can confide in their good intentions towards the United States."

Passports during the Napoleonic Era functioned differently from twentieth-century system that appeared in the wake of the Russian Revolution and First World War. Rather than being identity documents issued by a sending country to a host country, allowing for ease of deportation and surveillance of undesirable aliens and usually associated with border control, Napoleonic passports served as passes controlling internal movement within a state. Napoleonic-era passports did not serve as proof of citizenship. Excepting sailors' passports, which contained an attempt at description of their faces and bodies, passports during the War of 1812 assumed that the bearers were who they said they were. Moreover, although passports were usually issued by the host country they could also be issued by government officials from other foreign governments. Prior to orders indicating otherwise, a British subject in the United States could conceivably obtain a passport from the Portuguese consul. The national government did not maintain a monopoly on the authority to issue passports: Benjamin Silliman, the president of Yale College, received a passport from Jonathan Trumbull, the governor of Connecticut, in 1805. The restriction of permission to issue passports to the US Marshals and collectors of customs was a further extension of government power and monopoly over the surveillance system that had previously diffused authority among local community leaders.[25]

These new regulations were part of the federal government's growing attempts to control aliens and their internal movements. This change was a transatlantic import: the British government had imposed a passport system on aliens in 1793, and the American law was worded similarly to the 1793 British law.[26]

Madison administration officials felt that the restrictions had not yet dealt fully with the danger from British subjects in the United States. In the last major attempt to impose new restrictions on alien enemies, the State Department issued the following order on February 23, 1813:

> Alien enemies, residing or being within forty miles of tide water, are required forthwith to apply to the marshals of the states or territories in which they respectively are, for passports to retire to such places, beyond that distance from tide water, as may be designated by the marshals. This regulation, however, is not to be put in force without special notice against such alien enemies, not engaged in commerce, as were settled previously to the declaration of war in their present abode, or are there pursuing some regular and lawful occupation, unconnected with commerce, and who obtain monthly, from the marshal of the district in which they reside, permission to remain where they are.[27]

The proclamation divided British subjects in the US according to Republican economic concepts of productive labor. The proclamation's government authors placed alien enemies into two categories: those whom Madison administration officials wished to keep rooted in one place so that they could continue to contribute to the agricultural and manufacturing sectors of the economy; and a second, more dangerous class, either "engaged in commerce" or without "regular and lawful occupation." In other words, farmers and laborers were productive potential citizens: their work and the physical products they produced were clearly visible and contributed to the wealth of the country. Their labor supported themselves and their households, allowing them to interact with one another as proper independent citizens. In contrast, British merchants endangered the independence of fellow citizens and the country's wealth: the sales of their goods sapped the credit of hardworking Americans, making them dependent upon the merchants while directing the wealth produced by citizen labor out of the United States to its enemy, Great Britain. Thus merchants were in the same category as persons without regular or lawful occupations: thieves and the wandering poor, who also sapped the wealth of citizens through theft of goods or demands upon public relief.[28]

The government's actions and their successful enforcement also effectively abrogated the status of British and Irish migrants who considered themselves entitled to the rights and privileges of citizens regardless of whether they had naturalized. Suddenly, alien status carried significant penalties: not only did they lose rights of formal political participation, but many civilians born in the British dominions now found that they were required to register with the federal government (unlike their naturalized fellow migrants). Soon their movements were controlled and they were subjected, in some cases, to forced removal from their residences. Thus it was no wonder that Thomas William Holmes, the copper-plate printer discussed in the previous chapter, regretfully stated to US Marshal John Smith that to "his neglect he had not become naturalized & that he wishes to become a Citizen of the United States." Marshal Smith did not choose to treat Holmes like a citizen and refrain from including him in the list of alien enemies he forwarded to the Department of State in Washington, but he merely added Holmes's plaintive statement of regret to the remarks section of his report.[29]

The Relative Absence of Press Coverage: Government Policies Implemented without Public Criticism

Government actions, though officially publicized, were subjected to remarkably little public comment, providing officials leeway in determining policy toward alien enemies. Unlike discussions of impressment, war expenditures, invasion, and other news, coverage of regulations concerning alien enemies remained sparse in American newspapers. Madison administration officials consequently operated in an atmosphere of public permissiveness regarding their treatment of British subjects in the United States. There seems to have been a public agreement among Republican-leaning papers that national surveillance, particularly the passport system, was an amenable means of dealing with the perceived internal threat. Federalist papers were largely uninterested in the government's treatment of aliens, with the one prominent exception of a cause célèbre, the internal removal of the Boston musician George K. Jackson. The immigrant press for British subjects in the United States mainly consisted of the fledgling Irish immigrant press, which, while emphasizing the loyalty of Irish residents of the United States, refrained from openly criticizing alien policy. Irish immigrant newspapers instead provided their readers with practical advice about obeying regulations and attempting to further the path to naturalization when possible.[30]

Although the American press had initially refrained from significant praise or condemnation of alien policy, it divided along partisan lines in response to the removal order. Coverage of the order, however, was relatively light, especially compared to other war events and policies. Among those papers that did choose to address the issue, most initially attempted to look into existing current law and what laws remained in effect from the anti-immigrant panic of 1798. Several papers noted that although most of the Alien and Sedition acts had expired, the Alien Enemies Act remained in force. They also noted that existing laws forbade a change of allegiance in wartime. The only nonimmigrant paper to comment extensively on the laws saw them as necessary to prevent British infiltration of the country, consistent with its editors' Republican-leaning views:[31]

> . . . the time has arrived when the president may exercise the authorities vested in him by the act of '98 . . . and we trust that a system of police will be carried into execution, which is demanded by the quantity of British influence in this country, and without which spies may flock in upon us to watch our movements and blast our enterprises. When British officers themselves steal in disguise among us, it is time to arrest the evil. A system is apparently required of a similar nature with the British *alien office*; a system, which shall grant licenses for residence, *passports* for travel, and warrants for removal. We feel the importance of the subject, and we invited the attention of the constituted authorities of the nation to it.[32]

The editor of the *Enquirer* summed up much of what in fact seemed to be the thoughts and concerns of Secretary of State James Monroe, as well as concerns among the larger American public. The editor saw the British system of control as effective and worth copying in the United States, and he defended his reasoning by citing a fear of British infiltration. Aliens were to register with the government, not be allowed to move about the country without express permission from government officials, and dangerous aliens were to be expelled. The editor envisioned the courts' authority remaining in the process of obtaining warrants. Fear of infiltration created a desire to extend state regulatory power, gather information, sort through households, and categorize them according to their perceived threat to the nation.[33]

These fears also existed at the more local level, where Americans wondered about their British neighbors and their activities, even during the period leading up to the war. In a prelude to future concerns about the activities of the Masons, secret societies seemed to have been seen as chief vectors of British intrigue and infiltration. In New Hampshire, the presumably pro-Federalist *Keene Sentinel* published an explanation defending the inclusion of a British subject into a local "W. B. Society," explaining that although a British subject, he "came to this country when he was but *two* years of age," and that he was not yet twenty-one and ineligible to naturalize, but that he "intended to become an American citizen as soon as he became of age." Had he failed to support "the *American form of Government*" the society would not have allowed him to become a member. The announcement was also reprinted in the *Concord Gazette.*[34]

When the State Department issued the removal order, many papers simply published the order as a public notice but did not offer additional comment. Individual federal marshals for each district had the order published as much as they felt was necessary. Peter Curtenius, US Marshal for New York State, aware of the state's strategic value and its comparatively large foreign-born population, especially in New York City, ordered the order's publication in many New York papers. In Pennsylvania, there seems to have been comparatively less publication. New England papers also published the order, including the more inland *Bennington News-Letter*, although Federalist-leaning papers may have seen in the order further justification for opposition to high-handed policies.[35]

Those few papers that raised objections saw the removal order not as an affront to migrant rights per se, but rather as part of a broader opposition to the Madison administration and its unpopular war-related policies. Although coverage of earlier regulations had been scanty, some Federalist editors saw the order as an excess of federal power and a threat to individual rights. The issue was not always central to their concerns; rather, they saw it as part of an overreaching of federal executive power and threat to the right of due process. Harsh measures against British subjects were simply another reason to oppose a ruinous war. Among the condemnations was that of the *Federal Republican*, whose lengthier article was briefly excerpted in the *Bennington News-Letter*: "During the French war of '98, when there was a federal administration, and the alien law was in force, not a single Frenchman was ordered out of the country. Now when there is no law for it every Englishman is ordered forty miles from tide water."[36]

The original article in the Georgetown-based *Federal Republican* highlighted the case of the music teacher George K. Jackson, and further characterized the Madison administration's actions as an unnecessary witch hunt designed to distract the public from the war's lack of success. The *Federal Republican* also noted in a later article that Jackson's absence in Boston prevented a concert from taking place owing to the "ill-timed exercise of the despotic power given to the executive over aliens directed possibly . . . by the malice of party feelings." The *Federal Republican* was chiefly concerned with the treatment of aliens as a distraction intended to instill fear in the public and further support for the war, rather than a simple outrage against the right to due process. The *Bennington News-Letter* excerpted the original article to highlight the extreme measures taken by the Madison administration compared to the Adams administration, and noted that the regulations were put in force without an accompanying new law (an error in this case, as the administration grounded its actions in powers granted by the Alien Enemies Act of 1798).[37]

Enforcement of Alien Policy: Practical Success Despite Resistance of Officials

The Madison administration was largely successful in implementing compulsory registration and forced removal, despite resistance from US Marshals. Compulsory registration of all white aliens under the Naturalization Act of 1798 was unsuccessful, but this time enforcers of the State Department's orders concerning aliens ultimately obeyed them, though not without hesitation. Extant returns list a total of over 7,500 households headed by British subjects residing in the United States, from New England to South Carolina to the Illinois and Missouri Territories.

The federal marshals whose duty it initially was to enforce the laws at times required encouragement from the Department of State. They were particularly reluctant to fully enforce the removal order, which proved highly unpopular with British migrants in the United States. The Department of State found it necessary to repeat to US Marshals that orders were "*to be enforced.*" Despite delays in implementation, federal marshals largely complied with orders from the Department, causing much disruption in lives of British migrants "engaged in commerce" or "without regular or lawful occupation."[38]

The initial duty of alien registration was publicizing its existence, coordinating reports with county sheriffs, and gathering information on those who failed to register. Marshals were assisted by what seems to be a large number of aliens self-reporting soon after the announcement of compulsory registration. Marshals' information-gathering was also aided by mediation through the printed public sphere, since the largest American cities were too big to function as face-to-face communities. Notices began to appear in local newspapers informing British subjects that they were required to report themselves.[39]

The resistance of the marshals increased greatly when they were required to control the movements of British migrants rather than simply record their presence. When the circular dated October 13, 1812, informed the marshals that new residents were to be settled at least thirty miles from tidewater, which included all major port cities (and even the city of Albany, where the Hudson remained tidal), some of them wrote back expressing surprise at such measures. The department replied on October 29, two weeks after the initial order, informing the marshals that "I have to inform you, that you have very accurately construed *the intentions of the government,* in extending [the regulations] to all arrivals of persons of that description, subsequent to the war." Marshals had evidently judged some migrants as potentially dangerous, forcing them to settle away from coastal areas, and others less so, allowing them to settle in coastal areas where many of them had intended to find employment. Milling Wooley, a weaver who arrived in Pennsylvania in the fall of 1813, and was allowed to settle in Philadelphia where he found work in "Henry Hawking's factory" on Ridge Road, fell into this latter category.[40]

But it was the removal order of February 1813 that generated the most resistance from the marshals. The instructions accompanying the proclamation ordering the removal of the British subjects engaged in commerce or who otherwise happened to be persons of interest make clear that the department had planned action against those who resisted its orders, instructing marshals that "*all those . . . who do not immediately conform to the requisition, are to be taken into custody, and conveyed to the place assigned to them,* unless special circumstances require indulgence." The marshals were reluctant to fully enforce the proclamation, however, and refrained from deporting individuals to whom they planned to grant indulgence or about whom they planned to inquire with the department. As a result, the department wrote the marshals on March 12 that "the regulations . . . of the 23d ult. And your instructions of the same date, *are to be enforced.*" Moreover, marshals were told not to exercise individual judgment, but instead to "refer the question of indulgence to this Department, setting forth all the circumstances, on which the claim is founded." The orders further emphasized that "*in no instance is the removal of an individual to be delayed for an answer from Washington.*"[41]

Alien Resistance and the Deployment of Cultural Claims to Citizenship: American Households Produce American Citizens

The resistance of civilian British subjects that was most successful in obtaining more lenient treatment from officials also showed a weakening in the relationship of citizenship to the household and male authority. British aliens successfully obtained exemptions from removal in the case of British subjects "married to natives." They did so by arguing that (free, white) female American presences in their households made those households less foreign, and the alien enemies who headed them more like American citizens. These claims were aided by emphasizing the Patriot credentials of American women and the ties of binational couples to their local communities.

Claims based on household status were not the only ones made during the war. Also successful were liberal claims that successfully pushed for naturalization of alien enemies in wartime arguing that the allegiance of citizens could shift to reflect incorporation into their new communities. They also reflected a gradualist claim to citizenship: migrants who had taken the previous step of declaring their intent to naturalize prior to the war had already been on their way to becoming citizens. Other claims for differing treatment were less persuasive to officials enforcing orders relating to alien enemies: these claims sought to cast British subjects as "neutral" private persons uninterested in a conflict between states. Similarly, a court challenge asserting alien rights to habeas corpus may have been technically successful, but practically had no effect for the plaintiff or other British subjects similarly detained by US Marshals.

The virtual citizenship described in the previous chapter ceased to have practical benefits with the imposition of compulsory registration for most civilian British subjects in the United States. Legal status as citizen or alien was what mattered. Whether British subjects residing in the United States during the War of 1812 believed, like John Daly Burk in 1796, that they were virtual citizens, as discussed in Chapter 2, or if they wished to retain a formal political loyalty and remain subjects of the king of Great Britain and Ireland, migrants from the British Isles were subject to the emergency regulations. Overall, few aliens had begun the naturalization process. Using Pennsylvania as an example, only 104 out of the 761, or 13.7 percent, extant heads of household who appear in the marshals' returns had already declared their intent to naturalize. When the War of 1812 began and compulsory registration began to be instituted throughout the country, many migrants seem to have been caught off guard by how rapidly and suddenly their alien status became disadvantageous. A number of the previously apathetic migrants hastily began the naturalization process: of the ninety British subjects for whom the time between their alien registrations and declarations of intent can be calculated, twelve (or 13.3 percent) began the naturalization process within a day of registering as aliens. Still others expressed surprise at the alien registrations. Thomas Curran, a twenty-year-old "accomptant" with no wife listed, who resided at 37 South Water Street in Philadelphia, stated that he did "not know of its being requisite for him to apply, had omitted it but wishes to become a Citizen." Edward Clarke, a teacher living with his "Wife, 1 Child & 2 Servants" at 92 North Seventh Street stated that "he regret[ted] the delay of not making application to become naturalized," further emphasizing that he was "attached to the United States & pledge[d] himself to defend them with every energy he possesses against all violation." Others had begun the naturalization process but failed to follow through. Thomas William Holmes, mentioned earlier in this chapter, reported that to "his neglect he had not become naturalized," although he had declared his intent on June 21, 1803.[42]

Among the major successes for liberal citizenship was a change in legislation allowing for wartime naturalizations. Previously, a change of allegiance in wartime was seen as analogous to a betrayal of one's sovereign. Many migrants, however, saw wartime naturalization as an updating and formalizing of their integration into a new community. The push for liberalization of wartime naturalizations seems to have come at least in part from the Irish emigrant community.

Irish emigrants received early information about their legal options: they had access to emerging ethnic newspapers targeted at them. New York-based publications such as *The Shamrock* and the *Western Star* (or *Harp of Erin*) mainly carried articles concerning Irish politics and British-Irish relations. These papers provided information about US government policies of interest to them, as they fell under the category of alien enemies. The *Shamrock* began its coverage with a reprint of a legal commentary that had originally appeared in the Savannah *Republican*. The commentary stated that under international law ("the law of nations") allegiance could not be transferred from one sovereign or state to another in time of war. It averred that regardless of whether the required maximum residency of five years had been fulfilled, applications to naturalize could not be admitted. In the fall, the *Shamrock* published an article entitled "Informations to Aliens," which summarized the regulations in force regarding British subjects, noting that "a large majority of [emigrants] . . . are unacquainted with our laws respecting them." The article summarized the order requiring alien enemies to register with US Marshals, and also noted that the provisions of the Alien Enemies Act of 1798 remained in force and that state and federal courts had the right to deport British subjects or require "securities for their good behavior." The article then summarized the regulations of the Naturalization Act of 1802, emphasizing the residency requirements, the necessity of the declaration of intent to naturalize at least two years prior to the petition to naturalize, and finally noting that although the state of war prohibited naturalization, "aliens are not . . . prohibited from filing the declaration of their intention to become citizens."[43]

Migrants successfully lobbied to allow aliens who had filed a declaration of intent to fully naturalize. In a petition to Congress, migrants argued for legislation allowing the naturalization of those who had already taken oaths of allegiance prior to the war. On July 30, 1813, Congress passed legislation allowing such naturalizations, provided that declarations of intent had been made prior to start of hostilities.

The lobbying effort was successful because it was grounded in both a classically liberal idea of the mutability of citizenship and because of earlier, gradualist views of naturalization. The former was liberal in the sense that new residents could naturalize to reflect their incorporation into new communities and their change of allegiance; in this case liberalism and mutability superseded a view of citizenship/subjectship as fixed allegiance to a sovereign. The lobbying push was also gradualist in the sense that individuals would be gradually incorporated into the community as citizens in training, acquiring the rights of full citizens "step by step." Rather than a betrayal of one's sovereign in time of need, naturalization was a capstone in the process of community incorporation, the previous steps having been completed. This lobbying push, however, came in part because the migrants felt that they were "held in durance by the [US] Marshalls . . . deprived of the liberty of attending their personal concerns, as well as the means of procuring a subsistence for their families or themselves." Increasing burdens upon alien enemies, in particular forced removal, prompted the lobbying push—thus the passage of the law in the summer of 1813. Once virtual citizenship ceased to be a practical option, these migrants sought to make citizenship easier to obtain.[44]

CLAIMS THAT REPUBLICAN mothers or wives had Americanized British-headed households and that they should therefore be treated more leniently was a new and successful argument advanced by some British subjects in the alien returns. Robert Dunn, a "Principal of a Military Academy" residing in Philadelphia, noted that he was "married to an American Lady." As mentioned in the beginning of this chapter, William Nottingham pointed to his marriage to "a Lady a native of New Jersey Daughter of a Revolutionary Officer." Dunn and Nottingham's use of the term "lady" was also meant to indicate respectable, genteel status. These men not only made these claims, but the marshal recording them felt they were worth mentioning in his remarks. The Scottish-born shopkeeper Adam Donaldson of Fredericksburg, Virginia, did not report himself to the marshal, and a letter vouching for his conduct stated that "he was ignorant of having violated the law" because he "really thought himself a citizen in consequence of his marriage with a native." The letter-writer further cited evidence of Donaldson's acquisition of confiscable property as ignorance of his status. [45]

These claims paid off: in 1813, President Madison, "desirous of defining more particularly the treatment of Alien Enemies, and of extending as much indulgence to them, as may be compatible with the precautions made necessary," exempted from the removal order men who had already declared their intent to naturalize more than six months prior to the declaration of war and were "married to natives." Adam Donaldson was among the few Britons whom the administration granted an indulgence and "allowed to return on account of his wife."

On what basis could such claims be made? This was, after all, a time when women's legal identities and citizenship status were suppressed through a resurgence of the law of coverture, and a time of backlash against women's active participation in the public sphere. These men could make such claims for a variety of reasons: an ideology of Republican Motherhood or Wifehood, because of the day-to-day nature of marriages that husband and wife may have thought of as "equal"; the practical link that such marriages made that integrated the couple into the community; a Scottish Enlightenment conception of national culture as being transmitted by women; a longer Anglo-American legal tradition of a separate allegiance status for wives; and the inconsistency of the legal understanding of women's status.[46]

Republican Motherhood (or Republican Wifehood) provided major ideological support for claims made by binational couples. A true republican mother, who was often a "lady," infused her household with patriotism and instructed her children, especially her sons, in the principles important to republican liberty. More importantly, "she condemned and corrected her husband's lapses" from civic virtue. Madison administration officials seem to have found that republican mothers (or wives) had had a similar beneficial effect on their foreign-born husbands, whom they presumably infused with civic virtue and attachment to the United States. Proper social connections must also have helped. William Nottingham thought it advantageous to mention that his New Jersey-born wife was the "daughter of a Revolutionary Officer" when reporting himself as an alien.[47]

The claims that British men made could also be understood within a context of the differing roles for men and women in American society. The Scottish Enlightenment provided an understanding of social and cultural development that ascribed politics to men as their proper role and the transmission of culture and societal norms to women. This new understanding caused Americans to think of marriage as an equal partnership, with men and women having particular roles and duties.[48] Under the influence of the American ladies whom British migrants had married, the cultural transmission of American-ness was theoretically underway, while husbands, as alien enemies, had been removed from their ability to be politically active.

A foreign woman who married a man had historically retained her foreign allegiance. In practice this allowed the Crown to claim ownership over the husband's estate, reverting what were known as escheated lands to the state, but its flip side was a separate political identity for such women. Although *Martin v. Massachusetts* ruled that women's loyalty to their husbands trumped their birthright legal identity, British courts, at the same time, accorded French wives of British subjects a separate identity when it came to the confiscation of lands. For women in the United States married to British men, it was in their interest to stress their American connections in informal ways, and to appear cooperative. To push against their husbands too much, by asserting a separate, pro-American political identity could lead to the use of coverture by their husbands to check their wives' independence. Appearing as a linked unit was more advantageous.[49]

Some other factors allowed men in binational marriages to make the claims that they did: their role as important nodes within their personal social networks, and their wives' position as deputy husbands during a period of their husbands' legal disability. These rested less on women's status within the law than on their customary and day-to-day interactions, coupled with cultural understandings about women's roles.

The wives of British men could make claims because of their face-to-face interactions within their communities. Many Americans saw their communities as the place where real citizens interacted with one another. Elite women had a public presence and linked households through the bonds of womanhood with other members of the community. Formal, legal status was less central to this community membership, and it was possible to participate and live as a citizen of a town in an everyday way. Each town was connected more broadly through its public spectacles, and their reporting and mediated reproduction through early republican print culture, but the citizens of other towns were imagined citizens: within the community, citizenship was real, face-to-face, and embodied. In this context, it was possible to be a "citess," and maybe even a "female citizen."[50]

These claims could also be made because of the wives' places within their social networks. Status as a "lady" was genteel: it certainly relied on conspicuous displays of wealth and respectable deportment, but also on reputation and interaction and circulation within the community. American women were socially active: they attended church and mingled afterward; they attended dances and parties (even at taverns); they entertained visiting friends and family, and wrote letters at other times.[51] In this way they incorporated their husbands into their networks: literally, when attending events as a couple, and figuratively through mediated interactions, and even by their status and title of "Mrs.," using coverture as an extension of husbands' public and private presence in the community. Coverture in this instance was a simultaneous and seemingly contradictory restoration of male dominance for men who found themselves categorized as alien enemies.

Last, white American-born wives of British husbands could also make claims because of their role as deputy husbands when their husbands were unable to fulfill their roles as head of household.[52] Alien enemy status was a disability which prevented the husbands from representing their household in the legal and public sphere. Their wives could temporarily fulfill that role, albeit with limitations: they did not formally represent their husbands in a legal or political capacity, but served as the link to the community when the husband was ostracized. These women and their husbands were able to obtain formal, official recognition of their status because of the informal role of deputy husband as well as the other reasons previously discussed.

FORMER APPRENTICES MADE claims similar to those of binational couples, indicating that their time spent in American-headed households had made them into citizens, but the success of these claims is unclear. The men appearing in the marshals' returns for Pennsylvania indicate that a popular understanding of Americanization occurred through incorporation into an American household. Subsequent matriculation into the public sphere as an independent man conferred status as an American. As discussed in the beginning of this chapter, William Young, a "Carver & Gilder" residing in Philadelphia, stated that "he served 9 Years apprenticeship in the City of New York & that he was informed that [coming into] the country while a minor & serving an apprenticeship was sufficient to entitle him to the privileges of a citizen." Two wire-workers and a "Printer & Glazier" also noted their apprenticeships but did not explicitly claim citizenship. Adam Donaldson is the only such demonstrably successful claimant. In addition to his American-born wife, he noted that he "came to America as an indentured servant."[53]

These claims were less successful in changing treatment for several reasons. Artisanal status exempted these men from the removal order, if not from compulsory registration, so they could not claim damage to their economic livelihood as that those Britons who were subject to removal could. Lack of elite status also made these claims less effective because they were less likely to have personal connections to decision-makers. The British-born husbands of elite American women were able to exert influence and persuade central policymakers that their wives had made their households less foreign and the husbands less of a danger. Donaldson had risen from indenture to much more respectable shopkeeping. Nonetheless, artisans used the same cultural argument as binational couples: the presence of Americans in a household Americanized its other members.

Despite the success of binational couples, elite connections alone did not necessarily guarantee that the government would exempt migrants from removal, even when coupled with widespread public pressure for exemption. George K. Jackson was a Boston musician who faced forced removal to Northampton, Massachusetts. Despite his apparent non-merchant status, Jackson had been targeted for removal. He exercised his connections among the Boston elite to secure an exemption. Wealthy Bostonians wrote to the Commissary General of Prisoners requesting an exemption for Jackson, attesting to his character. As previously mentioned, the case became a cause célèbre in the Federalist press. Despite Jackson's legitimate claim that he was a non-merchant, and despite elite attempts to influence decision-makers in Washington, Jackson does not appear among the list of indulgences granted to those exempted from removal. Jackson's passport indicates that he was "ordered to Northampton, Hampshire Co.," in the interior of Massachusetts.[54]

Other claims were also unsuccessful: in particular, claims of private, personal neutrality in a public conflict between two nation-states (or sometimes the Republican and Federal Parties). Hugh Scott was a "son of [a] citizen of Glasgow" who owned a lumber business that supplied the US Navy Yard in Norfolk, Virginia. Additionally, he kept a "small store" because of which he was evidently categorized as a merchant. The removal order had been disastrous to him, and he returned to the Tidewater area because his "situation in the country for want of employment became Irksome." Arrested, Scott pleaded for more lenient treatment. He emphasized that he had "never interfered or taken part in the disputes of Political Parties." He further emphasized his connections to the United States and association with his local community, contrasting it with what he saw as unfair treatment for something he could not change: "my Crime is being born in a foreign country, although my Interests & affections are here," he wrote to General Mason. But such claims carried less power than an American-born wife. Scott did not win the exemption that binational couples had received and he was ordered to Augusta County in Virginia's interior.[55]

Collectively, the claims made by the British subjects described above were claims to virtual citizenship: Hugh Scott and William Young and William Nottingham claimed that they should be treated more like citizens and less like aliens. For most British subjects, virtual citizenship ceased to have value once the government decided to no longer treat virtual citizens as such.

Do Alien Enemies Possess a Right to Due Process? *Lockington v. Smith* and Aliens' Right to Legal Agency

Several migrants attempted to challenge the legality of the removal order and assert a right of legal agency. The cases attempted to preserve court and local jurisdiction over aliens, but decisions gave the federal government effective power to continue enforcing alien policy and forced removal. *Lockington v. Smith* was the most prominent of the court challenges, and the decision retained alien enemies' right to legal agency as well as state jurisdiction over aliens, while still keeping Charles Lockington, the British subject in question, in custody. Lockington was able to obtain a ruling that theoretically granted him legal agency and the right to petition for a writ of habeas corpus, but this ruling left key questions about the legal agency of alien enemies ultimately unresolved. It had little effect on British subjects subject to removal.

Courts successfully retained their authority in certain circumstances. William Bold, who had been placed in custody of the US Marshal in South Carolina, successfully argued that as a dependent, he became a naturalized citizen when his father naturalized in 1786, and so obtained a court order for his discharge.

Another case petitioning for a writ of habeas corpus for an alien enemy came before Virginia's circuit court. The opinion of the presiding judge, John Marshall, skirted the issue but retained some court authority over aliens by ordering Thomas Williams, the British subject in question, released on a technicality: he had not been ordered to remove to a specific place by the US Marshal.[56]

Lockington v. Smith stemmed from Marshal John Smith's arrest and confinement of Charles Lockington for violating the removal order. Lockington was an English emigrant who had settled in Philadelphia before the war, and he made his living there through "a mercantile pursuit." Although Charles Lockington was exceptional in his choice to pursue a court challenge to the removal order, his actions were otherwise typical of many men in his situation. He contemplated a return to Britain, but chose instead to remain in the United States, and followed the orders requiring his registration with the federal marshal. He even initially complied with the removal order, retiring inland to Lancaster, Pennsylvania. But his work, presumably involving import-export trade, was not a feasible means of subsistence away from port. Lockington's health, class status, and education meant that he felt himself "not fitted by condition or habit, for manual labor." Lockington "remained at Lancaster until his funds were exhausted, and being destitute of the means of support, he was compelled to return to Philadelphia, in order to obtain the means of subsistence." His presence came to the attention of US Marshal John Smith, who ordered him to leave for Reading, Pennsylvania, "where little or no commercial business is done." Lockington "represented his pecuniary inability to the Marshal" and asked for permission to leave the US, or to be sent to Reading, "if the means of doing so and supporting him when there should be furnished him." The marshal declined to do so and instead placed Lockington under arrest.[57]

Lockington had been arrested for being in violation of the State Department order of removal, but he had not been charged with a crime. Finding that his time in prison was becoming exceedingly lengthy, and the rations not to his liking, and that the marshal was unwilling to release him or allow him to return to Europe, Lockington initiated a suit with the Supreme Court of Pennsylvania. Lockington sued in a state court because of a federal circuit court decision, *Mumford v. Mumford*, that barred alien enemies from bringing suit in federal courts. The Pennsylvania Supreme Court agreed to hear his case, and the attorney Charles Hare represented him. The Pennsylvania Republican politician and lawyer Alexander James Dallas served as counsel for Joseph Cornman, "Keeper of the Debtors Apartment" where US Marshal John Smith had confined Lockington. Ironically, Dallas was a naturalized former British subject who had arrived in the United States in 1783 shortly after its independence, having previously lived in the British West Indies. He had also risen to prominence in Republican Party circles, becoming the de facto leader of the Pennsylvania Republican Party, and would soon serve as the US Secretary of the Treasury.[58]

The arguments centered on federal versus state authority and jurisdiction, as well as the rights of alien enemies—especially their legal agency. Dallas's arguments for denial of the writ of habeas corpus were that the US Congress had not granted state courts jurisdiction over alien enemies, nor the right of alien enemies to petition, nor the right to interfere with the marshal's execution of his orders. Additionally, Dallas argued that Lockington, as an alien enemy, did not have a right to petition the court; in other words, no right to legal agency.[59]

In contrast, Charles Hare, arguing for Lockington, emphasized a limited federal authority over aliens. He challenged the right of the federal government to regulate the internal movements and residences of alien enemies, arguing that the Alien Enemies Act granted the federal government the authority to seize aliens only to expel them from the United States. Hare also argued that state courts did indeed "have complete jurisdiction of an alien enemy . . . to issue a writ of habeas corpus," even if the detainment had been done under the authority of the federal government.[60]

Chief Justice William Tilghman rendered a decision that granted Lockington the right to petition for habeas corpus, but did not release him from custody. Although he did not consider alien enemies to be prisoners of war, he agreed that the federal executive retained sufficient emergency wartime powers and authority through the Alien Enemies Act to detain Lockington, even though orders came after the federal government had transferred authority from the Department of State to the Commissary General of Prisoners. This dispute over jurisdiction had yet to be fully resolved in the courts: although cases such as *Collet v. Collet* (1797) and *Chirac v. Chirac* (1817) increased federal authority over citizenship, *Spratt v. Spratt* (1830) gave state court decisions greater finality in decisions over citizenship status.[61]

ALIEN ARGUMENTS THAT an American presence in the household made those households less foreign were partially successful, at least combined with other forms of political influence and access. Lockington's challenge was also partially successful, but with limits. The court's decision ultimately did not change his situation, and left the access of alien enemies to courts as plaintiffs ambiguous, in part because of the continued ambiguous relationship between state and federal citizenship.

The strongest effect on the citizen/alien divide was the effective exercise of the national government's power to regulate its alien population. The federal government not only gathered information on alien residents (nationally implemented for the first time) and regulated their entry and exit, but it also controlled their internal movements and forcibly moved residents who had fallen into the category of potential political threats. Furthermore, the federal government recategorized residents as citizens or aliens. The implementation of the Alien Enemies Act resulted in all these powers accruing to the executive branch, and the Alien Enemies Act remains a part of the United States legal code.

Another British subject, John Johnson, was also affected by his treatment as an alien enemy during the War of 1812, but his South Asian heritage and Muslim faith placed him on the other side of the color line from the other British subjects discussed in this chapter. As he was sailing from Bengal to England to attend a boarding school, Johnson's ship was seized by American privateers, and he was abandoned on the island of Grenada to die of yellow fever. "A gentleman of the island" found Johnson and aided his convalescence. After recovering, Johnson sailed for Connecticut in hopes of obtaining passage to England. His attempts were unsuccessful, and he lived temporarily with a New England minister. Because he was an observant Muslim and a dark-complexioned grandson of a British man but otherwise of South Asian descent, his New England captors felt that he could not attend a school for white students. Instead, he was sent to the Foreign Mission School in Cornwall, Connecticut, where he, like other students, was subjected to Christian proselytizing and a strict disciplinary system. The engagement of such migrants from outside Europe with the color line, and their attempts to exercise citizenship and other political and social rights, are detailed in the next chapter.[62]

CHAPTER 4

Citizens Not Denizens

Desiré an alien a native of Jacmel in the Island of San Domingo a
french citizen of the Christian Religion a free man of colour aged
thirty years Reports himself as above according to law.

— Landing Reports of Aliens, No. 74, Desiré, December 17, 1798

B ENJAMIN MAINGAULT WAS CALLED in as a witness to explain why
he had voted in an 1806 Philadelphia election. He was part of a group
of allegedly unqualified voters—those who had come over from New
Jersey and did not live in Pennsylvania, those who had not paid taxes, and
those who were underage. Maingault, who himself may have been underage, was challenged for different reasons: a white witness, Samuel Ferguson,
described him as "a mulatto boy a native of Cape Francois" and a recently freed
indentured servant. Ferguson's actions indicate that he saw Maingault not as a
potential or naturalized citizen, but as a denizen whose legal abilities could be
rescinded by authorities, or even informally by men such as himself. Indeed,
after Maingault finished voting, Ferguson "disputed with him his right to
vote." Deposed by the governor's commission on the election, Maingault
countered Ferguson's challenge with evidence presenting his fitness for citizenship: Maingault's white father had been a citizen, and Maingault himself
owned several houses, though they were in the hands of a legal guardian. As a
former indentured servant, he exerted his free rights as a citizen regardless of
his place of birth. Many, if not most, white Pennsylvanians may have not seen
him as one, but Maingault was exerting the rights of a citizen in defiance of
their wishes.[1]

Maingault's actions are significant because when confronting a top-down
hostility to his ability to be a citizen, Maingault exerted his agency and obtained
citizenship rights for himself. Rather than being a passive victim of white racism,
Maingault and others like him pushed back and secured rights of citizenship
that others sought to deny them. The hold was tenuous, but it was Maingault's

own actions that caused him to have them. To what extent citizenship was dependent upon racial status and class position in the early American republic
has been a matter of some debate. Looking at the experiences and choices of
migrants from outside of Europe enriches our understanding of these factors
by showing both their entrenchment and, ironically, their mutability. The ability of non-European migrants to obtain citizenship depended not only on class
position but also on social ties and religion, because these factors influenced
perceptions of racial status.

When non-European migrants tried to act as citizens, either entering into
the naturalization process or exercising the rights of citizenship regardless of
their legal status, they confronted the ways white Americans culturally conflated
citizenship and racial status. Many white Americans assumed that those who
labored in a servile capacity were incapable of becoming citizens, and associated servility increasingly with nonwhite status. Although the state imposed
restrictions upon their eligibility for citizenship, non-European migrants in the
United States sometimes managed to carve out citizenship rights for themselves,
although they often faced considerable hostility and sharply limited options.[2]

As they navigated the legal system in the United States, non-European migrants encountered issues of status and citizenship in ways that differed markedly from those faced by European migrants. French European migrants who
were reluctant to culturally integrate into white American culture embraced
the legal aspects of citizenship as the best safeguard of their rights in a foreign
country. Migrants from the British Isles, by way of contrast, often ignored the
legal requirements of citizenship before the War of 1812 precisely because they
were comfortable culturally integrating into their communities. Non-European
migrants present yet another variation on this pattern. Some desired the integration that the French avoided, but they knew they could not count on the informal acceptance that the British and Irish took for granted. Thus their attempts
to gain formal citizenship were a means to obtain legal rights and security in
the face of community hostility. Assertions of legal citizenship could provide
them with forms of status and legal abilities French and British migrants took
for granted.

Early National Policies Regarding Race and Citizenship and White American Conceptions of Citizenship

One of the most important ways that issues of citizenship were tied to social
status for non-European migrants was through a key part of the Naturalization

Act of 1790. It stipulated that naturalization should be extended only to "free white persons." It did not explain, however, what it meant to be white. Was it simply a matter of skin color, or were other factors involved? Being nonwhite conjured up a host of civic deficiencies for many white Americans. When encountering these attitudes, migrants would have to work against them or around them.

Most white Americans in the early nineteenth century associated Blackness (and sometimes Indianness) with servile status and assumed that such people were unfit for citizenship. In addition to outright racism, this exclusion was due to the attachment of citizenship to the head of household and the concept of economic independence as a test for the fitness of citizenship. As white Americans increasingly attempted to equate blackness with servility, they pushed non-frontier American Indians into similar forms of indenture and servile labor; during the same time white indentured servitude declined. Consequently, white Americans increasingly associated other white people with independence and head of household status, and nonwhite people with dependence and servile labor.[3]

Additionally, as discussed in Chapter 3, the connection of citizenship to the head of household also rested on a concept of economic independence. Servants were not only household dependents, but economic dependents. Unfree servants required food, clothing, and shelter from the master; free servants required wages. Republicans and Federalists differed in assessing who met this qualification, but they agreed on the concept. The economically dependent were in danger of being influenced or compelled by those who held economic power over them: servants, dependent on their employers for wages and/or shelter, certainly fell into this category. Federalists also included artisans within this category, because they depended on the propertied people within their communities as a customer base.[4]

Migrants seeking citizenship would have to confront these views and evaluate which strategies might be effective in securing them legal rights as citizens as well as informal protections and community acceptance. The color line between white and not-white needed to be negotiated during this process, because white Americans sought to restrict naturalization to whites only. Leveraging social capital, avoiding religious practices deemed too foreign or uncivilized, and displaying personal wealth could all result in different racial and citizenship statuses for migrants from the same region. Migrants recognized that they could influence their racial reception through these means, and acted in ways that secured them further rights and community acceptance or support.

Agency Despite Exclusion from Citizenship:
Polynesian and South Asian Sailors

As the US whaling industry grew, teenagers and young men from Pacific Islands and New Zealand began to arrive on American shores in small numbers; missionary accounts indicate a small number of Polynesian youths living in port towns such as Boston and New Haven during the 1810s. US trade with East and South Asia also brought sailors from those regions to American shores. These migrants had neither the wealth nor the social capital necessary to pursue naturalization, so they chose instead to either cultivate a permanently foreign identity when interacting with the government, or present themselves as persons of color when interacting with neighbors. Polynesians found that African Americans and Indians could provide them with social and economic support in their daily struggles. Polynesians are almost nonexistent in naturalization records, indicating that they saw legal citizenship as either unnecessary or unattainable. Indeed, they probably made citizenship even more unlikely by creating social networks through African Americans and Indians, thus identifying themselves as nonwhite people. Despite white discrimination against them, many of them may have felt that the advantages of a nonwhite support network outweighed the disadvantages of alien status and white hostility.

Polynesians arrived via ships that were part of expanding American global commerce. Once those voyages ended and put into port in the United States, Polynesian sailors found that they had to seek employment in order to support themselves. Most ended up as servants or in trades increasingly dominated by African Americans. Thomas Hopoo "hired himself out in several families as a servant . . . and removed with one family into the interior of the country." William Kanui (Tennoe) and his brother traveled from Boston to Providence "in quest of employment," and William continued this search in Hartford and New Haven after his brother's death in Providence. This work may have further reinforced their place in the racial hierarchy and excluded them from the possibility of citizenship, as white lawmakers saw servants as lacking independence from their masters. Similarly, missionaries recorded Polynesians associating themselves with African Americans. In New Haven, William Kanui "went into a barber's shop [a traditionally African American trade] to learn the trade, and soon became very expert at his new occupation." At this point, he was contacted by students of Yale College, who offered to assume some of his debts in return for being "put to school under the direction of his Christian friends." Another Hawai'ian, Benjamin Carhooa, "joined a Baptist Church in Boston composed of people of colour." Hawai'ians and other Polynesians' activities employment as servants appeared to white Americans as economic dependence.[5]

Polynesian migrants sought to integrate culturally, but that integration was not with white Americans. With a lack of extant naturalizations, and only a few dozen extant Polynesian migrants in total, if even that many, the available evidence indicates that Polynesian migrants found citizenship either unattainable or sufficiently lacking in benefits, and preferred permanent status as aliens ineligible for citizenship if it afforded them support from African Americans and American Indians. Since they overwhelmingly did not pursue legal citizenship and/or did not persuade white people to accept them as potential citizens, they sought an alternative source of support, strongly economic and religious, among people of color in the United States, even as accounts by white missionaries claimed to provide similar support.

Although missionaries sought to transform Polynesians through Christianization and adoption of Western customs, there was a limit to white acceptance of Polynesian migrants as their social equals. Polynesians lacked the resources that other migrants were able to employ to successfully push for equal treatment. White missionary accounts demonstrate the common dilemma that came from bringing what they saw as civilization and Christianity to savage heathens: once civilized and converted, white reluctance to see them as such and admit them into the white community as equals created a set of people whose existence contradicted the civilizing and Christianizing process. White missionary accounts avoided this dilemma by playing down those migrants who remained in the United States for a length of time. In contrast, migrants who returned to Polynesia to further missionize under white supervision were given much coverage, those who died young and tragically even more so. Henry Opukahai'a (or Obookiah in missionary accounts) adopted Christianity, dressed in Western clothing, learned not just English but Hebrew and some Latin as well, and traveled in New England to promote missionizing activities, where missionaries presented him as a successful example to the townsfolk. His early death in Connecticut in 1818, not yet twenty-five years old, avoided the issue of his remaining in the United States as a fully civilized Polynesian.[6]

SOUTH ASIAN SAILORS who sailed to the United States also experienced discriminatory treatment and categorization as nonwhite people. They sought to redress discriminatory treatment through the US government, but did so by presenting themselves as foreigners wishing to return home. There does not seem to be any evidence of these sailors attempting to obtain citizenship, although later parts of this chapter show that genteel South Asian migrants were capable of obtaining full citizenship while still acknowledging their ancestry.

Sailors' encounters with racial categorization could begin before they set foot in the United States. When describing his voyages on early nineteenth-century whaling ships, the sailor Ned Myers spent considerable time with South Asian sailors, and "learned [to speak] a little Bengalee." But Myers also reinforced a racial divide that existed between himself as a white man, and the Bengali sailors, whom he referred to as "darkies."[7]

South Asian migrants, in addition to being racially associated with African Americans, had occasionally been enslaved by white Americans. In part, this perception of enslavability was fostered by the presence of slavery in South Asia, and British colonial participation in slaveowning. It was further normalized by the existence of an Indian Ocean slave trade. For instance, during the colonial period in 1737, "a Black Fellow born in Bengal called Pompey" who was "Detain[ed] as a slave" in Virginia wrote to the East India Company, and successfully brought the Company's intervention on his behalf to allow him to return to India. As we shall see, such attempts at enslavement also occurred after US independence.[8]

Despite such prejudice, migrants still sought legal redress in cases where they had been wronged. South Asian sailors participated in voyages into the Atlantic world that often ended in labor disputes. At times they successfully relied on semigovernmental institutions such as the British East India Company to obtain redress from Atlantic world governments. When encountering difficulties in the newly independent United States, South Asian sailors hoped to continue using what had been at times a successful strategy. In the best documented example, the stranded sailors remained in the United States for close to a year prior to obtaining passage back to Asia.[9]

The crew of the ship *Pallas* had sailed from Canton (Guangzhou) and through Batavia (Jakarta) before arriving in Baltimore in 1785, where the *Maryland Journal and Baltimore Advertiser* noted that "It is no unpleasing sight to see the crew of this ship, Chinese, Malays, Japanese and Moors, with a few Europeans, all habited according to the different countries to which they belong." The sailors themselves, however, had a more difficult journey. Like many Asian sailors in the Atlantic world, they found themselves in a dispute with the ship's captain, Irish-born John O'Donnell, over pay: "their wages on the *Pallas* were a paltry sum compared with what the American seamen received." Moreover, the sailors were stranded: the *Pallas* was not slated to make any new voyage, and so they traveled to Pennsylvania, where they petitioned the government of Pennsylvania for assistance in returning to Asia.[10]

But the petition also contained a second request: the return of Adam Keesar, "a Lad about twelve years old," the son of ship's lieutenant, Sick Keesar, "who was Stole from him by a certain Marylander John Hamilton." Furthermore, Captain O'Donnell had "lately threatened to kill" the sailors if they returned to Baltimore and had "kept the above mentioned lad in his possession." Although Captain O'Donnell wrote a letter offering a differing account of the dispute over wages and the sailors' decision to seek return passage from Philadelphia, there is no extant defense of his role in the abduction of Adam Keesar. O'Donnell's behavior is consistent with the actions of whites who saw free children of color as enslavable but refrained from enslaving white children. That indicates that whites saw South Asians, especially of lower social status, as in the same category as people of African descent, and as such, ineligible to become naturalized citizens. Low social status and lack of ties made enslavement thinkable and possible to men such as O'Donnell. This lack of political, social, and legal leverage mean that sailors appeared in the historical record not as aliens eligible for citizenship but as people dependent on elite benevolence, and as foreigners seeking to leave. Unlike the migrants appearing the following section, the South Asian sailors did not act as potential citizens, at least in this instance.[11]

Dominguans of Color: Countering Denizenship by Asserting the Rights of Citizens

People of color from revolutionary Saint-Domingue, soon to be Haiti, comprised the largest group of nonwhite migrants in the United States, arriving in the thousands, including a well-documented wave of over 3,000 people of color and over 3,000 enslaved people arriving in New Orleans in 1809, following their expulsion from Cuba. In eastern regions, a large number also came with the predominantly white refugees who fled the battle and conflagration of Cap-Français in 1793. Several accounts document Dominguans' active path to obtain citizenship rights and counter white attempts to discriminate against them. While their African ancestry disqualified them from naturalization according to the Naturalization Act of 1790, they leveraged their wealth, social connections, and association with the French Republic to carve out citizenship rights for themselves. Their frequent exposure to both French and Haitian revolutionary rhetoric gave them a fuller transatlantic understanding of citizenship, and they deployed that understanding in their struggle to obtain legal rights and protections in the United States. Their experiences contrast with those of Polynesian and South Asian migrants, whose limited social connections and lack of direct experience with revolutionary republicanism resulted in strategies such as asserting foreign status or seeking support among other people of color. Migrants from Saint-Domingue did not necessarily avoid such actions, but expressed them in terms of citizenship that forced whites to acknowledge citizenship status.[12]

Dominguans of color confronted white prejudice and discrimination against them by exerting rights of citizenship, or even citizen status itself. They did so by engaging in activities increasingly associated with citizenship, such as voting, but they also did so in less conventional ways: Dominguans sometimes presented themselves as citizens, not of the United States, but of France, or even as citizens who were fellow participants in the transatlantic revolutions of the eighteenth century. These assertions of citizen status forced whites to acknowledge that people of African descent could exercise the rights of citizenship. Dominguans' engagement with citizenship was part of their struggle against the legal disabilities placed upon people with African ancestry in the United States. Migrants of color also countered instances of discrimination against them through acts of political civil disobedience: registering as aliens when that "privilege" was reserved for white aliens only, or attempting to vote after obtaining freedom, despite birth outside the United States. The tenuous hold on rights and legal abilities of Dominguan migrants of color is part of the shift to denizenship for people of African descent in the United States. Dominguans also pushed to be potential citizens and sought fuller citizenship and legal rights.

Denizenship has historically been a status wherein the rights of citizens or subject were conditionally granted to noncitizens. Some scholars have argued that the rights extended to free people of African descent in the United States were, in effect, denizenship: rights extended by the grace of the state, but subject to unilateral revocation at any time. I agree that this is an accurate description of African American legal rights during this period. White attempts to impose denizenship were countered, however, by migrants of color seeking to obtain citizenship or its rights, or to be seen as potential citizens, even if it meant being defined as legal aliens. If denizenship was an attempt by whites to exert legal power over people of African descent, attempting to function as a citizen or potential citizen was the form that resistance took by definition.[13]

One case of a Dominguan asserting his status as a citizen in the face of discriminatory treatment is an alien registration made after the federal government instituted compulsory alien registration in 1798, as described in Chapter 2. Despite the 1798 provisions stipulating that only white aliens should register with the federal government, one head of household of African descent did register as an alien in federal court in 1798. This was an attempt to acknowledge that although free migrants of color could not become citizens of the United States, the federal government had to acknowledge their status as citizens, albeit of other republics, nonetheless. Desiré, a "free man of colour" and "an alien a native of Jacmel" in southern Saint-Domingue, registered as an alien in a federal court in Philadelphia. Desiré was denied the privilege of a last name, and unlike all the other registrants except for the one immediately preceding him, identified himself not only as a "a french citizen" but also "of the Christian Religion." Desiré also needed to have a presumably white man, George Bond, sign as a witness. His statement clearly indicates that if federal officials would not allow him to become a citizen of the United States, they nonetheless had to acknowledge him as a citizen of France. Assertion of citizen status was also a challenge against the attempt push people of color into denizenship.[14]

Desiré may also have been accumulating evidence should his free status be challenged. He experienced some difficulties with his former mistress, Mme. Beverneau, who had Desiré prosecuted for vagrancy, claiming that he had "having at divers times embezzled money and spent the same in lewd houses." Since freedom without the good will of a former master or mistress could often be precarious, Desiré may have been interested in documenting his free status and securing his right to remain in Philadelphia. He had a number of different motives, but in using the means of an alien report to his ends, Desiré also was forcing the federal government to acknowledge the presence of another class of citizens who suffered from unequal legal penalties and disabilities owing to their race. Desiré's strategy differed from other (usually white) men emerging from bondage, who claimed that their matriculation into the public sphere was akin to naturalization. In Desiré's case, his mistress's foreign birth, in addition to his racial reception, may have prevented such an argument.[15]

Desire's assertion of foreign citizenship is echoed in the actions of Pierre Toussaint, another Dominguan of color who emphasized his foreign status. Brought in slavery to the United States from Saint-Domingue, Toussaint was able to leverage his personal connection with his widowed mistress, whom he had economically supported in New York, to obtain his manumission. He chose to do so, however, not through American courts, but through the French consulate; doing so granted him status as a subject of the emperor of France, the same citizenship status as his former mistress. Thereafter, he worked as a hairstylist, cultivating a wealthy clientele and building a highly successful business. Consequently, Toussaint was able to become one of the few wealthy New Yorkers of African descent. He drew on his social prestige and cosmopolitan connections in France to construct an identity as a Frenchman, and for many years planned to move with his family to France.[16]

STILL OTHERS DEPLOYED citizenship in a manner intended to be vague about their allegiance to a particular state or regime, finding that that ambiguity could be used to avoid discriminatory treatment while maximizing connections to local communities, differing nations, and the idea of revolutionary republicanism. For people of color from revolutionary Saint-Domingue, an ambiguous citizenship could be used to demonstrate loyalty and simultaneously push for radical social change. Dominguans of color, especially as recent migrants, often viewed their political identities as tied to both metropolitan France and the colony of Saint-Domingue/emerging nation of Haiti, rather than as migrants intending to settle permanently in the United States. For migrants of color, the American racial system that failed to accord them an intermediate racial identity between black and white proved galling, and many saw their treatment in the United States as another reason to reject an American identity. Many also saw the United States as a temporary residence until conditions in either Saint-Domingue/Haiti or metropolitan France would allow their return to their place of true political allegiance. When the political situation was uncertain and could shift rapidly, refugees could find it expedient to deploy citizenship in a multisided way that exploited the ambiguity of their political status and allegiance.

One particular document demonstrates how Dominguans simultaneously presented themselves as local citizens, French citizens, and believers in transatlantic revolutionary republicanism. In 1793, the "citizens of color of Philadelphia" drafted a memorial to the French National Assembly supporting the revolutionary order abolishing slavery in northern Saint-Domingue, in anticipation of the formal abolition of slavery throughout the French empire in 1794. For the Dominguans who drafted the petition, they lobbied as citizens residing in Philadelphia but politically associated with the French Republic, an identification that blurred national boundaries and the distinction between local and national citizenship. Dominguans of all colors were not shy about lobbying for their political and economic interests in differing sovereign states, and presented themselves in a manner they felt would most benefit their interests. At this early juncture in the Haitian revolution (and the French Revolution), political identities were in flux. Was civil equality to be spread by the French Republic, or would Dominguans of color find an independent or autonomous Saint-Domingue a better place to secure their political rights while maintaining the plantation economy that was often the source of their wealth and economic and political power? Would republicanism and civil equality for people of color spread throughout the world? It seemed likely as French armies scored victories throughout Europe and the French commissioner Léger-Felicité Sonthonax negotiated an uneasy alliance with the leaders of the 1791 slave revolt, leading to the conquest of all of Hispaniola. The citizens of color of Philadelphia may have found that emphasizing a local citizenship when addressing the French Assembly carried a vagueness about loyalty that encompassed revolutionary dreams of the universal spread of republicanism yet avoided directly taking sides in the increasingly complicated Haitian revolution. Furthermore, the spread of republican governments across the Atlantic world meant that they may not necessarily have viewed themselves as citizens fixed to particular sovereign state, but rather as public citizens loyal to the idea of republican government wherever it might rise against monarchy. Citizenship did not necessarily have to be connected to a nation-state or a sovereign state—in the giddy days of 1793 when republican possibilities seemed limitless, the citizens of color of Philadelphia could present themselves as universal citizens loyal to republicanism everywhere. Universal citizenship was thinkable because of the virtual citizenship described in Chapter 2—wherever they might be, as long as newspapers circulated, citizens could participate in public debate and practice republicanism.[17]

The citizens of color of Philadelphia were attempting to link official citizenship with citizenship as it circulated in the public sphere. Unlike Desiré's appearance in the archive, here the main route of persuasion was through the printed public sphere of the Atlantic world rather than through face-to-face interaction: the original handwritten document was intended to circulate publicly and was ultimately printed in at least one newspaper. The actions of these citizens are also similar to those of John Daly Burk, whose virtual citizenship is discussed in Chapter 2. They differ in that they felt considerably less secure in their ability to participate in their polities as citizens, and in their choice of the government with which they should align themselves, or whether their citizenship was necessarily state-based or community-based.[18]

OTHER DOMINGUANS ATTEMPTED to exert the rights of citizenship as a form of resistance to white power manifested by the imposition of denizenship upon people of African descent. While those migrants asserting alienship often associated their status with the French national state or empire, other migrants of color, Dominguan or otherwise, attempted to exert a more local citizenship. This assertion of local citizenship is exemplified by the actions of Benjamin

Maingault, discussed earlier. His participation in the election was described in
a deposition given by white witness Samuel Ferguson:

> "a mulatto boy a native of Cape Francois, who served his time with Andrew
> Seguin, went up in the evening to the election with one James Mahan....
> His name is Benjamin Mingole [Maingault.] He has been in this country
> ten or eleven years—lived with Mr. Seguin—was free the 19th of July last."
>
> "...did not see him deliver the tickets to Mr. Bender, when the boy came
> down from the window he disputed with him his right to vote—Does not
> know whom the boy voted for."[19]

Ferguson's deposition was followed by Maingault's own deposition. Maingault admitted that he had "never been made a citizen of the United States,"
but noted that his presumably white father, who died in the mid-1790s, "was
a citizen of Pennsylvania," and that his father had left him some property, "a
brick house and some frames." Maingault also admitted that he did not "rightly
know his age," but believed himself to be over twenty-one, even if his guardian
"Mr. Chaudron" still held Maingault's property. In his testimony, Maingault's
defense of his eligibility was geared toward addressing specific qualifications for
voting and citizenship. His ownership of property indicated that his economic
status was sufficient to pay taxes, although he did not say so directly. In keeping
with white attitudes toward the eligibility of people of color to vote, his propertied status indicated that he was a better candidate for suffrage than people
of color of lesser means. Furthermore, as a dependent of a deceased citizen of
Pennsylvania, he might be eligible to obtain his father's citizenship status: he
could be a state citizen even if federal law prevented him from becoming a US
citizen. Pennsylvania allowed the adult sons of citizens the right of citizenship
in Pennsylvania.[20]

Maingault may have felt indifferent or hostile to the political system that consistently limited his access to political participation and not felt any compunc-
tion about what hostile whites would call voter fraud, or he may have viewed
suffrage as his right in the face of the laws that denied him that, or some combination of the two. The emergence of political machine-style politics, along with
a still functioning two-party system, allowed Maingault a political foothold
and space to emphasize his rights and change perceptions of "French negroes"
among the white American public. In Maingault's case, he could successfully
argue that he was simply a citizen of Pennsylvania, or that the franchise was not
restricted to citizens only, or even that, owing to his time served under indenture, his freedom was akin to a naturalization as an opportunity to choose his

own political destiny. Other former apprentices, albeit white, would claim that their time served in an American household had naturalized them during the War of 1812.[21]

Maingault's actions differed from the actions of British and Irish migrants, as well as those of white French Dominguans like his presumably white father. Unlike typical white Dominguans, Maingault sought a local, rather than national citizenship. Also, despite Maingault's intimate connections with white Dominguans, he seems to have found the emerging party-based electioneering a more effective means of acting politically than the bipartisan lobbying that white Dominguans pursued in the 1790s. Maingault's citizenship was virtual in that he never formally sought naturalization; he attempted to exercise the rights of a citizen by voting. Unlike most British and Irish migrants, he found his virtual citizenship directly challenged by hostile whites. Maingault's African ancestry was a possible disqualification that whites needed to carefully monitor continually, rather than a sudden, temporary response as occurred in the War of 1812 when the US government imposed harsh controls on British subjects.[22]

Maingault's presentation of personal respectability and participation in local citizenship are indicative of the issues that free migrants from outside Europe often faced when negotiating a place within American politics and the American racial system during the early American republic. Maingault understood the tenuousness of his citizenship status. To combat the prejudice that he experienced, he drew on other factors likely to make him more appear more fit for citizenship, factors that indicated elevated class status and connection to respectable white persons. Therefore he emphasized his propertied status and the transfer of wealth from his presumably white father, as well as his guardian, Mr. Chaudron, who may be Jean Simon Chaudron, the prominent silversmith and acquaintance of Thomas Jefferson discussed in Chapter 2.

Migrants also worked with the broader international system of identity documentation, but this, too, was not fully a top-down process. Maingault's actions and those of other migrants show how they reworked the system of identity documentation to their advantage. Maingault's bureaucratic citizenship demonstrates the imperfect, contradictory, and fictive nature of official documentation: his status was vague and not fully decided. Instead of a realm in which everyone is accounted for and categorized, and lawbreakers are duly found out and punished or corrected, instead there is ambiguity, and "fraud" from the perspective of whites hostile to citizenship for people of African descent.[23]

Similarly, Desiré was aware of the eighteenth-century system of identity tracking and worked through it to support his claims to freedom and citizenship.

Desiré successfully persuaded federal court clerks to record his citizenship status, producing an official record. That documentation became part of the global system of documentation that officials in the modern states of the Atlantic world relied on to verify identity. Other officials seeking to verify Desiré's status as a free person and a citizen would assume he had an extant document trail, and Desiré, assuming that asserting foreign citizenship status would be advantageous in some future instance, could direct them to the federal court records in which he appeared. The "fictional realm" described as a "second world that existed only on paper and in files" and was "imperceptible to ordinary mortals" was not only a top-down creation solely at the disposal of the state or solely resisted through personal fraud; individuals represented in the second world used those documents to their advantage, even as those documents reinforced hegemonic norms such as white supremacy.[24]

Maingault's and other migrants' actions are important because they demonstrate that non-European migrants attempted to counter white attempts to deny them the rights of citizenship, thereby influencing the development of citizenship rights. The abrogation of rights may have been a top-down imposition from American lawmakers, but migrants like Maingault resisted its enforcement and carved out rights for themselves, participating in the debate about what rights and qualifications should be associated with citizenship. In contrast, Desiré asserted a citizenship, not of the United States, but of France, and successfully persuaded federal clerks to record him as such. Such successes were limited at best. Other migrants were able to leverage their wealth and social connections to be accepted functionally as white people, and consequently as citizens.

The Law Family: South Asian Leverage of Social Capital to Obtain Citizenship

Some migrants persuaded their communities to see them as fit for citizenship. They were further able to mobilize this status to successfully appear in bureaucratic and official records as citizens, virtual citizens, or potential citizens, and as legally white persons. Persuasion of the community and successful representation in the official document system did not have to be total: not everyone had to be thoroughly convinced of a migrant's status as potential citizen or as a white person. What mattered was the ability to circulate in respectable white society as an equal.[25]

Success at becoming a citizen was affected by numerous factors: social capital or social ties, economic capital, adherence to Western religious norms and other norms such as dressing in Western clothing. The importance of these factors is demonstrated in the contrasting experiences of several biracial migrants of British and South Asian ancestry who resided in the United States during the years after independence. John and Edmund Law leveraged their ties, wealth, slaveowner status, and religious conformity as Anglican-Episcopalians to become citizens: one obtained citizenship legally, the other virtually. Their experiences contrast with that of John Johnson, the South Asian student described at the end of the previous chapter, who had been abducted by a privateer when traveling from India to Britain and eventually arrived in the United States.[26]

The Laws' transition was eased by significant social and economic capital, particularly in the form of strong family ties to wealthy whites. Edmund and John Law were the illegitimate sons of Thomas Law, an Englishman living in India, and a South Asian woman; they were able to naturalize and incorporate themselves into white society in Washington, DC. This transition was eased by their father's acknowledgement of paternity, active guardianship, substantial personal wealth, slaveowner status, Anglican faith, ties to men in top government positions, and further building and solidification of ties to their local community. These ties also meant that the Laws were able to acknowledge their South Asian ancestry and not engage in a secretive attempt at racial passing.

THE LAWS WERE aware of differing systems of racial prejudice, and saw in the United States an opportunity to circulate as equals in white society. In an 1829 letter, Thomas Law wrote that he saw the United States as a place where his sons would encounter less prejudice than in Britain: "By coming to America one object was to settle my natural children where a variety of climate reconciles differences of complexion & where there are not such strong prejudices." Law's letter shows an adherence to the popular early modern view of "complexion" as being environmentally determined rather than as an inherited trait. His second comment, "strong prejudices," requires some further interpretation for someone who settled in a society where racially based enslavement provided a cornerstone of social order and hierarchy, as it did in the area around Washington, DC, at the time. Although Law might have been expected to display some early naiveté concerning the racial order in the United States, this letter was written over thirty years after Thomas Law's arrival in the United States. Furthermore, he wrote after his sons' successful integration into Washington's white elite, including marriage with white women and successful business careers. Law's letter shows how family wealth, prominence, religious practices, and social connections allowed his sons a liminal space of either being within the range of acceptable white "complexions" or appearing as sufficiently nonblack or non-American Indian to interact with elite whites as social equals. American elites found the Law sons' openly acknowledged Asian ancestry as a tiny exception that did not upset the racial and social order of the United States. Some leading families of Virginia claimed American Indian ancestry while identifying as racially white, a claim that cemented their authority as a ruling elite. Perhaps the possibility of other elite whites claiming to be part "East India Indian" was consequently less disturbing to them. In contrast, Law felt that elite Britons more carefully policed the South Asian/white racial boundary and saw biracial Anglo-Indian people as a threat to the metropolitan monopoly over wealth and trade, and a disturbing byproduct of the process of civilizing and colonizing India.[27]

Not only did the Law brothers successfully integrate themselves into Washington society, but Edmund Law also successfully began the naturalization process. There are no extant naturalization records for John Law. Their baptismal records indicate a 1784 birth for John, and a 1786 birth for Edmund, both in India. The family moved to England in 1791, and Thomas Law took John to the United States in 1794, while Edmund arrived in 1802. The timing of Edmund's naturalization in June 1812, shortly prior to the US declaration of war against Great Britain, along with Thomas Law's own naturalization in January 1815, shows that the Laws behaved in a manner consistent with other British migrants: they did not bother with naturalization until they faced strong wartime alien penalties. While other British migrants found out about those penalties too late, Edmund Law's Washington connections may have made him aware of the problems British subjects might face, and so he successfully obtained his naturalization before the war began. Thomas Law missed that opportunity, but availed himself of legislation allowing wartime naturalization for British subjects who were long-standing US residents. His naturalization actually dates from after the signing of the Treaty of Ghent but several weeks prior to the arrival of news of peace in the United States. Despite his alien status, John Law served alongside Edmund in the DC militia, and took part in the defense of Washington during the British raid in 1814. Like most British subjects, they found that they were often able to obtain most of the benefits of citizenship and incur few of the penalties of alien status, and so did not pursue naturalization until they were threatened with restrictions on movement and compulsory registration of aliens.[28]

In contrast, Johnson found that his circumstances made the issue of citizenship less important than his ability to reestablish contact with his family or exert control over his life in general. Missionary accounts focused on his tale of dramatic rescue and hinted at the possibility of a successful conversion from Islam. They do not indicate that the missionaries had much interest in reuniting Johnson with his family or fulfilling his father's wish for his son to receive an education in England. It is possible that Johnson might have later succeeded in persuading Americans to think of him as a potential citizen, but his placement in the Foreign Mission School indicates that this was not likely: the school intended for its students to receive an education with the purpose of evangelizing in their native, insufficiently Christian lands. In contrast, the Laws experienced an easier flow into community acceptance as potential citizens, ultimately leading to the official naturalization process.

Citizenship and American Religious Identity: Despotic Oriental Islam, Savage Heathenism, Tolerable Judaism

Migrants from the Near East were often successful at obtaining citizenship so long as they were not seen as Muslim, though there is a dearth of evidence articulating why Americans made this distinction. One explanation is an American association of Islam with the concept of Oriental despotism, and consequently an incompatibility with republican institutions. Alternatively, many Americans may have had a more general sense of Islam as un-Western or too "foreign." Still other Americans may not have understood Islam as a distinct religion, despite encounters with Islamic religious practices among enslaved Africans, but may have viewed such religious practices as "foreign" rather than a religious identity per se. In contrast, Middle Eastern or North African birth was not necessarily a barrier to naturalization.

Of the students at the Foreign Mission School, one in particular was especially successful at integration into white society. Photius Fisk, an ethnic Greek originally from Izmir in present-day Turkey, who had spent most of his childhood in Malta, attended the Foreign Mission School and shared experiences with the Polynesian students that pushed him away from whiteness, even though he was able to exercise white status later in life. Shortly after his arrival in New England in 1822, Fisk traveled with missionary promoters to New England churches, where he and another Greek-Maltese student were put on display "'like a couple of young baboons,' to gratify the curiosity of the faithful" and replenish the cost of their transatlantic passage. Fisk graduated and served as a Navy chaplain during the antebellum period and the Civil War, while also associating with the leaders of the abolitionist movement. Fisk was able to make this transition in part because of a willingness among whites to evaluate his complexion as "white," but he also had the advantage of having been born into (Eastern Orthodox) Christianity and subsequently adopting, if not orthodox Calvinism, an acceptable New England Protestantism.[29]

For still other migrants, emergency political conditions excluded them from citizenship, and also resulted in the imposition of new state-level alien penalties, such as deportation. Several North African Jews arrived in Virginia in 1785. Although they were probably from Morocco, the Virginia governor Patrick Henry suspected that they were spies from Algiers, then at war with the United States, and the Virginia legislature granted the governor the authority (for the first time) to expel dangerous foreigners. Henry believed that their possession of documents written in non-Roman script, which was probably Hebrew, was evidence of their spy status, although he does not appear to have made any attempts to contact Virginia's Jewish community for assistance in translation. Their expulsion was not explicitly on racial grounds, but rather as potentially alien enemies. The expulsion did not occur through the judicial process but instead through the executive branch, denying these aliens the right to due process. The Virginia legislature's actions presaged the construction of executive-run deportation that the US Congress passed as part of the Naturalization Act of 1798 and the 1798 Alien Act. Once again, under those laws, a legislature granted the executive powers at the expense of the judiciary, while imposing deportation as a new legal penalty on aliens. In both cases, emergency conditions were the cause, but in the Virginia case, the law was not designed to expire, unlike the Alien Act.[30]

Moses Elias Levy, a later arrival from Morocco, had a more successful path to residency and citizenship: he settled permanently in the United States and naturalized. Levy's transition was possible because of an investment in social capital as well as family and personal experience in lobbying political leaders. Although family members faced anti-Semitism in the United States, it was not a barrier to their naturalization. Moses Levy was a successful candidate for citizenship because he presented himself as an ally to white supremacy rather than an enemy, even as he made no secret of his interest in establishing a Jewish colony in northern Florida. Levy did publish an anonymous *Plan for the Abolition of Slavery* in London in 1829. The plan was published not to further the cause of abolitionism, but rather to counter it as it gained strength in the British Empire. Levy's plan was extremely gradualist and sought to stem calls for immediate emancipation. He differed from supporters of colonization in advocating widespread interracial marriage after the abolition of slavery, which was an unconventional argument in the early American republic and one likely to encounter strong white hostility in the antebellum era.[31]

Levy's transition was smoothed by a residence in the Caribbean and integration into slave society as a wealthy business owner and the husband of a daughter of a prominent family in Saint Thomas in the Danish Virgin Islands. Levy declared his intent to naturalize in a Philadelphia court in 1821, having planned to establish a Jewish settlement in northeast Florida in the waning years of its Spanish rule—he would not settle there until after Florida was ceded to the United States. His son, David Levy Yulee, born in Saint Thomas, became a US senator from Florida. Levy and Yulee successfully negotiated, through their acceptance into Caribbean white society, acceptance into American white society—but the acceptance was not entirely smooth. Full citizenship for former residents of Spanish Florida was increasingly policed along the color line in the years leading up to the mid-nineteenth century; Florida shifted from a sparsely populated frontier region to a more settled plantation economy, the borderland receded, and political divisions heated up in the 1840s. During this time, David Levy Yulee's citizenship and racial status were called into question. Levy ran successfully for office as Florida's territorial Congressional delegate (despite the challenges to his eligibility) and a final attempt occurred as he was sworn in, as recorded by John Quincy Adams:[32]

> . . . [Congressman Francis Wilkson] Pickens [D-SC] introduced David Levy as delegate from the Territory of Florida. [Christopher?] Morgan [W-NY] objected to his being sworn, and presented papers contesting his election and denying that he is a citizen of the United States. The Speaker called for credential, and, upon inspection of it, swore him in. The papers presented by Morgan were referred to the Committee of Elections. Levy is said to be a Jew, and, what will be, if true, a far more formidable disqualification, that he has a dash of African blood in him, which, sub rosa, is the case with more than one member of the House.[33]

As Adams recorded, the challenge foundered, and although Adams would continue to refer to him as "the alien Jew delegate from Florida" in his diary, his remarks also show how it was necessary to treat the questionably white as white, even as gossip about their racial ancestry might continue in private. To do otherwise would upset the racial system that placed white people in positions of gentility (as well as power).

The rumors of David Levy Yulee's African ancestry reflected antebellum concerns about racial mixing and white respectability that assumed that African ancestry was always passed matrilineally. These borders were policed in part because such unions combined African descent with the potential transfer of wealth, and therefore upset the racial order in ways that white Americans assumed patrilineal African descent did not. Thus the rumors about Yulee centered on his Caribbean-born mother rather than on his father, who was literally born on the continent of Africa, but whom Yulee's detractors did not see as the source of "African blood." Moses Levy had successfully become a citizen, whether it was through the handover of Spanish Florida or through a petition to naturalize in an American court. He had successfully presented himself, and been accepted, as a free white man.

Yulee's claims during the 1841 election to make him palatable to voters also were related to his satisfactory claims of US citizenship. Levy stressed his conversion from Judaism to Christianity, and the family estrangement that resulted from it; he had not converted merely for the sake of convenience. In Yulee's case, his father's 1829 *Plan for the Abolition of Slavery* that advocated interracial marriage as a solution to the post-abolition problem of racial tensions did not come up for public debate. If it had, Yulee's racial evaluation might have placed him beyond the possibility of whiteness. In fact, challenges to Yulee's citizenship do not appear to have openly alleged nonwhite status. Rather, challenges related to Moses Levy's Florida residency status at the time of the handover from Spanish to US control.[34]

Migrants from Latin America: Historians, Essentialism, and the Unknowable

This discussion has not challenged the essentialist assumption that white Americans assigned a racial status to all the migrants that they encountered, even if that status was one of racial ambiguity. To complicate matters, the racial status that present-day readers might wish to assign to certain migrants may differ from the status of that migrant's time of appearance in the historical record. As scholars of queer theory have demonstrated, at times individuals defy the certainty with which historians, scholars, and readers view their subjects. In other words, it would be erroneous to assume that there necessarily exists some firm, clear truth about the race and naturalizability of each free migrant from outside of Europe in the early American republic. Migrants from Latin America are an excellent example that should disabuse readers of such notions: people in the United States assigned Latin American migrants a racial status in legal documents, but to evaluate that status in light of a "true" present-day status is to engage in ahistorical thinking.[35]

Latin American migrants' naturalization documents illustrate that they are among those who defy easy and anachronistic categorization. In East Coast cities, migrants from Cuba predominated during the early republic, but a number of migrants also came from elsewhere in Latin America. Some of them obtained naturalization documents stating that they were "free white men." Their legal claims to whiteness, which may have rested on the racial hierarchy in Latin America that considered them white in their places of origin, were successful. White Americans were probably also willing to receive some of these migrants as white, and perhaps others would be able, like the Law family, to present themselves as white despite their complexions. Many of these migrants were also aided by wealth and gentility. They included a number of merchants and a prominent composer, Antonio Raffelin, who migrated between Havana, Philadelphia, and Paris. When Antonio Antelo, born in "St. Iago" in 1779, arrived in Philadelphia in 1816 after a journey from "Havanna" and declared his intent to naturalize six weeks later in a federal court, the court agreed that he was "a free white person."[36]

Also missing is evidence of rejected claims. Examinations of the large body of extant naturalization records indicate that clerks at times began to fill out naturalization petitions only to stop and reject them, but the only extant cases are for minors whose petitions clerks marked as rejected because of age. If there were any migrants who appeared before the US District Court of the Eastern District of Pennsylvania in an attempt to naturalize but were rejected because of racial disqualifications, the existing archive leaves no record. Many migrants in the early republic naturalized not on their own but with the assistance of lawyers or politicians courting their votes. A migrant who sought naturalization not as an act of civil disobedience but with the intention of succeeding would have prepared accordingly. Similarly, Desiré, the migrant of color discussed earlier in this chapter, took care to be accompanied by a witness, who was probably a white man.[37]

THE PRODUCTION OF citizenship was a complex process in which the migrants themselves participated. Although they often faced strong barriers and struggled against racial and class prejudices, they worked toward their own interests. When faced with a denial of rights through the imposition of denizen status, their resistance took the form of exercising citizenship and/or the rights associated with it. The rights and abilities that they managed to carve out for themselves complicate a fully top-down model for the development of citizenship in the early American republic.

By engaging with citizenship in the ways that they did, these migrants laid a groundwork for succeeding migrants who would negotiate American naturalization policy and its racial system. By leveraging social connections and personal wealth, and disassociating themselves from Islam and low-status occupations, some were able to obtain citizenship and legal white status. In contrast, those migrants who found employment in service often found themselves in different racial categories than their countrymen with more genteel occupations. Some migrants were still able to force hostile whites to view them as foreign citizens, acknowledging their citizenship status. Although white Americans attempted to impose a racial qualification for citizenship, migrants, especially Dominguan migrants, resisted and at times successfully exercised some rights of citizenship. In so doing, they forced white people to extend some citizenship rights, or acknowledge the foreign citizenship status of other migrants.

CHAPTER 5

From Servants to Equals

He knew the law in America, he said, and I had better realize that
he was my equal.

— Ludwig Gall, in Trautmann,
"Pennsylvania through a German's Eyes"

ON NOVEMBER 29, 1818, twenty-two German indentured servants
decided they would no longer accompany their master to Alabama.
James Brown had purchased their time in Philadelphia, and was
transporting them down the Ohio River when they disembarked at Marietta,
Ohio, and refused to reboard. Brown organized a group of men to retake them
by force, but the servants were able to win the support of local law enforcement
and remain in Ohio. In response, Brown took out a notice in Marietta's newspaper, the *American Friend*, warning Ohioans against aiding the servants in
their attempts at freedom. He closed his advertisement with an additional claim
over their legal status: "I forbid them or their children from becoming citizens
of the United States, as they are not free. . . ." Brown claimed control over their
citizenship status during the term of their indenture.[1]

Several overlapping understandings of citizenship coexisted in the early nineteenth century. Citizenship began to be associated with white social independence, an association that included European immigrant servants. At the same
time, an older Federalist conception of citizenship that adhered to leaders of
economic, social, and political standing within a community remained. In addition to this elite understanding, a local, face-to-face version based on crowd
actions—embodied collective actions by communities, often with the involvement of prominent local leaders—also persisted into the nineteenth century.

German indentured servants understood these concepts and deployed them
in their extant autobiographical writings. The early nineteenth century was a
period when citizenship, national identity, and white racial status began to be
more closely, but not yet completely, entwined. White indentured servants from

Germany might emphasize one of these identities but only imply the relevance of the others. Their migrant status also meant that they did not always fully emphasize American-ness, but sometimes asserted a legal status independent from their masters that gave them rights within the United States: they were not necessarily Americans, but they were socially and legally independent people in America.

German migrants encountered complex sociopolitical changes in the decades after US independence into the antebellum period: the denization of African Americans and the elevation of white citizenship, the role of white racism in legitimating labor regimes and dignifying white labor, and the role of racism in preventing the development of cross-class solidarity, as well as the possibility of political participation for those outside of formal venues of power.[2] In response, indentured servants theorized citizenship and functioned as citizens in their communities in a way that that asserted greater independence and equality with native white Americans despite their indented status. This chapter explores why indenture persisted in a society that increasingly emphasized egalitarian citizenship between white men and dominance over others. The persistence of earlier models and understandings of citizenship did not preclude the conflation of citizenship with white male adult status.

The evidence in this chapter is drawn from a number of sources. In contrast to French migrants, and even to some extent Irish migrants, German migrants are difficult to track because of frequent Anglicization of names, successive waves of German immigration and consequent duplicate names, and a tendency of indentured servants to rename themselves. Consequently, this chapter relies on newspaper accounts, political writings, records of political debates, state and legal documents, and court cases. It also draws from several autobiographical works, among the few cases where we hear indentured servants speak in their own voices, and directly express their views regarding their political identities.

The American Revolution and the Destabilization of Indenture

The American Revolution, while not a radical reordering of society like the French and Haitian revolutions, nonetheless destabilized hierarchical social institutions, and indentured servitude was no exception. Indentured servants had resisted the power that masters attempted to assert over them in a variety of ways, and servants who served their contracted time received their freedom. The American Revolution provided opportunities for servants to leave and join the armed forces of either side. The rhetoric of the Revolution also created a space for servants to assert their status as citizens or potential citizens. In extant public debate, however, assertions that white indentured servitude was incompatible with the Revolution seem to have appeared only post-independence.[3]

Virginia's royal governor, Lord Dunmore, granted freedom to indentured servants in his 1775 proclamation, stating: "I do hereby declare that all indentured servants, Negroes, or others, (appertaining to Rebels), free that are able and willing to bear arms." Dunmore's proclamation was limited: it applied only to servants indented to people in rebellion. The Patriot side also recruited indentured servants, but there were limits to these offers: the Continental Congress forbade enlistments without permission from masters. Virginia exempted "imported servants" from its 1777 recruitment law while establishing a draft and permitting free African Americans to enlist. New York required masters' permission for indentured servants to enlist, and instructed Gen. David Wooster to return runaways "provided their masters pay to him the disbursements, deducting therefrom the pay, if any be due." Considering Washington's decision to enlist African Americans into service, and the offers of freedom to enslaved African Americans in states such as Rhode Island in return for service (also with the permission of masters), it is likely that official provisions against recruiting runaways were sometimes ignored as the recruitment of soldiers became increasingly desperate, and fewer white Americans wished to enlist as the war dragged on.[4]

The recruitment of people fleeing from bondage also coincided, and was related to, a changing conception of political membership during the American Revolution: that of volitional allegiance. American colonists had been British subjects. Subjecthood was a condition of loyalty to the monarch, and a permanently fixed identity. From enslaved women on Carolina rice plantations to the wealthiest and most powerful men in the colonies, all were still subjects to His Majesty. As tensions increased throughout British North America and spilled into open conflict, everyone in the colonies was forced to make a choice: to side with the Patriots or to side with the Loyalists. Rather than being born into citizenship, Americans chose to become citizens.[5]

This choice of status was made more complex by heads of household intending to compel their subordinates both in the public Patriot-Loyalist divide and in private household matters. Moreover, while popular memory views the personal choice to embrace the Patriot side as earnest, brave, and permanent, other people in the Revolution chose and re-chose, going back and forth for practical reasons. For wives, children, servants, and enslaved people, personal freedom competed with political ideology when the time came to pick one side or another. German indentured servants were no exception.

The factors affecting those choices are clearly recalled by Johann Karl Büttner. Büttner had been an indentured servant, arriving in 1773 and bound to a master in New Jersey. In May 1775, he ran away, was captured, returned, and began to work several months later for a new master, Abraham Eldridge, an innkeeper, member of the local militia and supporter of the Patriot cause. Büttner received permission to attend Lutheran services in Philadelphia, and in 1777 Maj. Nikolaus Dietrich, Baron von Ottendorf, came to the services to recruit soldiers for the Patriot side. Büttner joined, writing that German servants willing to enlist were promised "thirteen acres of government land free of charge, to be taken possession of as soon as peace was declared." Büttner claimed to be motivated by personal rather than political reasons, mainly hoping to be able to return to Germany, stating: "I was less concerned about the freedom of North America, than about my own." But he was persuaded by local public opinion: "When I saw the great enthusiasm for the cause of freedom manifested in Philadelphia, I straightaway forgot Germany and plans for my own freedom, [and] took service in Major Ortendorff's [sic] corps." Freedom, however, was not complete: his master was supportive of his enlistment, but demanded from Büttner a monthly payment that would allow him to recoup the cost of the indenture.[6]

Volitional allegiance was indeed flexible, as Büttner's experiences as a soldier in the Revolutionary War attest. He initially served in Ottendorf's Patriot forces, but soon found that "the service of this corps was very hard" and decided to desert. When Ottendorf's forces clashed with Hessians at the battle of Short Hills in the summer of 1777, Büttner hid in the woods and waited until the battle ended to see who won. As it was a Hessian victory, he approached the Hessians, expressed a desire to return to Germany, and was enlisted after providing them with intelligence about the Patriot forces he had deserted. This change of allegiance was not permanent; he would, according to his narrative, change sides twice more: once more in the aftermath of the battle of Red Bank in October 1777; after an injury on the battlefield he worked in a Continental Army hospital for the future Surgeon General Theodore Tilton. His final shifting of sides described in his narrative occurred after joining an American privateer: Büttner conspired with British prisoners to help them take over the ship, after which he returned to the Hessian forces and left with them to return to Germany at the war's end.[7]

While for some indentured servants the war was a path to freedom, the war led others into bondage. A number of Hessian mercenaries were captured by Patriot forces and were given the option of indenting themselves instead of remaining interned as prisoners of war. For these indentured Hessians, formal naturalization could also matter. During the American Revolution, George Shaffel had served as an infantry private in the forces sent by the state of Hesse-Hanau. His regiment was among those that surrendered at the Battle of Saratoga, and while being held prisoner of war at Reading, Pennsylvania, he was indentured on October 12, 1782. The American government, which had previously been fairly lenient in its treatment of prisoners of war, changed to a policy designed to encourage naturalization and enlistment but also to reduce its financial burden. American captors cut rations and moved prisoners out of a barracks and into more prison-like conditions. The way out was to enlist in the Continental Army or sign an indenture. Shaffel chose the latter.[8]

Shaffel's actions indicate a preference for settling permanently in the United States. Other Hessians signed indentures but quickly absconded to New York with the intention of returning with Hessian forces to Germany. While many wished to return home, others found that the United States offered greater economic opportunities than Hesse, also sweetened by American government incentives. Relationships with and marriages to local women added further inducement to remain in the US.[9]

For these Hessians, there may have been a connection between indenture and a desire to obtain formal, legal citizenship. Shaffel is the only former soldier painted by the local Pennsylvania artist Lewis Miller with an extant record of naturalization, and also the only clearly extant record of an indenture. Shaffel's portrait also demonstrates citizenship in other ways: he is depicted with a flail to indicate his status as a farmer, and through that, a productive member of the community. Miller painted several other tradesmen, all former Hessians, with their tools, including plastering tools for the plasterer Heinrich Hattendorf, a brush and bucket for the house painter David Craumer, and knives for the butcher Johann Hubly. The more prosperous blue-dyer Friedrich Stein was shown with a blue coat, symbolizing the product that he made rather than his tools: none of the artisans were so depicted. Thus less prosperous artisans defined their membership and value to the community as productive citizens, emphasizing their labor, while the more well-off dyer asserted the value of the finished product, eliding his labor and those in his employ: a consumerist citizenship of the emerging market revolution of the post-independence period. There is some ambiguity in whose conceptions of citizenship are being painted: it is not clear whether these inclusions are at the direction of the painter or subject. However, the frequency of artisans emphasizing their productive work as part of their citizen identities in public parades and other forms of self-representation indicate that those painted wished to have those tools included.[10]

Reconciling Indenture with a Newly Emerging White Republic

The Confederation period saw a resumption in the migration of European indentured servants but also some republican rumblings against the institution,
including a few tentative plans for the compensated liberation of indentees arriving in the United States. Those plans also envisioned a republic of free, independent, white citizens.

There had been important changes in the demography of indenture during
the Revolution. The disruptions of the Revolution cut off traditional sources of
European migrants, causing a temporary demographic depression in the number of indentured servants. The other major change was the growth of African
American indentures in Northern states as they began to end slavery and pass
gradual emancipation laws, most notably in Pennsylvania in 1780. With the arrival of peace and the end to disruptions of transatlantic trade and travel, indentured servants from Europe began to arrive again in larger numbers.[11]

In November 1783, the ship *Irish Volunteer* arrived in Charleston, South Carolina, with "Sixty-nine passengers, Tradesmen and Labourers, indented for 4
years" and "subject to a clause of Redemption for twenty days." After its first
advertisement ran, a subsequent issue of the *South Carolina Gazette* carried a call
to purchase the manumission of the passengers. "THE GENTLEMEN AND
LADIES OF SOUTH-CAROLINA" were urged to begin a "subscription for
the emancipation of the indigent natives of Ireland, now in our port." The Irish
passengers were deserving of "the genuine lustre of Virtue and Charity" owing
to their being "mostly forced from their native country, by the cruelty and oppression of rich, and unfeeling *Landlords*." They were further deserving because
of the support the Irish public had given to the American cause: they had "been
so remarkably instrumental in promoting our present freedom, happiness, and
independence," and furthermore had "such a glorious thirst for rational liberty."
Unsurprisingly, this call for emancipation did not extend to people of African
descent, and in late 1783, the *South Carolina Gazette* was filled with advertisements for the sale of enslaved people and attempts to recover runaways seeking
their freedom.[12]

In January 1784, the New York *Independent Gazette* issued a similar call:

WHEREAS the traffick of WHITE PEOPLE heretofore countenanced
by this state, while under the arbitrary controul of the *British government*,
is contrary to the feelings of a number of respectable Citizens, and to the
idea of liberty this country has so happily established: And whereas it is

necessary to encourage emigration to this country, upon the most liberal plan, and for that purpose a number of the Citizens of this state, have proposed to liberate a *cargo of* SERVANTS, just arrived by paying their passage, and repaying themselves a small rateable deduction out of the wages of such Servants.—Such of the Citizens of this state, as wish to encourage so laudable an undertaking, and (if necessary) petition the Legislature for a completion of their humane intentions, are requested to meet at Mr. DAY'S, the sign of the HYDER ALLY, the lower end of King-street, this evening, at six o'clock.[13]

The announcements had several major similarities: both called for an organized attempt to raise funds for the purchase of the indentees' time. In both cases, the calls followed the arrival of a shipload of indentured servants, instead of being addressed generally to the community for the purchase of servants' time or a case-by-case fund. In the New York example, the meeting place was close to the slave market, perhaps a mere block away. There does not seem to have been any action taken beyond the call for the meeting: despite the nascent ideological attack on indenture, there is no extant evidence that either of these attempts to free indentured servants from their contracts transpired, either through purchase or other means.[14]

These advertisements also imagined a particular racialized vision of the nascent republic: one composed of free white citizens, liberal in its openness to immigrant membership, benevolent in purchasing their freedom, and stripped of all old monarchical institutions. In South Carolina, the vision was a transfer of servants' debts to virtuous citizens, leaving them as free wage laborers, albeit with their wages garnished (as had been the case for indentured soldiers such as Büttner). In New York, the new citizens were to be free of debts and economically independent. There were also other ways that the status of indentured servants could be understood in this period.

One closely related alternative was a conception of indenture as an institution through which European migrants could become citizens: the end of indenture meant a matriculation into the public sphere, and then citizenship. J. Hector St. John de Crèvecoeur's *Letters from an American Farmer* discussed this idea. Indenture would provide "both technical training and moral cultivation" to become a virtuous republican citizen. In particular, Crèvecoeur's Letter 3 was both liberal in its understanding of citizenship as mutable and possible through naturalization, reflecting a Scottish Enlightenment understanding of citizenship as a status that came with duties, and incorporated a republican understanding of citizenship as the public face of the household, dependent upon public representation to be effective.[15] Crèvecoeur's citizen was implicitly white, male, economically and socially independent, and demonstrated the racial limits of this citizenship: Crèvecoeur did not envision it for native people, and while his letters condemned slavery, they did not envision black citizenship as a possibility either.

The question of the status of indentured servants also appeared in debates over representation at the Constitutional Convention, leading to the infamous clause by which enslaved people would be counted in the census as three-fifths of a person (indentured servants would count as whole persons in that instance.) These debates also showed how the members of the convention viewed the relationship between race, bondage, freedom, and citizenship: they associated whiteness, citizenship, and free status, and where indenture might diverge from such an association, they placed it closer to citizenship.

When debating the clause, Gouverneur Morris equated citizenship to free status for men: "Upon what principle is it that the slaves shall be computed in the representation? Are they men? Then make them Citizens and let them vote." As the scholar Hoang Gia Phan has noted, the delegate William Paterson, describing a hypothetical scenario of direct democracy, stated that enslaved people would not vote, and therefore were not part of the general will, as their enslavement compelled them to obey the will of their masters.[16]

Citizenship was also equated with a labor theory of value during debates over taxation and representation in the Confederation Congress. The members of Congress viewed enslaved labor as less productive of wealth, and therefore counted free labor as more valuable to the nation. Although the congress was made up of the nation's elite, this view reflected the emerging artisanal radicalism that equated political membership, and therefore citizenship, with products produced by labor. Citizens contributed to the commonweal through their labor, and those who did not contribute were, conversely, not worthy of political membership.[17]

The Constitution's final form provided another way that indentured servants were placed into the category of free people and, implicitly, citizens. "Indians not taxed" were excluded entirely from counting toward representation, enslaved people ("all other persons") counted as three fifths, but "the whole Number of free persons, including those bound to Service for a Term of Years" would otherwise count for representation. Indentured servants would be counted as citizens, and their status was clearly understood as separate from "Servitude," which the convention altered from the original draft. No explicit mention was made of immigrants for purposes of representation, even though the convention had previously debated the number of years that a member of the House of Representatives would have to have been naturalized in order to hold office.[18]

Overall, the debates at the Constitutional Convention showed the legal and political atmosphere that indentured servants would confront when contemplating their social and political identities, one that held out citizenship as a possibility after their terms of service were complete. This understanding would affect them as they used court cases to push for greater freedom. But many servants had to confront the reality that even after their terms ended, they would continue to rely on their former masters in ways that made asserting an independent political identity challenging, especially as the conflicts of the first party system began to intensify in the 1790s.

THE STORY OF one particular indentured servant illustrates servants' own views on politics and participation as citizens after the completion of their indentures, if not necessarily a universal one. In an account written in 1795, John Frederick Whitehead (Johann Friedrich Wittkopf) placed himself outside of citizenship, which he reserved for local elites or politically motivated factions—although his writings and observations show that he was not without opinions on political and social power. Whitehead's memoir, as other scholars have noted, emphasizes the "victimization of the innocent or vulnerable by those in power or authority" and contains little discussion of "relationships with people who would not have demanded deference or subordination—his siblings, friends, fellow servants, his wife and children, and even the friend to whom he dedicates his work, Thomas Pearson." His writing also contains a "radical insistence on the essential equality of masters and subordinates."[19]

Whitehead's public and civic identity was infused by relationships with the more powerful. Written in 1795, his account demonstrates a view of citizenship put forth by Federalists: to be a citizen was to be a prominent person within the community, whose status was further asserted through public presentation of elite status. This view existed alongside a view of citizenship as being politically active within the public sphere. During a brief period of trying work as a shoemaker, Whitehead hoped that he would acquire the skills to make elegant footwear such as "Cordevan boots, Morocco slippers," and "the cork heel of a Citizen." In his narrative, discussing his writing style and the topics he covered, Whitehead characterized himself as an "inhabitant of the Country," in a rural sense, and warned readers that they "must not expect to find in me the politeness and high complimential Strains of a first rate Courteor [courtier] or a high bred Citizen." His post-emancipation experience included continued reliance upon his former master, and he stated that the he was not so quickly "metamorphosed or . . . refined from a Country Pumpkin into a Citizen." As this transition occurred at the same time as Cornwallis's surrender at Yorktown, his return to his master allowed him to "escape the Hands of the Citizens," further stating that there was "a great deal of mischief which was performed by a foolish inconsiderate mob whereby many that were worthy and peaceable Citizens greatly suffered." Whitehead was almost certainly referring to the large Quaker community in his region of Pennsylvania. Whitehead was able to slowly transition to greater economic independence, but his narrative does not display a clear assertion of civic identity throughout. Instead (as other scholars have noted) its emphasis is on the exploitation of the weak by the powerful, especially between men, while advocating for female chastity.

Citizens, as they appear in the narrative, are local elites, whose refinement and business relationships with persons of lower status accord them the title. This bourgeois citizenship, defined by conspicuous consumption and public display, was accurately represented in Whitehead's writings by the overlapping meanings of bourgeois and citizen in German: it was *bürgerlich*. Existing in parallel to this understanding in Whitehead's narrative is a description of citizens functioning as an organized political group (e.g. Patriots) whose coercion of loyalty within the community accorded them the status of citizen. To Whitehead, citizenship functioned as a status of exerting power over others in the community—political, economic, and social.[20]

During the post-independence period, courts also confronted the status of indentured servants in cases brought by servants asserting independence and demanding release from their contracts. Northern judges increasingly applied scrutiny to the contracts of white indentured servants, while allowing masters to retain power over servants of African descent. By the 1830s, this scrutiny would combine with employers' needs in the emerging industrial revolution to result in the collapse of indenture as a common labor system through the effective unenforceability of indenture contracts, with a few odd cases persisting until the eve of the Civil War. These cases were not primarily driven by German indentured servants, but they acted to secure greater independence and equality as the legal system became more amenable to their interests.[21]

A 1793 state court case illustrates this shift, and servants' choices and actions. Benjamin Hannis, a fourteen-year-old indentured servant, ran away from his mistress, Katherine Keppele, was caught, and was held in jail. Hannis appealed his case and the Pennsylvania Supreme Court ruled in his favor. In fact, the court ruled that no native-born whites could be bound as servants because the indenture of native-born whites was incompatible with republican government.[22]

But that did not mean that other forms of bound household labor were incompatible. Apprenticeship of native-born whites remained legal, with the understanding that apprenticeship produced artisan citizens, whereas white minors bound as servants would become "degraded" white adults. The court did not see such as status as unfit for nonwhite people in Pennsylvania: although in subsequent court cases, white people bound into labor were increasingly able to obtain favorable rulings on legal technicalities, for people of color the technicalities resulted in rulings in favor of people claiming mastership over them. This included a rejection of freedom claims by two people enslaved by a white Dominguan refugee, Mrs. Chambre, who had returned to Philadelphia after she forced them to accompany her to New Jersey in order to avoid Pennsylvania's manumission law. In 1795, the court issued a ruling in *Respublica v. Richards* regarding another white slaveowner's attempt to evade the manumission law by forcibly taking a man to Virginia through deception and kidnapping. In that case, the court allowed the slaveowners to retain ownership, concluding that because the seizure occurred in New Jersey it was outside Pennsylvania's jurisdiction, and that the anti-kidnapping provisions in the manumission law applied only to free people. The court was dismissive of evidence that Toby, the formerly enslaved person, had his documentation of free status taken by the master, while viewing claims of his enslavement as valid.[23]

There was also another difference between native servants and white immigrant servants: non-native Europeans, particularly German redemptioners, could still be subjected to an indenture contract (redemptioners differed from other indentured servants in that their contracts could be "redeemed," or bought out by a family member or other benefactor—they also could negotiate contracts directly with potential employers.)[24] The courts viewed such contracts as legitimate means of paying the cost of passage, and implicitly providing time for an acculturation into possible citizenship. Redemptioners and other European immigrant indentured servants benefited from the legal scrutiny given to those contracts and could obtain favorable rulings owing to clerical and other errors. A subsequent case, however, shows the scrutiny that courts began to apply to transatlantic contracts.

In 1797, the Pennsylvania Supreme Court again encountered a case relating to indentured servitude. The indentured servant John Connor refused to work for his master, Hugh Black, who "claimed him by an indenture, executed in Europe, on 13th June 1797." Consequently, Black lodged Connor in the Philadelphia prison, and Connor petitioned for a right of habeas corpus. In this case, the court ordered Connor to be freed because in his indenture contract "the word 'servant' had been inadvertently omitted." When indentured people of color brought suits to courts in Northern states, such legal technicalities were of no matter to court, and those indentures were permitted to continue until the post-Jacksonian rise of a free-labor understanding that servants should only be wage laborers. The one exception was in cases where Northern states eliminated indenture under abolitionist pressure.[25]

The result of the changed legal environment was a strengthening of legal advantages for native whites at the expense of people of color. But another difference was the increased value of native status, and with it citizenship. Citizens should not be bound into a "degraded" life of serving others but should become productive, independent citizens of the republic. White foreign migrants were different: they had, in theory, contractually consented to their arrangements, and were not citizens, although they could become citizens in time.

THIS SHIFT IN court attitudes was part of a move away from a strict, narrow, patriarchal model in which citizenship attached to the head of household. Instead citizenship began to be associated with adult white men, in part through a redefining of what it meant to be free and independent. Indenture fit uneasily into this understanding, but German redemptioners, seeing the advantages of American concepts of independence and social equality, seized their opportunity. The bonds of mutual obligation between master and servant dissolved as free wage labor became increasingly dominant, but what remained was a significant amount of economic power for former masters (now employers). Redemptioners such as John Frederick Whitehead, mentioned earlier, remained economically dependent after the end of their indentures: they often found that they needed to rely on former masters for their connections. In the 1830s, courts would be less welcoming to indentured servitude, applying sufficient scrutiny to conditions of housing and food as to render contracts unenforceable, and a brisk labor market made most newly arrived immigrants uninterested in continuing to abide by their contracts. Migrants continued to arrive and would have to negotiate this shifting legal environment. During this transition, European concern about the treatment of migrants grew and would lead the commissioning of a report on their status.[26]

Fürstenwärther's Report: An Aristocrat Finds Vulgar, Democratic Citizens and Fears Possible "White Slaves"

German indentured servants were among those who arrived in significant numbers during this period of changing legal attitudes toward their contracts and status. The Post-Napoleonic years were a period of severe hardship for many people in Europe: environmental disaster and postwar chaos led to a wave of indentured migrants arriving in the US from the German states in the later 1810s. The volcanic eruption of Tambora in 1815 was large enough to affect the global climate and cause a year without a summer in Europe. Cold temperatures resulted in crop failures and forced many people off their land. They began to migrate down the Rhine and congregated in Amsterdam, where, desperate, they signed indentures in exchange for food and passage to the United States.[27]

In 1817, the German Diet, concerned about migration from the Rhine Valley area, commissioned an investigation into the issue. Moritz von Fürstenwärther was tasked with visiting the United States and informing the German Diet about emigrant conditions there. He was given a list of questions and areas for investigation. Some of these questions implied a goal of replicating traditional German social hierarchies and installing a gentry over German tenant farmers with inheritable loan contracts (*Erbleihcontracte/Erbvertrage*), while others reflected concerns facing German migrants and the threat of exploitative indentures. The initial questions also reflected concerns about relations with native whites and European immigrant groups, and asked, "How does the German farmer get along with the savages?" The initial questions did not inquire about relations between African Americans and Germans.[28]

Fürstenwärther's report differed in some key ways from his original instructions. Comparing the original instructions and what he chose to emphasize, the report painted a broadly positive picture of German redemptioners' experiences in the United States, while expressing some concern about the loss of German cultural identity. Fürstenwärther did, per his instructions, include descriptions of the process by which redemptioners disembarked and sold their time to local masters in the United States. His aristocratic status seems to have led him to view American republicanism critically, if not negatively, and his report devoted relatively little space to the idea of citizenship: Fürstenwärther was no Alexis de Tocqueville. His report followed his instructions to comment on the functioning of the redemptioner system, and he expanded his instructions to focus, not on citizenship, but on German immigrant relations and status relative to enslaved African Americans. When he did discuss citizenship, Fürstenwärther emphasized cultural assimilation into American vulgarity and coarseness, and the loss of German culture.[29]

Fürstenwärther's report betrayed an inconsistency when discussing perceptions of Germans and their experiences as indentured servants: when comparing Germans to free whites only, the report painted a rosy picture, but in passages comparing Germans to African Americans and slavery, the report showed considerable anxiety about white perceptions of Germans and the similarities between indentured servitude and slavery.[30]

Fürstenwärther addressed a major point of concern: the binding of passengers on arrival. He emphasized the regulations in place, the oversight by German aid societies, and the practical benefits of indenture for passengers, while dismissing concerns about exploitation by cruel masters after the process of arrival and sale of time. The report contained extensive description of the process of binding servants and the conditions upon arrival in the United States, as well as demographic and socio-economic information about the servants themselves. This information was probably taken from the register of indentures in Philadelphia, the main port of entry for German migrants. The report concentrated on migrants leaving from Amsterdam, the chief port of embarkation at the time, and arriving in Philadelphia.

Fürstenwärther reported that migrants concluded contracts, written in German, with ship captains in Amsterdam. Ships arriving in Philadelphia were first subjected to quarantine and "visited by a doctor representing the board of health, and at the same time by the interpreter from the German Association." The interpreter would also inquire "concerning treatment on the voyage and [investigate] grounds of possible complaints in this regard." After this process, the arrivals would be advertised in local newspapers, and the ship would land. Those passengers who paid full fare would depart, and the rest remain on ship with the captain or "local consigners [would] take them on the basis that the Americans will take these people into service." Negotiations for contracts would ensue, and would be "concluded in the dwelling of an authorized person," fluent in German and English, and who would act as a mediator between parties in addition to recording the contracts. Contracts were generally for two to four years, "according to differences in fare, age, sex, health, and capabilities," and would contain stipulations for living arrangements and clothing, as well as schooling for children. Laws also restricted bindings outside Pennsylvania or family separation, except with the consent of the servant. Those whose time was not sold would remain in debt to the captain or consigner, although the report noted that such situations were "highly unusual." Fürstenwärther also noted that 1817 was a year of unusually heavy migration, and that the migrants, usually poorer and without means of support, overwhelmed the emigrant aid societies' resources for assistance and had to compete for limited employment opportunities. [31]

The report argued that a short term of indenture was often the best option for migrants, as they could invest what money they might have brought with them with their masters, and "draw interest until the end of their service." Doing so would give them time to familiarize themselves with "the language, the customs," options in employment, and "obtain for themselves necessary local knowledge." Their savings would allow them to "be able to [begin] a self-supporting trade," or "buy a few acres of land on which to settle," while improving the land in increasing its value. The report emphasized that "Almost all who come here . . . after ten or twelve years . . . become skilled in this manner," and that "instances are known" where after "20 or 30 years, they are now capitalists."[32]

Furthermore, Fürstenwärther claimed that "in Pennsylvania and the western bordering states where the population is mainly German" treatment of indentured servants was "as a rule humane and good." Those maltreated or deceived could lodge a complaint with "the solicitor of the German Association," and that "more frequently, there are complaints on the part of the employer against the employee." According to the report, those who opted not to do a year of service were "often misused by their own fellow countrymen for their own purposes" and likely to "squander [their money] until they find an opportunity to work."[33]

Fürstenwärther did temper his positive remarks to describe specific abuses. In part, he attributed these abuses to "lack of following the law which produced the great suffering and disorder in former years." At the time of his writing he identified other issues that migrants faced: commission agents who "transmit money to respective heirs in both parts of the world" were often dishonest. Ship captains in Amsterdam would "make arbitrary alterations," often illegal, to passengers' contracts, "which the people in their inexperience let go by." The German aid society in Philadelphia suffered from "little money to relieve the great needs."[34]

When comparing Germans and enslaved African Americans, Fürstenwärther painted a grimmer picture. In areas with significant enslaved populations Germans lost status. In areas with fewer enslaved people the report was largely sanguine and fears of sinking in a shameful comparison with native whites appeared, supported by anecdotes acquired secondhand.

The report illustrated these concerns by including several English-language newspaper extracts, all from 1817, one containing the headline "German slaves in Ohio," (although it clearly stated that the so-called slaves were in fact indentured servants). Another article was summarized: "Deceived young German artisans

become white slaves in this manner." Fürstenwärther also included an article
that mentioned an important difference between slavery and indenture, freedom
from sexual exploitation by masters. That article noted that "The Germans in
Ohio forced a scoundrel to give a fifteen year old Swiss girl freedom and 500
Reichsdollar for disgracing her."[35]

Government or German immigrant action was swift when white indentured
servants were purchased by people of color, cases where there is extant evidence
suggest. In Baltimore in November 1817, according to Fürstenwärther, "Two
families [traveling from Amsterdam] were bought by free Negroes" without the
initial knowledge of the German community. Fürstenwärther himself cited a
letter from "H. Graff, one of the rich local businessmen" in recounting this incident. According to this secondhand account, the German community "brought
the families back and pledged to prevent further such disgraceful abuses."
Fürstenwärther contradicted the details of the story in a later section of his report, referring to the same letter, stating instead that it was a single family purchased by a single free African American buyer. In Louisiana, another incident
(not appearing in the report) occurred in the spring of 1818, where free people of
color purchased German redemptioners from a recently arrived ship. In this case,
the response came from the Louisiana legislature, which banned such sales.[36]

LAST, FÜRSTENWÄRTHER DID describe redemptioners' and other Germans'
views on citizenship and political identity. Here his aristocratic background
and distaste for republican government caused him to paint their attitudes in a
negative light: "I cannot remain silent about some of the dark sides," he wrote.
The United States lacked Germany's elegance and high culture, "one misses everything that can make life on earth more beautiful and refined." Refinement
in life was so absent that there was "no notion" of its earthly existence in the
United States. Instead, "Lack of sociability, disdainful pride, reserve and coarseness distinguish the masses and repel the European of culture and sensitivity."
Americans had "civic freedom" but not "that higher spiritual freedom which is
found only in Europe—and I say it boldly—mostly found in Germany." Despite
republican government, Americans were "with all their freedom more or less
slaves to their national prejudices, to their narrow-mindedness, their ignorance
of everything that is not practical or parochial."[37]

German immigrants were not immune to this transformation into vulgar
American citizenship. According to Fürstenwärther, the German in the United
States was "an ardent Democrat, and at the same time a quiet citizen." He singled
out former Hessians especially as "a good example.... Beside[s] being especially

democratic in outlook, they are given to bluntness, crudeness, and obstinacy." Speaking of more newly arrived immigrants more generally, he wrote that "After a time, [they] become accustomed to [the US] once they find suitable surroundings, or by degrees an awakening feeling of pride as free citizens, [that] the memories of the advantages of their Fatherland vanish."[38]

As his writing revealed, Fürstenwärther's aristocratic views were not shared by his fellow Germans in the United States. The report demonstrated a politically active population, if not one so famously forceful as the Irish immigrants described in a previous chapter. His notes on race relations provided a window into the anxieties and choices made by indentured German servants when asserting status and independence in a society that increasingly equated citizenship with a white, adult male identity in contrast to blackness.

Redemptioners, Renewed Anxieties, and Runaways

During the period of Fürstenwärther's travels, the controversy over indentures erupted again in American newspapers when a ship with redemptioners aboard docked at Annapolis, and "their time was purchased . . . by some western members of Congress" who then attempted to transport about fifty redemptioners to Tennessee. They passed through Washington, DC, and then Kentucky, where the editor of the *National Pulse* expressed "remarks on that kind of soul-selling business in all its various branches," addressing both the conditions of passage and the system of redemptioning and indenture, with a particular focus on the customs of hospitality to journeymen artisans in Germany and its use in luring the unwary to the US. The editor noted that "an express law of Kentucky not only sanctions such bargains, but even enforces the servitude, by the same cruel means by which African slaves are mellowed down to absolute obedience to a master." The editor stated that he wished to "lay before the public an unhallowed speculation in white free men's liberty, which is in the highest degree derogatory to the exalted character of the American republic." The editor further claimed that the trade in indentured servants was "a flagrant breach of the law of nations, and abhorred by every civilized government," was "absolutely unconstitutional" in the United States, and that such laws should be "speedily and eternally repealed."[39]

The recent sudden rise in poor German migrants and continuing migration along the Ohio River valley into the interior of the United States meant that officials and members of the public in Ohio would have to confront the status of redemptioners in their state. This came about because of the actions of the migrants themselves: their choices and actions precipitated the discussion over their status and political engagement in Ohio communities. It was in this context that another group of German redemptioners would work to secure their freedom in Ohio in the fall of 1818.

THESE REDEMPTIONERS ARRIVED in Philadelphia in October 1818, and negotiated indenture contracts with the American James Brown. According to Brown's later memorial to Congress, he "purchased . . . a number of German redemptioners" including "vine-dressers and mechanics." Brown intended to transport them to Tennessee, where they would serve for a term of three years and five months. His memorial also stated that he "described to them the climate . . . and the kind of business they would be required to follow." Brown and the redemptioners left Philadelphia on November 2—there does not seem to have been a significant issue or dispute as the party traveled overland through Pennsylvania, but things changed after Brown purchased a boat at Wheeling and they all began to sail down the Ohio River on November 26, and approached the growing town of Marietta "on the evening of the 29th." When they were about seven or eight miles away, they had to land the boat "in consequence of high wind." They stayed there for the night, and in the morning James Brown and a free employee, George Ross, "left the boat in a skiff about three miles above Marietta and proceeded in advance to said town." Brown purchased provisions and got them ready to put aboard the skiff, "when he discovered his boat landing some distance above." Brown went up with the skiff, put the provisions on the boat, and came back into town, where he encountered his servants—he told them everything was ready "and that they must go on board immediately." Brown claimed that the redemptioners at this point "made several frivolous excuses," and when he followed his earlier request to board with a direct order to get back on the boat, "they refused to obey." Brown believed this was "in consequence of advice given" to the redemptioners "by the people of Marietta."[40]

Having encountered the refusal of the servants, and the lack of sympathy for his views from the people of Marietta, Brown turned to local law enforcement "for the purpose of putting down insubordination of citizens and servants." On the advice of his lawyer, he went to the house of Enoch Hoff, constable at Marietta—but Hoff "was not at home, and would not be until late in the evening." Brown returned to the courthouse and met again with his lawyer, John P. Mayberry, who recommended that Brown "get men enough in the town of Marietta to put his servants on board his boat," and Mayberry was willing to accompany him in this endeavor. The people of Marietta, however, were not so willing: "after repeated trials, not more than one man could be got who would lend any aid or assistance." They would have to wait for Constable Hoff to return home that night. While waiting, Brown spoke with another local lawyer and county solicitor, Caleb Emerson. During their discussion, Emerson learned that Brown was "preparing aid to take them away by force that night." Emerson warned him that "such a procedure would be a violation of our laws, and would not be submitted to by our citizens." Brown's plans would be delayed until the following day: he had crossed over into Virginia to meet one Levi Wells, recommended by Mayberry, as someone who "no doubt, would afford the necessary aid" in seizing the redemptioners.[41]

In the meantime, the redemptioners had "taken lodging" in a house in Marietta and stayed the night. Emerson visited them the next morning and "through an interpreter, had partly heard their story," when they were interrupted by the arrival of a posse comitatus organized with the help of Levi Wells: "Certain men came with Mr. Brown, from the Virginia side, armed with bludgeons, &c." A crowd had organized in Marietta to challenge the posse, including the house's "landlord and a young man by the name of Willard, as well as many others." In the meantime, Emerson and the redemptioners closed the doors of the house to prevent entry and they waited "until [the posse] dispersed." After this experience, the redemptioners decided to flee "into the country as a body" the following morning, with help from two local men, David Ward and John Taylor. They made fast progress, covering "fourteen miles up Duck Creek," but "they were requested to return," or in Brown's account, "arrested" for a hearing before "Mr. Justice Booth, in order to obtain a certificate to remove them under United States law, respecting fugitives from labor." This hearing would "occupy a great part of two days."[42]

Brown soon found events turning in an unexpected direction. Once the redemptioners had come back into town on the evening of December 3, Enoch Hoff "came down to [Brown's] boat, and informed" him that Hoff "wanted [Brown] to go up immediately." Hoff took him not to the courthouse, the implied destination, but they "had to pass near Captain John Mills's storehouse" where Brown "discover[ed] a number of persons collected together at the door, [and] he was induced to approach," at which point Brown further "discover[ed] that they were armed." Brown was puzzled. What was going on?[43]

The answer came after a short wait: Sheriff Timothy Buell "came out of the store accompanied by Captain John Mills, and informed [Brown] and Enoch Hoff constable, that they were prisoners." Hoff and Brown were marched to "Justice Booth's office . . . with Captain Mills's company of militia armed at their heels."[44]

James Brown's arrest was the result of claims made by the redemptioner John Gold, who alleged "assault and battery and false imprisonment, damages five thousand dollars; that [Brown] was ruled to bail." Brown expressed skepticism that this came from Gold himself, suspecting that the charges came from Emerson or his ally David Putnam, or so he "was informed by the clerk." The charges, Brown further claimed, were put forth to elicit public sympathy for the redemptioners and help in collecting funds to pay off their indentures. He quoted David Putnam as saying "that the money and the cost and expenses of [Brown's] servants could be made up," and if Brown "did not take that, he could whistle for them."[45]

It seems there was both a trial and a simultaneous negotiation for the paid release of the redemptioners from their contracts. Caleb Emerson stated that Brown paid "$1,275 for 22 [redemptioners] in Philadelphia. It was proposed to him in Marietta to redeem these Germans, paying all reasonable charges; but he refused to take less than $3,500." Brown had implied in his statement that the purchase price would pay his fine, while Emerson's account omitted this aspect, firmly focusing on the payment and presenting Brown as unreasonable in his negotiations by demanding nearly the triple the original amount he paid. Brown's deposition indicated that the trial included a "lapse of nearly thirty-six hours"—it may have been during this period that the negotiations took place, and when they failed to come to arrangement pleasing to Brown, the court would make its ruling without any provisions for a paid remuneration.[46]

The trial deliberated the status of the redemptioners (what Brown called "a trial of property") and not Gold's allegations against Brown. It began with two justices: James Booth and probably Buell as well; justices of the peace seem to have served as judges uncontroversially. In the trial, discussions hinged on the Fugitive Slave Law of 1793 and whether it applied not only to enslaved people but to indentured servants as well. Brown claimed that one of the justices left, and implicitly it was Justice Booth who delivered the final verdict: "the court set the servants at liberty." This was a popular decision in the courtroom: "the servants were congratulated by the court, most of the bar, and nearly all the spectators." James Brown himself felt that he was "unable to obtain justice" but he did not know nor "was able to learn where the United States district judge for that district resided" and so decided to leave Marietta.[47]

There was still the matter of his own arrest to contend with. Brown "made application to judge Sharpe for a writ of *habeas corpus*" in order to determine on what charge he was held and who was behind it. Emerson "had directed the writ to be discontinued on the 4th day of December," but Brown was held until the seventh. During that time, "stones were frequently thrown" at his boat, still moored in town. Shortly afterward, Brown slunk out of town with his damaged boat.[48]

James Brown was not done. He planned to return, but in the meanwhile he took out an advertisement in the local newspaper, the *American Friend*. There he wrote to "hereby caution and forewarn all persons in the state of Ohio, and elsewhere, from harboring or employing, aiding or assisting, or contracting with or trusting" the redemptioners, whom he listed by name. It was in this advertisement that he announced that he "forb[ade] them or their children from becoming citizens of the United States . . . until they go to the Alabama Territory and serve me there" for the term of their indentures.[49]

LET US PAUSE in this narrative to address what it meant for the idea of citizenship. The controversy over the redemptioners showed several conceptions in conflict, with Brown's understandings and claims on one side at odds with the redemptioners' and Mariettans' on the other. Brown's understanding of the law indicated a conception of citizenship linked to the head of household and rooted in patriarchal control over dependents. In his view, indentured servants lacked the legal power to choose allegiance, and could not have a political allegiance separate from the head of household. The naturalization process would have to wait until their matriculation as free people.[50]

In contrast, the Mariettans' view rejected patriarchal control over other white adults. Their focus was not on naturalization but rather on the ability of the redemptioners to reject their indentures and act independently as separate households and legal persons. In particular, their view was expressed in legal arguments rejecting the obligation to assist in the seizure and remanding of white bondspeople. They also showed a local understanding of citizenship and political culture, in which community leaders could organize and direct crowd actions. It may have been elite-directed, but it relied not just on passive consent but on active public affirmation and political participation by the community.

Let us return to the redemptioners' two-day court case and their legal status and rights. At its heart, the case centered on the right of access to the courts: under what circumstances were alleged runaways to have access to the courts? And how should this law be interpreted? Caleb Emerson and Justice Booth thought that the 1793 Fugitive Slave Law applied only to people born in slavery: "It may well be doubted whether this provision can in any case apply, excepting as to persons born slaves." Emerson recalled the status of indenture as it appeared in the debating and drafting of the US Constitution: the pains taken to distinguish indenture from slavery; the view of indentured servants as potential citizens resulted in a divide in racial treatment. Enslaved African Americans leaving masters to seek freedom could be denied that opportunity, but white indentured servants received protection under the law. Emerson also followed his statement on legal interpretation with a tale of misery: the Germans stated that they had been forced to abandon their ship in the Azores after "losing many of their children and companions" at sea, and then further obliged to "re-ship, as redemptioners, for America." Once again, these travails can reflect a divide in racial sympathy: surviving the transatlantic slave trade would not be grounds for exemption from the 1793 Fugitive Slave Law.[51]

Caleb Emerson also presented a vision of the law in his statement, and with it, a notion of citizenship that emphasized rights and protections for white people within the bounds of the state of Ohio. Emerson pushed against Brown's claims that Mariettans had talked the redemptioners into defiance of his will. Rather, Emerson stated:

> The citizens of this place would have been better satisfied, had the Germans been content to go with their purchaser. But the Germans having claimed the benefit of our laws, for the protection of their persons, the citizens could not, in justice to themselves, tamely suffer one of the most essential maxims of our constitution to be violated.[52]

The Germans were foreign, and not citizens like their rescuers. But they were (white) people in Ohio, and therefore had rights of access to the law and its protections—this was Emerson's argument as written in his reply in the *American Friend*.

Emerson's reply also offered a Federalist interpretation of citizenship. He, along with leading citizens such as David Putnam, James Booth, and Timothy Buell, made decisions as community leaders. They were citizens in the fullest, Federalist sense. The crowd that they assembled to prevent the seizure of the redemptioners, and to arrest James Brown, was composed of citizens, but the crowd was acting in an orderly manner in accordance with the wishes of the leading citizens of Marietta. This view also countered the accounts of Brown and his fellow deponents of disorderly mobs preventing the proper enforcement of the law. Both Brown and Emerson emphasized "law and order" and presented their opponents' crowds as illegitimate.

The incident also showed that naturalization followed an earlier pattern of attaching to the head of household but increasingly was being tied to a status of free economic agent. Since the court in Marietta ruled in favor of the

German migrants, it did not address the issue of whether Brown had control over his servants' ability to naturalize. Brown continued his campaign to persuade government officials to take action, but dropped the naturalization issue. His initial forbidding of naturalization was in part based on a fear that if they did naturalize, or even begin the process, his case for control over their labor would be greatly weakened. The more the German migrants acted like citizens, the less likely Brown would be to assert control over their time, labor, and free movement. After his initial push to use brute force via a posse comitatus failed, Brown increasingly relied on other legal channels. His actions revealed the shifting landscape of freedom, citizenship, and bondage that was developing in the early American republic.

Brown was attempting to treat the white redemptioners like African Americans, and found that Ohioans were unwilling to let him. Black Americans could be subject to interpersonal, private violence and force without the intervention of the legal system, but white migrants could use the system to their advantage, removing themselves from bondage, and asserting a citizen-like status based on their economic agency and white racial status. This was the case in the North: so-called "Dutch slaves" were increasingly an impossibility in Ohio and Pennsylvania, while masters retained more power over indentured servants in the South, though indenture remained a temporary form of bondage distinct from slavery. This initial incident also highlighted sectional and partisan division in what was supposed to be an era of good feelings, at a time when harder feelings were developing over the Missouri Compromise. Brown would encounter this system again in his second attempt to seize the redemptioners several months later.[53]

JAMES BROWN HAD made a tactical retreat in leaving Marietta, but he made plans to return, and began to lobby powerful people in the Ohio Valley. Brown traveled to Tennessee, where he persuaded Governor Joseph McMinn to write "a letter of remonstrance" to Governor Ethan Allen Brown of Ohio, delivered by a William Craighton Jr., of Chillicothe, Ohio. Brown then came back to Ohio and successfully obtained "a warrant to arrest . . . his servants" from Federal District Court Judge Charles W. Bird. With this warrant, Brown returned to Marietta, arriving on February 27, 1819, having stopped first at Parkersburg "to procure physical aid to assist in arresting his servants."[54]

The redemptioners were still in the area, and Brown was able to seize six of them on the 28th. Brown also found "two of his servants in the employ of Caleb Emmerson [sic] . . . who had been the zealous advocate for their emancipation."

Emerson persuaded Brown to hold off, making "a matter of conscience about delivering them on Sunday." When Brown came back, however, he "found the door closed, the family at home, and no admittance to be had." That night a "number of persons crossed over the river to Levi Wells's, on the Virginia side, for the purpose of rescuing the six servants," but they apparently were unsuccessful. Still determined, Brown came back to Emerson's house "the next morning . . . and was informed by" Emerson's wife, Mary Dana Emerson, "that neither he nor the servants were there; that they had left town."[55]

Temporarily foiled again, James Brown nonetheless heard of more redemptioners: "he was informed where ten or twelve of them had been seen the day before." Once again, Brown turned to Parkersburg and "procured . . . four men to go with him" and crossed the river again at Marietta and "proceeded immediately to the place where his servants had been seen." He did not receive a warm welcome or much sympathy or aid: "none of the neighbors appeared disposed to give . . . any information" and they "pretended not to know of any such people having been seen in the neighborhood." Brown thought "they were making off to get into the interior of the country" and he kept looking for them "until two o'clock next morning, when he stopped at a house." There he learned that the redemptioners "were not far off, and being much fatigued, called a halt." Brown would start again "by sunrise."[56]

Brown "was roused from bed by a visit from one of the neighbors" with more information about the whereabouts of the redemptioners, but he soon found himself in a trap. Sheriff Buell and Caleb Emerson "had collected between one and two hundred men, and had stopped in the woods until the preconcerted signal could be given." They marched out of the woods, "variously armed," and constable Silas Cook arrested Brown "for an alleged assault and battery . . . on [his] servants while acting under the [federal] warrant" Brown had been issued. Brown was tried and Emerson "was the prosecuting attorney"—but as the trial began Emerson quickly "abandoned the prosecution" and Brown "was dismissed" from the court—but only for an hour or so. Brown "was again arrested . . . upon the affidavit of Charles Sylvester." This second time, Brown appeared for trial "before Justice Whitney," and "he was again dismissed, no one appearing to prosecute."[57]

It had taken him a while, but James Brown was finally realizing that the community of Marietta had organized against him and would not let him seize any more of the redemptioners. Still, he had managed to capture six of them, and so he began his voyage down the Ohio in a flatboat, with the six forced to accompany him.

THIS SECOND ROUND of conflict over the status of the redemptioners displayed several new aspects: a federal government more amenable to Brown's claims, coupled with the ineffectiveness of the federal order facing a broader public mobilization. Additionally, the local courts were willing to entertain claims of violence exerted by a master against his servants: claims that enslaved people could never bring before a court across the river in Virginia and that an Ohio court would be highly unlikely to entertain. And although Brown had temporarily succeeded in seizing the unlucky six, he would encounter yet another crowd of citizens in Cincinnati.[58]

Brown and the remaining redemptioners "embarked the on the fourteenth day of March," arriving one week later at Cincinnati. According to the boat's owner, William Eastham, Brown left the boat for several hours while the servants remained on board. When he came back, however, a "considerable assemblage of persons" had crowded around the boat, coercing the disembarkation of the German servants. Roderick Osborn, a boat hand, described the crowd as a "mob . . . preceded by five men, who called themselves citizens." Eastham claimed that Brown arrived as the last one was disembarking to freedom, at which point the crowd "[threw] away the stones they had with them" and "dispersed." A larger crowd soon reappeared and forced the boat to land, and the crowd "took such things as they chose, stating them to be the property of the aforesaid German servants." Osborn told a slightly different version of events: the "citizens" requested to board the boat, while Brown, still on board, refused. Brown himself stated that the men who approached the boat had heard one of the redemptioners speaking to another "in the German language." The citizens "disclaim[ed] any evil design towards the master or servants," convincing Brown to let them board, but it soon became clear that they intended to "seize" or "seduce off his servants." By all accounts, the servants were able to leave with assistance from the crowd. But they were not done: according to William Eastham, "an increased number of persons reappeared" on the banks of the Ohio, "with every appearance of hostility." Brown's witnesses corroborated the account from this point: the crowd demanded that the boat be landed, and, meeting with refusal, "forcibly seized the cable and the oar" of the boat and towed it shore. The crowd boarded and "took from the boat what they were pleased to call the property of the . . . servants." Evidently satisfied, they then "retired to shore with their booty." Thus the two different accounts of the same series of events in Cincinnati differed in some details, but agreed on the main picture: a crowd assembled and liberated the servants. [59]

Once again, we see a local citizenship in action in support of the redemptioners, and James Brown at a loss: he would have to rest his hopes on a memorial submitted to the United States Congress, since "owing to the temper and feel-ing of the people generally . . . he would be unable in the state of Ohio to have [Brown's version of] justice done." Cincinnati's practice of citizenship resem-bled Marietta's in this account: local leaders were supportive of and perhaps organized crowds to engage in action. In Cincinnati, local citizens included German-speakers, as evident from the initial negotiations. The entirety of action was informal in Cincinnati: no appeal to courts is mentioned in the accounts, but by this time Brown was probably skeptical of using local Ohio courts to maintain command over the redemptioners.

OTHER ACCOUNTS OF master-servant tension reflect assertions of legal and social egalitarianism, with accompanying implications for citizenship. Ludwig Gall, a German intending to travel and perhaps emigrate to the United States, experienced similar difficulties as part of a generally disastrous journey to the United States. During his voyage to the United States one of the other passen-gers "attempt[ed] to throw him overboard." Gall had paid the passage of several other travelers, with the expectation that they would serve as redemptioners in the United States, but they "r[a]n away from him by the time he was cleverly landed." Others continued to "drop off, one by one, on the way from Philadel-phia to Harrisburg."[60]

Gall also had to contend with renegotiation of household relations in the context of household service. As his servants came to understand the cultural meaning of white servility, they advocated for a greater equality of social rela-tions, with a focus on communal meals, not doffing one's hat, speaking with "un-wonted familiarity," and being provided with "a Sunday suit as good as" Gall's own. This renegotiation bears similarity to the reimagining of companionate marriages as marriages between equals in a Scottish Enlightenment sense, as discussed in Chapter 3. Gall's servant Peter Wissel demanded social equality between master and servant, grounded in legal rights: "He knew the law in America, he said, and I had better realize that he was my equal." When Gall had him imprisoned, Wissel countered that the conditions there were preferable to working under Gall's terms. Gall also noted that this assertion of equal status was more common among his male servants. German redemptioners reevaluated their relationships in the transition to republicanism as well as their economic negotiating power and access to a legal system that was increasingly uninterested in tolerating white indentured servitude, even among foreign migrants.[61]

These incidents extended beyond indentured servants to white waged labor-ers, and into the Jacksonian Era. The English novelist Frances Trollope, seeking to hire and retain white women servants while living in Jacksonian Cincinnati, linked their expectations to citizenship: "The greatest difficulty in organizing a family establishment in Ohio, is getting servants, or, as it is there called, 'getting help,' for it is more than petty treason to the Republic to call a free citizen a *servant*." When she instructed a servant to eat separately in the kitchen, she was told: "I guess that's cause you don't think I'm good enough to eat with you. You'll find that won't do here." The idea of equality also extended to clothing: according to one of her servants, white women employers regularly lent their dresses to their servants, but when Trollope balked at such a suggestion, her employee replied: "I guess you Inglish thinks we should poison your things, just as bad as if we was Negurs." Trollope also noted that one of her servants employed an enslaved woman who traveled from Kentucky to work in "free" Ohio. After further difficulties, Trollope eventually settled on "a very worth French woman, and soon after a tidy English girl to assist her." Both continued in Trollope's employ for most of the rest of her stay in the United States, and to her satisfaction in the employment of servants, she had "no more misfortunes . . . to relate." Trollope also contrasted such behavior with a greater public deference when she crossed the Niagara River into Canada, and encountered "British Oaks, British roofs, and British boys and girls. These latter, as if to impress upon us that they were not citizens, made bows and curtseys as we passed, and this little touch of long unknown civility produced great effect."[62]

Overall, these incidents allow us to think about the place of citizenship for people as the United States moved toward Jacksonian democracy, elevating the status of free white men and emphasizing adult white economic and legal independence. Citizenship mattered for these migrants, but only as one of many markers of personal independence from masters. Their own choices and seizing of freedom were important in this process, but they were greatly aided by shifts in public opinion and the friendliness of the courts, prosecutors, and the legal community, which frequently made white indenture contracts unenforceable. Economic arguments about the collapse of indenture need to take into account the shift in legal thought, the practical choices open to migrants, and the reframing of household economic relations and hierarchy as part of the shift toward a commercial, free-labor market that created a growing space for "independent" wage labor.

Formal citizen status in Jacksonian society still coexisted with an alternative meaning of citizenship, grounded in the political conflicts and tensions of the final decades of the eighteenth century. "Citizen" continued to mean persons of high standing the community who could function as community leaders. There was some flexibility in this term, as it could by 1819 extend to German-Americans even as they acted in ways that seemed to destabilize social, economic, and political order from the perspective of people such as James Brown and William Eastham. Indeed, the "citizens" of Cincinnati shared the ability to mobilize inhabitants to violence with the Patriot citizens of Whitehead's Pennsylvania. The incident at Cincinnati demonstrates a Federalist conception of citizenship without xenophobia, or at least one that did not view German immigrant political organizing as a threat.[63]

Akin to this tiered conception is an understanding of community membership, leadership, and narrative. Full citizens were those who intervened with heroism, while a crowd of lesser citizens lent them support. But those rescued were framed as outsiders: potential citizens, perhaps, but definitely not members of the community at the time of their rescue. Americans increasingly consumed Romantic novels and watched melodramatic plays. White women learned that republican citizenship could be threatened by aristocratic seducers. Gothic horrors of revolutionary violence spilled out from the speeches of counterrevolutionary politicians excoriating France and proslavery writings denouncing the Haitian revolution. In this instance, the drama came back into real life.[64]

GERMANS CONTINUED TO be politically active after 1798, and fully active participants in law and society when it came to perceptions of German indentured servants. Germans were similarly active in shaping race and racial categories during the early American republic, driven by their need (and that of Americans of all races) to rethink the relationship between race, labor, freedom, and citizenship as unfree German servants labored in parallel with a growing number of indentured and free African Americans. Germans attempted this reshaping by vigorously policing the possible exploitation of German servants while emphasizing the temporary nature of indenture. Even as a Jacksonian model became more dominant over time, different conceptions of citizenship, including those associated with the Federalists of the 1790s, persisted into the 1820s.

Coda

Haunting this tale of white freedom is another one: of Black death and slavery. Thirty-five years after the German redemptioners escaped from their master, Margaret Garner, an enslaved woman, joined a group of seventeen people who crossed the frozen Ohio River in January 1856. They hoped to escape slavery and secure their freedom by traversing the state of Ohio and reaching Canada. Some of the group were able to evade the gauntlet of white surveillance and secured safe hiding places in Cincinnati, but Garner and the majority of her companions were not so fortunate. Alerted, their masters came, "with officers and a posse of men." Unlike the German redemptioners, Garner and her companions had no assistance from a large white crowd, only the backing of a handful of abolitionists working discreetly to help them. With the passage of the Fugitive Slave Law of 1851, they had no support in securing freedom from the legal system. Garner and her companions decided to fight nonetheless, but were overpowered. The abolitionist Levi Coffin described Garner's next choice of action:[65]

> At this moment, Margaret Garner, seeing that [her] hopes of freedom were [in] vain seized a butcher knife that lay on the table, and with one stroke cut the throat of her little daughter, whom she probably loved the best. She then attempted to take the life of the other children and to kill herself, but she was overpowered and hampered before she could complete her desperate work. The whole party was then arrested and lodged in jail.[66]

There followed a trial at which Garner petitioned for freedom, citing earlier residence on Ohio's "free" soil. Her claims were unsuccessful, and she was ordered to be returned to Kentucky and to slavery. According to Coffin, "A crowd followed them to the river," but Garner and "the masters were surrounded by large numbers of their Kentucky friends . . . and there was great rejoicing among them, on account of their victory." What the Germans gained, Garner lost—or never had in the eyes of the American legal system. The psychological scars and legacy of such events, both personal and social, are more deeply explored in Toni Morrison's *Beloved*.[67]

Conclusion

T HE GROWTH OF NATIONAL citizenship and its importance as a legal
status occurred alongside the growth of the power of the national government in the early American republic. This expansion was not necessarily a top-down imposition, however: the growth of national citizenship did
not always proceed smoothly, as migrants themselves challenged laws they found
to be restrictive, and frustrated the enforcement of others, while offering alternative ways of constructing citizenship.

National crises were important points in the formation of national citizenship during this early period. The Alien and Sedition Acts laid a groundwork
for further national legislation pertaining to citizenship and naturalization. The
acts also pushed the United States in the direction of a nation-state and away
from a state that functioned as a decentralized republic or confederation. The
War of 1812 was the first test of the Alien Enemies Act, and it resulted in an
enormous growth of state power over foreign residents: compulsory registration,
the imposition of an internal passport system heretofore restricted to borderland
areas, and forced internal removal.

The War of 1812, like other periods of emergency, led to the growth of executive power. But this change was contingent on historical circumstances: Republicans did not trust the court system where too many Federalist judges could
impede Republican policies, so they relied on the executive instead. Pragmatism
also mattered; the orders were impossible to carry out without the cooperation
of local sheriffs and other government officials. The surveillance of aliens was
centralized through the collection of information, but achieved through the cooperation of local community surveillance of British subjects.

In addition, while periodic crises of nationality surfaced at discrete, brief
times, migrants of color faced a durable political climate that saw the idea of
citizenship for people of African descent as a continual threat. That hostility
would continue, if not grow, during the Jacksonian era.

Migrant agency and resistance gave shape to citizenship law in the early American republic. Policies, even when harsh and strictly enforced, were nonetheless
affected by migrants' resistance and attempts to influence the policymaking process. Non-citizen rights were not merely the result of what policymakers might

condescend to give them. Instead, these rights often were wrested from the grasp of hostile officials and Americans generally, especially in the case of race-based restrictions. For white migrants, even indentured servants, citizenship became easier to obtain, but it was part of a broader web of status and coincided with varying definitions of citizenship that persisted into the Jacksonian period.

During the War of 1812, migrants indirectly subverted the law of coverture when they challenged existing policies that considered American women who married British subjects to no longer be American citizens. They were successful in winning exemptions because of several factors relating to how elite marriages were viewed at the time: American-born women were transmitters of culture, able to persuade their husbands of their proper civic duties and able to act as the temporary public representative of their husbands in this instance of their legal disability. They further cemented their claims through their everyday face-to-face interactions with the community. When challenging official attempts to exclude and control them, they did not offer destabilizing radical claims, but rather presented themselves as pillars of community order and as members of the community. Their actions resulted in a victory for migrants in the face of harsh government measures such as forced internal removal. The relationship between head-of-household status and citizenship mattered not only for the wives of citizens but for those who labored for them, be they enslaved, indentured, or contractually obligated. Migrants in these situations found that the path to citizenship was difficult and challenging and its benefits sometimes elusive. Some foreign migrants chose to reject citizenship, preferring to cultivate personal support networks among people of color, while others chose to exert citizen rights or foreign citizen status.

National citizenship would continue to gain strength in the nineteenth century, despite the continuation of state and local citizenship into the antebellum period. Notable among the actions of the national government were the Passenger Act of 1819, which sought to limit pauper immigration while encouraging white migrants of somewhat better means, indirectly affecting the pool of potential citizens. This regulation of European immigration emerged simultaneously with the colonization movement, which aimed to remove free people of African descent from the borders of the United States. Similarly, the Supreme Court case of *Chirac v. Chirac* (1817) gave greater strength to national citizenship, even if *Spratt v. Spratt* (1830) kept state jurisdiction over naturalization. As other scholars have described, it was the period leading up to, during, and after the Civil War when citizenship gained truly national reach. The case of *Scott v. Sanford* (1857) attempted to reserve citizenship for whites and exclude people of African descent from citizenship at the national level. During Reconstruction, frustrated with white Southern intransigence, the Republican-led passage of the Fourteenth Amendment created a national citizenship: it defined who was a citizen, and prevented states from curtailing national citizens' rights. The Fifteenth Amendment specifically connected voting rights to citizens. Even so, full federal bureaucratic control over naturalization would not arrive until 1906, when Congress created a Bureau of Immigration and Naturalization and stated that only federal courts had control over naturalizations.[1]

The relationship between citizenship, public identity, and the household would continue to cause tension along the citizen/alien divide. The Fourteenth Amendment was not only a gain in rights for African Americans but a rejection of the paternalist view of slavery that recast its fundamentally exploitative nature as an ordered, hierarchical household. Similarly, the changes in the Alien Enemies Act during the First World War, which extended its provisions to women, reflected a change in the relationship between citizenship and the head of household. In acknowledging that women could act politically in a manner separate from their husbands, it weakened the association between citizenship and head-of-household status.[2]

MUCH HAS HAPPENED since I began writing this book. It began in graduate school as I became a graduate teaching assistant for a twentieth-century immigration course. My then-partner was in the United States on a student visa, and the American public and government seemed determined to never recognize our same-sex relationship. I began to look into the deep roots of immigration policy as I researched its origins in the early American republic and its definitions of family, citizenship, and membership in the nation, even as those definitions shifted in the first two decades of the present millennium. I completed my dissertation as Barack Obama was campaigning for re-election against the Republican challenger Mitt Romney. On the left, the original enthusiasm for Obama had dimmed somewhat: deportations continued, and the government was targeting people abroad in warfare, including US citizens.[3]

In the course of researching this book, it became clear that debates in the early 2010s over citizenship, and the understanding of citizenship and belonging, had roots in the events from the period after US independence, particularly the relationship between the household and citizenship. Both historically and into the present, the federal government has used naturalization as a tool to shape households, citizens, and the nation, while excluding those whose household arrangements did not conform to prevailing norms. Historically, migrants have challenged these strictures in a variety of ways, most notably the deployment of the concept of Republican Wifehood in the case of binational couples challenging their forced removal during the War of 1812. These couples used popular understandings of women's status along with the effect of their everyday integration into their communities to make successful claims to remain in their residences. Migrants in the twenty-first century still challenge normative views of households and have faced discrimination in naturalization when doing so. Some campaigns have been able to influence policies more effectively than others. Campaigns by same-sex couples to stop deportation and challenge the 1996 Defense of Marriage Act had some limited short-term success, and were able to mobilize a base of public support, even as many Americans viewed such couples as a danger to American society and heteronormativity. Following the *Obergefell v. Hodges* decision (2015), which compelled the federal government to recognize same-sex marriages, LGBTQ couples achieved formal equal footing with heterosexual couples, although LGBTQ couples and migrants still face challenges when dealing with the US immigration system. Other migrants have faced greater challenges in gaining public support, and some may not choose to operate in a manner intended to sway the broader American public.[4]

Migrants must still make claims in a normative fashion to experience success. For example, the DREAM Act, a cause that undocumented college-age migrants championed during the Obama presidency, grounded its claims of citizenship through normative ideas of who deserved to be a citizen: college graduates and those who have served in the armed forces. Like the migrants discussed in this book, Dreamers faced a dilemma; in order to engage with policymakers under pressure, they could either argue that they fit the normative criteria for citizens, or they could seek to change how citizenship and naturalization functioned. In this case, undocumented DREAM Act supporters did both. They sought to change the law by presenting themselves as good citizens, but at the same time engaged in acts of civil disobedience by pursuing goals and careers many US citizens take for granted. To be undocumented and publicly announce that status is itself an act of civil disobedience that calls attention to the freedom from deportation that US citizens gained in 1798 at the expense of noncitizens, as described in Chapter 1.[5]

Although this book has emphasized the concurrent growth of national citizenship and the centralized state, such changes should not necessarily be taken for granted. One case in point: in 2012, US Attorney General Eric Holder justified the targeted killing of US citizens abroad. This policy was a growth of state power, but one that removed a privilege of citizenship and placed citizens and aliens on an equal footing. In this case, neither has a right to trial, and either may be designated for targeted killing by the United States government. Additionally, that policy is a new power that has accrued to the federal government not at the expense of internal state or local governments, but at the expense of international institutions and foreign sovereign governments.[6]

The period and issues covered by this book also have troubling implications for this policy change. How much due process would there be? What precedents would be drawn upon? In explaining and justifying this policy, Holder differentiated between the issue of due process and the right to trial, a policy choice remarkably similar to the enforcement of the Alien Act described in Chapter 1, when Secretary of State Timothy Pickering oversaw the enforcement of alien deportations, which included a due process but no right to trial. He and President John Adams clashed over differing visions of how extensive the process should be. Adams was unwilling to provide blank warrants to Pickering, who wished to fill in the names himself. This incident highlights the issues of centralized power, authority, and decision-making that make such policies troubling to many US citizens and the wider public.[7]

AS I WRITE this conclusion, Donald Trump has been US president for nearly four years, having ridden a wave of xenophobia as part of his campaign for the presidency in 2016. I have since struggled to make sense of, interpret, and fully understand the historical roots of Trump-era xenophobia, its mindset and consequences. The rapid shifts in policy and contestations from a large and active protest movement mean that making effective predictions about even the short term are quite difficult, especially in light of the 2020 election. What policies will the administration attempt to roll out? How will Trump's Supreme Court appointments affect the interpretation of citizenship status and immigration law? And will they survive a challenge from supporters of immigrants in the public sphere? If Trump does not hold onto the presidency after 2020, what policies would a new administration keep in place?[8]

The Trump presidency has pursued policies that have targeted undocumented immigrants in the United States while also seeking to halt or diminish migration from certain countries or regions, notably through attempts to eliminate the global visa lottery and attacks on family reunification. Other historians have connected the current administration's policies to tactics intended to suppress Asian immigration in the late nineteenth and early twentieth centuries. This push attempted to limit families to a nuclear definition, and while nonwhite migrants were often subject to harsh enforcement, white migrants received tolerance and exemption.[9]

The Trump administration's policies and attitudes look back to one of the incidents at the beginning of this book: Benjamin Maingault's attempt to vote in 1807. Americans at the time saw his action as a threat that could corrupt the republic. In the eyes of white Americans, his family status was irregular; he appeared to be the son of a deceased white Dominguan refugee and an enslaved woman of African descent. The current administration and supporters of its immigration policy share a similar view: to grant immigrants and their descendants voting power so that they can sway elections is a threat to American national identity. Built into this view is a narrative that defines white racial status as pure and the presence of people of color as inherently corrupt, especially when they exercise political power or have a voice in civic matters. This is also described as immigrants "cutting in line" in front of "true Americans" who deserve more of a voice, power, and political access. Maingault confronted the same issues and problems that immigrants and their supporters face today.[10]

The current political climate has made clear the importance of activism in forming immigration and citizenship policy. For historians, broadly defined, this is a call to engage more broadly in writing, with the public, in the classroom, and as private individuals. Many of us are already doing this: of particular note is the creation of the #ImmigrationSyllabus, a resource put together by a number of historians of immigration, but I encourage you all to build civic engagement in your classes, to connect students with people in positions of power, and to engage with the public and the press. These are things that can help you professionally despite the initial time investment. They can raise your profile, get more students to think about taking your classes, and lead to invitations to submit publications or contribute to scholarship. At the same time, it is important to recognize that some face greater consequences for speaking out than others, and those consequences can be terrifying and severe for women, trans people, and people of color. Historians have other skills that are important for social movements: the ability find and research information, access and look through government records, compile information and create databases, apply for grants, and find local, national, and international contacts and to build ties with them. These activities require time and often money; once again, many of us face a variety of demands upon our time, and this can be the case particularly for women and people of color.[11]

For the broader public, let me emphasize the importance of sustaining the movement and building lasting connections. This book emphasizes the work that immigrants did in securing their status in the face of widespread hostility. This is also not always easy: many of the issues facing historians engaged in activism and public engagement also apply to activists. This work to change and historicize the understandings of immigration in the present is work that will likely require a long and sustained push by broad swaths of the public. I am sure we are up to the task.

But perhaps, dear readers, you want a plan. Here it is, put together by someone with much more direct experience than I have. First, do some reflective thinking: what are some things you want to change? What are some ways you might assist a broad social movement? Can you provide help, such as housing and meals? Are you in a place to advocate within institutions? Or maybe you are better positioned to organize outside the system? Perhaps your frustrations make you determined to speak out and act, even at risk to yourself. Reach out to others and draw up a plan: what are the pillars of support that uphold oppression, the actors and deciders who need to be engaged with? Work on an action, and feel free to join an existing campaign (reaching out to strangers is hard, I know!). Finally, victories are hard-won and hard-fought, but they have historically been the result of post-action deliberation and recalibration, the testing of tactics and strategies, and gearing up for new action. You will find Daniel Hunter's guide (noted at the end of this paragraph) to be an excellent resource as a guide to action.[12]

AT A TIME when an increasing number of people residing in the US are not citizens, and when US power continues to be projected beyond its borders, the issue of legal rights of citizens versus that of non-citizens is of great contemporary importance. Policymakers who seek to make and enforce laws and policies without considering how their actions affect those whom they act upon should take note. Readers, I urge you to engage and act, and have given you some tools and suggestions on how to do so. You have finished this book; put it down (or turn away from your screen), take up a notepad, and get started sketching out what you have decided to do.[13]

Introduction

1. *United States Gazette* (Philadelphia), April 15, 1807, 2; Marshals' Returns of Enemy Aliens and Prisoners of War, 1812–1815, National Archives Record Group 59: General Records of the Department of State, 1756–1999, microfilm publication M588: "War of 1812 Papers" of the Department of State 1789–1815; Kenneth Scott, comp., *British Aliens in the War of 1812* (Baltimore: Genealogical Publishing Company, 1979), 322; Notice of the Department of State, February 23, 1813; John Mason to Marshals of the United States, "Respecting Aliens," May 31, 1813, in *The Case of Alien Enemies, Considered and Decided Upon a Writ of Habeas Corpus, Allowed on the Petition of Charles Lockington, An Alien Enemy* (Philadelphia, 1813), appendix v–vi; James Mercer to John Minor, March 31, 1813, Letters Received Regarding Enemy Aliens, War of 1812 Papers, NARA Microfilm M588; Scott, *British Aliens in the United States*, 322, 384.

2. Karin Wulf, "Vast Early America: Three Simple Words for a Complex Reality," *Humanities* 40, no. 1 (Winter 2019).

3. William J. Novak, "The Myth of the 'Weak' American State," *American Historical Review* 113, no. 3 (2008): 752–772; Laura F. Edwards, *The People and Their Peace: Legal Culture and the Transformation of Inequality in the Post-Revolutionary South* (Chapel Hill: University of North Carolina Press, 2009); Douglas Bradburn, *The Citizenship Revolution: Politics and the Creation of the American Union, 1774–1804* (Charlottesville: University of Virginia Press, 2009.)

4. This book uses the term "Republican Party" to refer to the political party led by Thomas Jefferson that emerged in opposition to the Federalist Party in the 1790s. It is sometimes referred to as the Democratic-Republican Party, in part to distinguish it from the Republican Party that arose in the 1850s. The exclusion of nonwhite residents from citizenship extended beyond alien status, most notably in the denization of African Americans as well as continued exclusions for Native Americans. See Bradburn, *Citizenship Revolution*, 235–271, for a discussion of African American denization.

5. Those scholars who have attempted to challenge this top-down view have focused on foreign migrants as close allies of the Republican Party rather than as independent actors. Other scholars have described active migrant lobbying but have concentrated on the role of slaveholders fleeing the Haitian Revolution, and their attempts to retain power over the enslaved people they attempted to bring to the United States. Bradburn, *Citizenship Revolution;* Kenneth W. Keller, "Rural Politics and the Collapse of

Pennsylvania Federalism," *Transactions of the American Philosophical Society* 72, part 6 (1982); James H. Kettner, *The Development of American Citizenship, 1608–1870* (Chapel Hill: Published for the Omohundro Institute of Early American History and Culture, Williamsburg, Virginia, by the University of North Carolina Press, 1978); Rogers M. Smith, *Civic Ideals: Conflicting Visions of Citizenship in U.S. History* (New Haven, CT: Yale University Press, 1997); Ashli White, *Encountering Revolution: Haiti and the Making of the Early Republic* (Baltimore: Johns Hopkins University Press, 2010); Aristide Zolberg, *A Nation by Design: Immigration Policy in the Fashioning of America* (Cambridge, MA: Harvard University Press, 2006).

6. In particular, the role of ordinary people in state-building and the construction of citizenship is examined by Martha S. Jones, *Birthright Citizens: A History of Race and Rights in Antebellum America* (New York: Cambridge University Press, 2018); Novak, "Transformation of American Citizenship"; Kettner, *Development of American Citizenship*. Although I argue for and use an analysis that goes beyond liberalism, the scholar Patricia Williams has made clear the importance of rights for marginalized people in the legal system in *The Alchemy of Race and Rights: Diary of a Law Professor* (Cambridge, MA: Harvard University Press, 1991).

7. Saskia Sassen, "The Repositioning of Citizenship and Alienage: Emergent Subjects and Spaces for Politics," *Globalizations* 2 (2005): 79–94.

8. Karen Orren and Stephen Skowronek, *The Search for American Political Development* (Cambridge, UK: Cambridge University Press, 2004); Richard R. John, "American Political Development and Political History," in *The Oxford Handbook of American Political Development* (Oxford, UK: Oxford University Press, 2016); Anna O. Law, "Lunatics, Idiots, Paupers, and Negro Seamen—Immigration Federalism and the Early American State," *Studies in American Political Development* 28 (October 2014): 107–128.

9. Smith, *Civic Ideals*, 1–3, 44–45, 110; Kettner, *Development of American Citizenship*, 173–209, 213–214, 246–247; Marilyn C. Baseler, *"Asylum for Mankind": America, 1607–1800* (Ithaca, NY: Cornell University Press), 252–256; Gary Nash, *The Unknown American Revolution: The Unruly Birth of Democracy and the Struggle to Create America* (New York: Viking, 2005), 267; Orlando Patterson, *Slavery and Social Death: A Comparative Study* (Cambridge, MA: Harvard University Press, 1982), 38–45. Although Patterson does not specifically discuss modern Atlantic slavery of people of African descent, its legacy for people of African descent is further explored in Erna Brodber, "History and Social Death," *Caribbean Studies* 58, no. 4:111–115. There was an exception: enslaved people could be prosecuted for a crime. Attempts to fully expel enslaved people and people of African descent were complicated by government issuance of seamen's protection certificates stating that the bearer was an American citizen. These certificates are discussed in greater detail in Nathan Perl-Rosenthal, *Citizen Sailors: Becoming American in the Age of Revolution* (Cambridge, MA: Harvard University Press, 2015.)

10. John M. Murrin, "Fundamental Values, the Founding Fathers and the Constitution," in *To Form a More Perfect Union: The Critical Ideas of the Constitution*, ed. Herman Belz et al. (Charlottesville: Published for the United States Capitol Historical

Society by the University Press of Virginia, 1992), 1–37; John Gilbert McCurdy, *Citizen Bachelors: Manhood and the Creation of the United States* (Ithaca, NY: Cornell University Press, 2009). Gilbert also notes that adult white male sons without a household of their own were nonetheless able to exert full citizenship.

11. Holly Brewer, "The Transformation of Domestic Law," in *The Cambridge History of Law in America*, ed. Michael Grossberg and Christopher Tomlins (New York: Cambridge University Press, 2008), vol. 1, 288–323; Rosemarie Zagarri, *Revolutionary Backlash: Women and Politics in the Early American Republic* (Philadelphia: University of Pennsylvania Press, 2007); Rosemarie Zagarri, "Morals, Manners, and the Republican Mother," *American Quarterly* 44, no. 2 (June 1992); Barbara J. Todd, "Written in Her Heart: Married Women's Separate Allegiance in English Law," in *Married Women and the Law: Coverture in England and the Common Law World*, ed. Tim Stretton and Krista J. Kesselring (Montreal: McGill-Queen's University Press, 2013), 163–191; Laurel Thatcher Ulrich, *Good Wives: Image and Reality in the Lives of Women in Northern New England 1650–1750* (New York: Knopf, 1982) 39–43.

12. Smith, *Civic Ideals*, 110–113, 185–186; Todd, "Written in Her Heart," 163–191; Linda K. Kerber, "The Republican Mother: Women and the Enlightenment—An American Perspective," *American Quarterly* 28 (1976): 187–205, 202. Jan Lewis has noted the limits of wives' persuasive, political, and legal power in "The Republican Wife: Virtue and Seduction in the Early Republic," *William and Mary Quarterly* 44 (1987): 689–721; Susan Lee Branson, *These Fiery Frenchified Dames: Women and Political Culture in Early National Philadelphia* (Philadelphia: University of Pennsylvania Press, 2001), 1; Rebecca J. Scott, *Freedom Papers: An Atlantic Odyssey in the Age of Emancipation* (Cambridge, MA: Harvard University Press, 2012).

13. Smith, *Civic Ideals*, 2–4; Douglas R. Egerton, *The Atlantic World: A History, 1400–1888* (Wheeling, IL: Harlan Davidson, 2007), 361–389; Rachel Hope Cleves, *The Reign of Terror in America: Visions of Violence from Anti-Jacobinism to Antislavery* (New York: Cambridge University Press, 2009) 62–65, 73; James Morton Smith, *Freedom's Fetters: The Alien and Sedition Laws and American Civil Liberties* (Ithaca, NY: Cornell University Press, 1956); Laurent Dubois, *Avengers of the New World: The Story of the Haitian Revolution* (Cambridge, MA: Harvard University Press, 2004), 300; White, *Encountering Revolution*, 171–173; Pauline Maier, "Popular Uprisings and Civil Authority in Eighteenth-Century America," *William and Mary Quarterly* 27, no.1: 4–35 (1970); McCurdy, *Citizen Bachelors*; Murrin, "Fundamental Values."

14. John Bodnar, *The Transplanted: A History of Immigrants in Urban America* (Bloomington: Indiana University Press, 1987), 52–54. For more in-depth discussion of specific groups and their attitudes, see Michael Durey, *Transatlantic Radicals and the Early American Republic* (Lawrence: University Press of Kansas, 1997); Doina Pasca Harsanyi, *Lessons from America: Liberal French Nobles in Exile, 1793–1798* (University Park: Pennsylvania State University Press, 2010); Kerby A. Miller, *Emigrants and Exiles: Ireland and the Irish Exodus to North America* (New York: Oxford University Press, 1985); Ashli White, "The Politics of the 'French Negroes' in the United States," *Historical Reflections* 29, no. 1 (Spring 2003): 103–121; White, *Encountering Revolution*.

15. Articles of Confederation, article 4, section 1; *US Statutes at Large*, I, 4 (1845); Kettner, *Development of American Citizenship*, 219–22. Smith, *Civic Ideals*, 162, has noted that residents of the Northwest Territory were citizens of the United States rather than a particular state. Smith cautions that this citizenship was not uncontested in the 1790s. The Federalist governor Arthur St. Clair felt that the white inhabitants of the Northwest Territory, both Anglo whites and French inhabitants of longer standing, should be considered not citizens but subjects of the United States, owing to their lack of gentility and Republican voting sympathies.

16. US Constitution, article 1, section 8, clause 4. *US Statutes at Large*, I, 13, 103; Baseler, *"Asylum for Mankind,"* 255–260; Kettner, *Development of American Citizenship*, 235–239, 250–251.

17. The year 1795 in fact began with a proclamation from George Washington, instructing thanksgiving and prayer to "render this country more and more a safe and propitious asylum for the unfortunate of other countries" in addition to other safeguards of peace, prosperity, and republican virtue. The inclusion of the statement supporting the United States as an asylum was drafted by Alexander Hamilton, who insisted that it remain over Edmund Randolph's objections. Presidential Proclamation, January 1, 1795, https://founders.archives.gov/documents/Washington/05-17-02-0239; Baseler, *"Asylum for Mankind,"* 251–252; Smith, *Civic Ideals*, 138–140.

18. Baseler, *"Asylum for Mankind,"* 260–266; Smith, *Freedom's Fetters*, 22–23.

19. Kettner, *Development of American Citizenship*, 243–245; *US Statutes at Large*, I, 566–572, 577–578, 596–597. The Alien Enemies Act did not come into force during the quasi-war with France, which ended in 1800, because it was undeclared.

20. Baseler, *"Asylum for Mankind,"* 313–315, 21; Bradburn, *Citizenship Revolution*, 285–286; D. M. Dewey, *Naturalization Laws of the United States: Containing also the Alien Laws of the State of New York: A Synopsis of the Alien Laws of Other States, with the Forms for Naturalizing Aliens, Important Decisions, General Remarks, &c., &c., &c.* (Rochester, NY, 1855) 34–35, 37.

21. Zolberg, *Nation by Design*, 33–37, 63. For an extensive study of migration from the British Isles immediately preceding the American Revolution, see Bernard Bailyn, *Voyagers to the West: A Passage in the Peopling of America on the Eve of the Revolution* (New York: Knopf, 1986). See also Aaron Fogleman, *Hopeful Journeys: German Immigration, Settlement, and Political Culture in Colonial America, 1717–1775* (Philadelphia: University of Pennsylvania Press, 1996), 7; Farley Grubb, *German Immigration and Servitude, 1709–1920* (New York: Routledge, 2011), 172; Farley Grubb, *German Immigrant Servant Contracts, Registered at the Port of Philadelphia, 1817–1831* (Baltimore: Clearfield, 2013), iii–x.

22. Baseler, *"Asylum for Mankind,"* 140–142; Ken Miller, *Dangerous Guests: Enemy Captives and Revolutionary Communities during the War for Independence* (Ithaca, NY: Cornell University Press), 96–98; Zolberg, *Nation by Design*, 63.

23. Kerby A. Miller et al., *Irish Immigrants in the Land of Canaan: Letters and Memoirs from Colonial and Revolutionary America, 1675–1815* (New York: Oxford University Press, 2003), 193–198; Grubb, *German Immigration and Servitude*, 7–9, 160–161, 172.

24. Baseler, *"Asylum for Mankind,"* 166–171; Zolberg, *Nation by Design*, 102–105; Herbert Heaton, "The Industrial Immigrant in the United States, 1783–1812," *Proceedings of the American Philosophical Society* 95, no. 5 (1951): 519–527, 524–525.

25. Paul F. Lachance, "The 1809 Immigration of Saint-Domingue Refugees to New Orleans: Reception, Integration and Impact," *Louisiana History: The Journal of the Louisiana Historical Association* 29, no. 2 (1988): 109–141, 111; White, *Encountering Revolution*; Ashli White, email message to author, November 2, 2011.

26. R. L. Brunhouse, "Lascars in Pennsylvania: A Side-Light on the China trade," *Pennsylvania History* 7, no. 1 (1940): 20–30; E. W. Dwight, *Memoirs of Henry Obookiah: A Native of Owhyhee, and a Member of the Foreign Mission School* (Philadelphia, 1830); *A Narrative of Five Youth from the Sandwich Islands: Now Receiving an Education in this Country* (New York, 1816). The history of the Foreign Mission School itself has been more recently discussed in John Demos, *The Heathen School: A Story of Hope and Betrayal in the Age of the Early Republic* (New York: Knopf, 2014.)

27. US Law Code, title 50, chapter 3, paragraph 21; US Constitution, article 2, section 1, clause 4.

Chapter 1

Epigraph: National Archives Record Group 21 (Records of District Courts of the United States, 1685–1991): Landing Reports of Aliens, 1798–1828. U.S. District Court for Eastern Pennsylvania, Volume I. Digitized and available through the National Archives and Records Administration Archival Research Catalog: https://catalog.archives.gov/id/279083 . Last accessed January 24, 2008. Report No. 161, Marie Dominique Jacques D'Orlic and Marie Laurence Carrere D'Orlic, 14 January 1799.

1. Médéric-Louis-Élie Moreau de Saint-Méry, Kenneth Lewis Roberts, Anna M. Roberts, and Stewart L. Mims, *Moreau de St. Méry's American Journey [1793–1798]* (Garden City, NY: Doubleday, 1947), 253.

2. *Statutes at Large of the United States* I (1845), 570–572; US Department of State, Passport Letters, October 27, 1795, Domestic Letters, X, 422–423, XI, 11, 61–63; Frances Sergeant Childs, *French Refugee Life in the United States, 1790–1800: An American Chapter of the French Revolution* (Baltimore: Johns Hopkins University Press, 1940), 189–191. A chart of the ships receiving passage to carry French citizens under flag of truce appears on page 191. Pickering's abstract counts fifteen, to which can be added at least one more ship, the *Benjamin Franklin*, master Lloyd Jones and owner Francis Breuil, both listed as American citizens. Pickering wrote, "If an American vessel is fairly designed to deport French citizens according to the [presumably Alien Enemies] act, as many passengers will be engaged as she can conveniently carry." Pickering to G. Latimer, July 14, 1798, quoted in Childs, 190n6. Here Pickering has clearly organized passage and secured safe transport during the undeclared quasi-war with France, and is anticipating, like many Federalists, an officially declared war that will trigger the appropriate provisions in the Alien Enemies Act, *US Statues at Large*, I, 577–578.

3. William J. Novak, "The Legal Transformation of Citizenship in Nineteenth-Century America," in The Democratic Experiment: New Directions in American Political History, ed. Meg Jacob, William J. Novak, and Julian E. Zelizer (Princeton, NJ: Princeton University Press, 2003), 85–119, 97, 109; Douglas Bradburn, The Citizenship Revolution: Politics and the Creation of the American Union, 1774–1804 (Charlottesville: University of Virginia Press, 2009), 140, 163, 171–172, 334; Rogers M. Smith, Civic Ideals: Conflicting Visions of Citizenship in U.S. History (New Haven, CT: Yale University Press, 1997), 137–164.

4. Smith, *Civic Ideals*, 137–164; Renato Rosaldo, "Cultural Citizenship and Educational Democracy," *Cultural Anthropology* 9, no. 3 (1994): 402–411.

5. Novak, "Legal Transformation of Citizenship," 85–119; Bradburn, *Citizenship Revolution*, 140–148.

6. Migrants of color or African ancestry also engaged in these activities, though as a means of overcoming the racial discrimination that was aimed at them. Their struggles are detailed in Chapter 5.

7. Novak, "Legal Transformation of Citizenship," 86–89; Bradburn, *Citizenship Revolution*, 192, discusses the state-centered citizenship that Republicans presented as a counter to Federalists' national citizenship. Douglas Bradburn, "'True Americans' and 'Hordes of Foreigners': Nationalism, Ethnicity and the Problem of Citizenship in the United States, 1789–1800," *Historical Reflections* 29 (2003): 19–41, 22–23, discusses Irish migrants' argument that they had a right to engage in their own different forms of organized political activity such as political meetings after Catholic mass. See also Smith, *Civic Ideals*, 153–154, 163–164.

8. Marilyn C. Baseler, *"Asylum for Mankind": America, 1607–1800* (Ithaca, NY: Cornell University Press), 271–273. The provisions of the acts are spelled out in *US Statutes at Large*, I, 566–572, 577–578, 596–597.

9. *Oxford English Dictionary Online*, s.v. "nativism," http://www.oed.com/.

10. Ashli White, *Encountering Revolution: Haiti and the Making of the Early Republic* (Baltimore: Johns Hopkins University Press, 2010), 57–59; Rachel Hope Cleves, *The Reign of Terror in America: Visions of Violence From Anti-Jacobinism to Antislavery* (New York: Cambridge University Press, 2009), 5–8, 28–30, 59–66; Bradburn, *Citizenship Revolution*, 155.

11. Cleves, *Reign of Terror in America*, 62–65, 73; William Cobbett (as Peter Porcupine), "History of the American Jacobins," in William Cobbett, *Peter Porcupine in America: Pamphlets on Republicanism and Revolution,* ed. David A. Wilson (Ithaca, NY: Cornell University Press, 1994), 200; "[Advertisement] Curiosités en Cire," *Philadelphia Aurora General Advertiser*, March 5, 1794.

12. *Gazette of the United States*, June 11, 1798.

13. *New York Daily Advertiser*, June 30, 1798. Reprinted from *Porcupine's Gazzette*.

14. Reprinted in the *New York Daily Advertiser*, June 30, 1798, 3; *New-Hampshire Gazette*, September 25, 1798; *Gazette of the United States*, November 12, 1798. An account of the prosecution of the *Croyable* for privateering appears in the *New York Commercial Advertiser*, July 25, 1798, 2.

15. *Portland Gazette*, July 30, 1798; *Charleston Evening Courier*, August 10. 1798; *Readinger Adler*, July 1, 1798; *Gazette Française*, July 25, 1798; *Claypoole's American Daily Advertiser*, August 15, 1798, 3. The story followed the aftermath as well; the Republican-leaning New York *Argus* noted that M. Gardie was buried in the potters' field, while Mme Gardie was "respectfully interred... in the Catholic burial ground," as reprinted in the *Connecticut Courant*, July 30, 1798.

16. *Porcupine's Gazette*, July 23, 1798; Brattleboro, Vermont *Federal Galaxy*, August 7, 1798.

17. *Porcupine's Gazette*, July 23, 1798; Concord, New Hampshire *Mirror*, February 18, 1798.

18. *Porcupine's Gazette*, July 23, 1798; Susan Branson, *These Fiery Frenchified Dames: Women and Political Culture in Early National Philadelphia* (Philadelphia: University of Pennsylvania Press, 2001), 73; Francis Grose, *1811 Dictionary of the Vulgar Tongue: A Dictionary of Buckish Slang, University Wit, and Pickpocket Eloquence* (Northfield, IL: Digest Books, 1971).

19. Stockbridge, Massachusetts *Western Star*, June 18, 1798, reprinted in the *Baltimore Federal Gazette,* June 29, 1798.

20. *Gazette of the United States*, July 23, 1798. The *Aurora General Advertiser*, July 21, 1798, reported more sympathetically about the Frenchman in question, noting that he had served in the Revolutionary War and "maintained the reputation of a peaceable and quiet citizen" in Philadelphia. *Moreau de St. Méry's American Journey*, 253.

21. Baseler, *"Asylum for Mankind,"* 271–272.

22. *US Statutes at Large*, I, 566–572, 577–578, 596–597.

23. James Morton Smith, *Freedom's Fetters: The Alien and Sedition Laws and American Civil Liberties* (Ithaca, NY: Cornell University Press, 1956), 7–10, 21, 25; Adams to Congress, April 3, 1798, in John Adams, *The Works of John Adams, Second President of the United States: With a Life of the Author* (Boston, 1850), IX, 158; 8 *Annals of Congress*, 1427.

24. 8 *Annals of Congress*, 1566–1567. Rather than dreaming up legislation on the spot, the committee saw the 1793 British Aliens Act as a model. It also contained provisions allowing the national government to deport aliens and keep records of their entry into British territory. 33 Geo. 3, ch. 4 (1793).

25. *US Statutes at Large*, I, 566–572.

26. 8 *Annals of Congress*, 1453–1454, 1574. The French passengers bill is discussed in greater depth later in this chapter.

27. 8 *Annals of Congress*, 1568–1572. Otis argued that the naturalization clause of the Constitution granted Congress the authority to distinguish between naturalized citizens and native citizens. Abraham Venable of Virginia and Nathaniel Macon of Georgia countered that this would require an amendment specifically making those distinctions in officeholding. If the Constitution said that a citizen could hold an office, any kind of citizen was eligible unless otherwise specified. See also Smith, *Freedom's Fetters*, 27–29.

28. "Albert Gallatin," in *Biographical Directory of the United States Congress*, United States Congress, http://bioguide.congress.gov/scripts/biodisplay.pl?index=G000020.

29. 8 *Annals of Congress*, 1568–1573, 1776–1779; Smith, *Freedom's Fetters*, 29–31.

30. *US Statutes at Large*, I, 570–572.

31. Joan R. Gundersen, *To Be Useful to the World: Women in Revolutionary America, 1740–1790* (New York: Twayne, 2006), 150–151; Josiah Henry Benton, *Warning Out in New England* (Boston: W. B. Clarke, 1911), 114–116; Ruth Wallis Herndon, *Unwelcome Americans: Living on the Margin in Early New England* (Philadelphia: University of Pennsylvania Press, 2001), 11–13. Herndon notes that by the 1780s and 1790s, warning out was declining in New England. See also Baseler, *"Asylum for Mankind,"* 197–198, 289–290; Ashli White, "The Politics of the 'French Negroes' in the United States," *Historical Reflections* 29 (2003): 103–121, 110; Thomas Mifflin to John Adams, June 27, 1798, in *Philadelphia Gazette*, June 28, 1798.

32. Smith, *Freedom's Fetters*, 159–160, 163–166; George W. Kyte, "A Spy on the Western Waters: The Military Intelligence Mission of General Collot in 1796," *Mississippi Valley Historical Review* 34, no. 3 (1947), 427–442; Moreau de Saint Méry, *American Journey*, 253; Thomas Jefferson to James Madison, April 26 and May 21, 1798, *The Papers of Thomas Jefferson*, ed. Barbara B. Oberg et al. (Princeton, NJ: Princeton University Press, 2003), vol. 30, 299–302, 360–362.

33. Smith, *Freedom's Fetters*, 166; Timothy Pickering to John Adams, October 11, 1798, Timothy Pickering Papers, IX, 453, Massachusetts Historical Society; Adams to Pickering, October 17, 1798, Pickering Papers, XXIII, 241.

34. Pickering to Adams, August 1, 1799, Pickering Papers, XI, 525, quoted in Smith, *Freedom's Fetters*, 166–167. Jefferson to Madison, May 3 and 21, 1798, *Papers of Thomas Jefferson*, vol. 30, 322–324, 360–362.

35. John Adams to Timothy Pickering, October 16, 1798, in *Life and Works of John Adams*, VIII (Boston, 1853); Smith, *Freedom's Fetters*, 162–169; George W. Kyte, "The Detention of General Collot: A Sidelight on Anglo-American Relations, 1798–1800," *William and Mary Quarterly* 6 (1949): 628–630.

36. Smith, *Freedom's Fetters*, 159–161; Childs, *French Refugee Life*, 189–191; Jefferson to Madison, May 3 and 21, 1798, *Papers of Thomas Jefferson*, vol. 30, 322–324, 360–362; US Department of State, Passport Letters, October 27, 1795, Domestic Letters, X, 422–423, XI, 11, 61–63; Childs, *French Refugee Life in the United States,* 189–191.

37. Bradburn, *Citizenship Revolution*, 140, 334.

38. *US Statutes at Large*, I, 103–104, 566–569, 570–572. Like other federal naturalization laws that Congress passed in the 1790s, the new law followed earlier gradualist views about how foreign migrants should be incorporated into citizenship—meaning that aliens would increasingly acquire the rights of citizens over time. The provisions of the Naturalization Act of 1798 lengthened the naturalization requirements for citizenship to fourteen years, but did not exclude any migrants beyond the racial restrictions already instituted in the Naturalization Act of 1790. In addition to the compulsory registration provisions in the Naturalization Act of 1798, the Alien Act also contained provisions to gather information on aliens coming into the United States through its ports. Smith, *Freedom's Fetters*, 34. For a discussion of Federalists' national vision for citizenship, see Bradburn, *Citizenship Revolution*, 140.

39. Jefferson to Madison, April 26, 1798, *Papers of Thomas Jefferson*, vol. 30, 299–302; Moreau de Saint Méry, *American Journey*, xviii–xix, 251, 253. Childs, *French Refugees*, 34.

40. Thomas Jefferson wrote that the original bill in the Senate was "worthy of the 8th or 9th century" but the House was "preparing a reasonable one." Several weeks later, Jefferson saw the House bill as "rather worse" but hoped that "it will perhaps be a little softened." Jefferson to Thomas Mann Randolph, May 9 and 24, 1798, *Papers of Thomas Jefferson*, vol. 30, 341–342, 365–366. In contrast, Albert Gallatin stated in the House debates that he had no objections to a "well-defined enemies bill," although this may have been political posturing. See also Smith, *Freedom's Fetters*, 35, 48–49; *US Statutes at Large*, I 577–578; US Law Code, title 50, chapter 3, paragraph 21. The only significant change in the law came in 1918, when its provisions were specifically extended to women. For discussion of alien enemies during the War of 1812, see Chapter 4.

41. Laurent Dubois, *Avengers of the New World: The Story of the Haitian Revolution* (Cambridge, MA: Belknap Press of Harvard University Press, 2004), 197–198; 8 *Annals of Congress*, 2063–2067.

42. *Chambersburg Farmer's Register*, July 4, 1798; Thomas Mifflin to John Adams, June 27, 1798, in *Philadelphia Gazette*, June 28, 1798. See also 7 *Annals of Congress*, 592–593, and Baseler, "*Asylum for Mankind*," 289–290.

43. 7 *Annals of Congress*, 592–594 (1851). Some changes were made in the bill prior to passage in the Senate. The Senate even rejected a motion, 17–3, to clarify that the law would not apply to the slave trade. Similarly, the Senate rejected an amendment excepting women and "children under the age of twelve years. . . in cases specially authorized by the President." The Senate also struck out a preamble blaming France and French migrants for abusing American "hospitality and protection" and rejected on a tie vote a preamble more specifically citing the evacuation of Port-au-Prince. The Senate then passed the bill, leaving it to be taken up in the House.

44. 8 *Annals of Congress*, 2064.

45. 8 *Annals of Congress*, 2064–2065.

46. 8 *Annals of Congress*, 2065–2067.

47. Bradburn, *Citizenship Revolution*, 171–172, 288.

48. Dubois, *Avengers of the New World*, 226–227, 251. Childs, in *French Refugees*, 189, notes that the early returned migrant Talleyrand, now the Directory's foreign minister, was key in assisting prominent émigrés in returning to France.

49. Childs, *French Refugees*, 189–190. Moreau de Saint Méry, *American Journey*, 253; Smith, *Freedom's Fetters*, 160.

50. National Archives Record Group 21 (Records of District Courts of the United States, 1685–1991): Landing Reports of Aliens, 1798–1828. US District Court for Eastern Pennsylvania, Volume I, has been digitized, and is available through the National Archives and Records Administration Archival Research Catalog: https://catalog.archives.gov/id/279083 (hereafter referred to collectively as Landing Reports of Aliens, and individually by landing report number). Other records of landing reports exist, but they do not necessarily list alien residents and may instead focus on new arrivals: see "Register of White Persons Being Aliens Who Have Come to Reside in the Territory of

the United States," October 1799–January 1, 1800, Collector of Customs, City Point, Virginia, and loose reports made to the clerk of the US District Court for the District of Virginia, June 1798–September 1799 in US District Court, District of Virginia, Ended cases 1799, Virginia State Library, Richmond, Virginia; "Records of Primary Declarations," vol. A, 1798–1845, US District Court for the District of Massachusetts, RG 21, National Archives and Record Center, Waltham, Massachusetts. The first seven pages of this volume constitute an alien register for July 23, 1798, through October 1799, with a notation after a January 12, 1799 entry, "Transcript sent to the Secretary of State to this date." Noted in Baseler, *"Asylum for Mankind,"* 308–309. Some migrants among the Philadelphia returns were either under British protection or naturalized British subjects, despite birth in France or Saint-Domingue; however, persons born in the British Empire do not appear until 1801.

51. Moreau de Saint Méry, *American Journey*, 253.

52. Baseler, *"Asylum for Mankind,"* 308–309; *US Statutes at Large*, I, 566–572. See also earlier note on landing reports.

53. Landing Reports of Aliens; Baseler, *"Asylum for Mankind,"* 308–309.

54. *New York Daily Advertiser*, June 30, 1798.

55. Hannah Cushing to Abigail Adams, October 8, 1798, in *The Documentary History of the Supreme Court of the United States, 1789–1800,* ed. Maeva Marcus and James R. Perry (New York: Columbia University Press, 1985), vol. 3, 296–299. See also Smith, *Freedom's Fetters*, 270–274.

56. Hannah Cushing to Abigail Adams, October 8, 1798, in Mark Edward Lender, *"This Honorable Court": The United States District Court for the District of New Jersey, 1789–2000* (New Brunswick, NJ: Rutgers University Press, 2006), 55–56. See also Smith, *Freedom's Fetters*, 270–274; *Aurora General Advertiser*, October 12, 1799; Newark *Centinel of Freedom*, November 6, 1798, October 8, 1799.

57. The following examples are taken from the Alien Landing Reports. Early registrants in particular were likely to give lengthier explanations.

58. Cap-Français, also spelled Cap-François, was also referred to as Le Cap. Report No. 1, Jacques Julien Robert Malenfant, June 24, 1798; Report No. 24, Francis (François) Mery, December 13, 1798; Report No. 146, Charles Collet, December 19, 1798.

59. Report No. 3, Joseph Marie Thomas, Jeanne Felicité Faugere Labarte Thomas, Jean Baptiste Labarte, and Pierre Hiacinthe Labarte, July 3, 1798. See also No. 137, December 18, 1798, Joseph Marie Thomas, in which Thomas identified his family as subjects of the king of France, excepting one stepson who had naturalized. Report No. 7, Lewis Francis (Louis-François) Morin Duval, November 28, 1798; Report No. 124, Jean Lefeve, December 15, 1798; Report No. 136, Etienne Paris, Pierre Nauze, and Louis Neau, December 15, 1798.

60. Report No. 161, Marie Dominique Jacques D'Orlic and Marie Laurence Carrere D'Orlic, January 14, 1799.

61. The wives of French citizens were legally French citizens regardless of the place of their birth under the common law tradition of coverture. Report No. 76, Louis Duvivier, December 17, 1798; Report No. 113, Joseph Aubaye, December 18, 1798; Report

No. 145, Petter Joubert, December 18 ,1798; Report No. 144, Lewis (Louis) Deseuret, December 18, 1798. Refer to Chapter 3 for a discussion of binational couples during the War of 1812, which also examines coverture in more detail.

62. Report No. 91, Francis (François) Rosset, December 17, 1798; Report No. 139, Jean Baptiste Lamdry, December 18, 1798; Report No. 44, Andrew Vanderherchen, December 14, 1798; Report No. 129, Jean Baptiste Thiry, December 18, 1798; Report No. 134, Henry (Henri) Roberjot, December 18, 1798.

63. Report No. 4, Charles Colbert, July 15 ,1798; Report No. 83, Thomas Badaraque, December 17, 1798; Report No. 76, Louis Duvivier, December 17, 1798.

64. Baseler, *"Asylum for Mankind,"* 303–305. Baseler's work is an investigation of the concept of asylum in the United States, and this phrase is taken from the title of her book.

65. Thomas Mifflin to John Adams, June 27, 1798, in *Philadelphia Gazette*, June 28, 1798; "Reply of the French Royalists," *Philadelphia Gazette*, July 2, 1798, 2.

66. "Reply of the French Royalists," *Philadelphia Gazette*, July 2, 1798, 2.

67. "Reply of the French Royalists," *Philadelphia Gazette*, July 2, 1798, 2.

68. "Reply of the French Royalists," *Philadelphia Gazette*, July 2, 1798, 2; *8 Annals of Congress*, 2065–2066.

69. These merchants were associated with the organization of French passengers returning to France, Saint-Domingue, and other Caribbean colonies. See Childs, *French Refugees*, 189–190.

Chapter 2

Epigraph: Letter of John Shaw to Robert Tennant, 10 December 1801, D1748/C/1/184/5, Tennent Papers, Public Record Office of Northern Ireland (PRONI.)

1. John Daly Burk, "Address to the Public," Boston *Polar Star*, October 6, 1796. Italics original.

2. Timothy Pickering to Richard Harison, July 7, 1798, Pickering Papers XXXVII, 315, Massachusetts Historical Society, in James Morton Smith, *Freedom's Fetters: The Alien and Sedition Laws and American Civil Liberties* (Ithaca, NY: Cornell University Press, 1956), 210–211. The statement that specifically incensed Pickering and New York's Federalist district attorney was Burk's accusation that President John Adams had altered a dispatch by the US diplomat Elbridge Gerry for partisan ends prior to its being passed to Congress, or in Burk's words, "a F— adapted to promote certain ends in this country." *New York Time Piece* 2 July 1798.

3. James H. Kettner, *The Development of American Citizenship, 1608–1870* (Chapel Hill: Published for the Omohundro Institute of Early American History and Culture, Williamsburg, Virginia, by the University of North Carolina Press, 1978), 239–247; Rogers M. Smith, *Civic Ideals: Conflicting Visions of Citizenship in U.S. History* (New Haven, CT: Yale University Press, 1997), 164, 190–192; Douglas Bradburn, *The Citizenship Revolution: Politics and the Creation of the American Union, 1774–1804* (Charlottesville: University of Virginia Press, 2009), 2–3, 206–209; Smith, *Freedom's Fetters*,

135–149; Jeffrey L. Pasley, *"The Tyranny of Printers": Newspaper Politics in the Early American Republic* (Charlottesville: University Press of Virginia, 2001), 118–124.

This chapter discusses freedom of speech *through* the press. When discussing individuals, I use the term "free speech," and more generally, when discussing the Sedition Act, I use "freedom of the press." As demonstrated in the case of Luther Baldwin and Lespinard Colie, addressed in the previous chapter, persons were prosecuted for spoken seditious utterances as well as written or printed seditious libels.

4. Marilyn C. Baseler, *"Asylum for Mankind": America, 1607–1800* (Ithaca, NY: Cornell University Press), 295–300. Baseler notes a rise correlating with the escalation of partisan politics in the 1790s, but even so, numbers remained comparatively small in relation to mid-nineteenth century political machines' use of immigrant votes.

5. John M. Murrin, "Fundamental Values, the Founding Fathers, and the Constitution," in *To Form a More Perfect Union: The Critical Ideas of the Constitution,* ed. Herman Belz et al. (Charlottesville: University Press of Virginia,1992), 11–21; Valentin Groebner, *Who Are You?: Identification, Deception, and Surveillance in Early Modern Europe,* trans. John Peck and Mark Kyburz (New York: Zone Books, 2007), 193; Bernhard Siegert, "Pasajeros a Indias. Biographical Writing between the Old World and the New," in *Talleres de la memoria—Reivindicaciones y autoridad en la historiografía indiana de los siglos XVI y XVII,* ed. Robert Folger, Wulf Oesterreicher, and Roland Schmidt-Riese (Hamburg: Lit, 2005), 295–306; Benedict Anderson, *Imagined Communities: Reflections on the Origin and Spread of Nationalism* (London: Verso, 1983).

6. National Archives Record Group 21 (Records of District Courts of the United States, 1685–1991): Landing Reports of Aliens, 1798–1828, US District Court for Eastern Pennsylvania, vol. 1. Digitized and available through National Archives and Records Administration Archival Research Catalog: https://catalog.archives.gov/id/279083; Marshals' Returns of Enemy Aliens and Prisoners of War, 1812–1815, National Archives Record Group Record Group 59: General Records of the Department of State, 1756–1999, microfilm publication M588: "War of 1812 Papers" of the Department of State, 1789–1815.

7. Charles Campbell, ed., *Some Materials to Serve for a Brief Memoir of John Daly Burk,* (Albany, NY, 1868), 43–44; Michael Durey, *Transatlantic Radicals and the Early American Republic* (Lawrence: University Press of Kansas, 1997) 114.

8. Joseph I. Shulim, "John Daly Burk: Irish Revolutionist and American Patriot," *Transactions of the American Philosophical Society* 54, no. 6: 1964, 5–6.

9. Michael Durey, *"With the Hammer of Truth": James Thomson Callender and America's Early National Heroes* (Charlottesville: University Press of Virginia, 1990), 1–4, 18.

10. Durey, *"With the Hammer of Truth,"* 9–17.

11. Durey, 4–5, 22–26.

12. Durey, 37–43.

13. Durey, 43–44.

14. Dumas Malone, *The Public Life of Thomas Cooper, 1783–1839* (New Haven, CT: Yale University Press, 1926), 4–10.

15. Malone, *Life of Thomas Cooper,* 13, 20–26.

16. Malone, *Life of Thomas Cooper*, 34–40; Rachel Hope Cleves, *The Reign of Terror in America: Visions of Violence From Anti-Jacobinism to Antislavery* (New York: Cambridge University Press, 2009), 62–65, 73.

17. Malone, *Life of Thomas Cooper*, 49–53.

18. Malone, 67–70. Walker "was accused of unlawfully trying to overthrow the constitution and government of the kingdom and of speaking seditious words against the king."

19. Malone, 75–82, 87–90.

20. Otis and Harper advocated birthright citizenship during debates over the Naturalization Act of 1798, 8 *Annals of Congress*, 1566–1568; Craik, 1779; Williams, 1781–1782 (1851). See also Smith, *Freedom's Fetters*, 27, and Baseler, *"Asylum for Mankind,"* 273–276; Otis also refused to acknowledge the possibility that citizens or subjects of foreign states might naturalize into citizens of other such states, as described in the previous chapter's discussion of debates over the French Passengers Bill. Otis argued that white refugees from the Haitian Revolution who had sided with British forces and become naturalized British subjects were still French.

21. Pasley, *"Tyranny of Printers,"* 120–124. Pasley also argues that moderate Federalists were concerned about the practical erosion of their power by an unruly electorate, contrasting with the extremist fears voiced by John Allen of Connecticut.

22. Ray Boston, "The Impact of 'Foreign Liars' on the American Press (1790–1800)," *Journalism Quarterly* 50 (1973): 722–730, 724–726. Boston further argued that the new style allowed editors greater independence because they were able to cultivate a readership.

23. Cleves, *Reign of Terror*, 89–90. Federalist views, particularly Congressman John Allen's orations on the floor of Congress in support of the Sedition Act, are discussed later in this chapter; see also 8 *Annals of Congress*, 2095–2099.

24. These migrants are discussed most extensively in Durey, *Transatlantic Radicals*.

25. Jürgen Habermas, *The Structural Transformation of the Public Sphere: An Inquiry Into a Category of Bourgeois Society,* trans. Thomas Burger (Cambridge, MA: MIT Press, 1989); John L. Brooke, "Consent, Civil Society, and the Public Sphere in the Age of Revolution and the Early American Republic," in *Beyond the Founders: New Approaches to the Political History of the Early American Republic,* ed. Jeffrey L. Pasley, Andrew W. Robertson, and David Waldstreicher (Chapel Hill: University of North Carolina Press, 2004), 209–250; Nancy Fraser, "Rethinking the Public Sphere: A Contribution to the Critique of Actually Existing Democracy," in *Habermas and the Public Sphere,* ed. Craig Calhoun (Cambridge, MA: MIT Press, 1992), 109–142; David Waldstreicher, *In the Midst of Perpetual Fetes: The Making of American Nationalism, 1776–1820* (Chapel Hill: University of North Carolina Press, 2004), 2–13, 110; Michael Warner, *Publics and Counterpublics* (New York: Zone Books, 2002).

26. Brooke, "Consent, Civil Society, and the Public Sphere," 228–230; Jürgen Habermas, *Between Facts and Norms: Contributions to a Discourse Theory of Law and Democracy,* trans. William Rehg (Cambridge, MA: MIT Press, 1996).

27. Durey, *"With the Hammer of Truth,"* 109. Callender is listed as having naturalized in the Philadelphia Court of Common Pleas on June 4, 1798, in P. William Filby, *Philadelphia Naturalization Records: An Index to Records of Aliens' Declarations of Intention*

And/Or Oaths of Allegiance, 1789–1880, in United States Circuit Court, United States District Court, Supreme Court of Pennsylvania, Quarter Sessions Court, Court of Common Pleas, Philadelphia (Detroit: Gale Research Company, 1982); Smith, *Freedom's Fetters*, 173, 217–218, acknowledges Burk's status as an alien in discussing the deportation proceedings against him. Smith also notes Pickering's plan to disregard Duane's claims to citizenship and initiate deportation proceedings against him as well, although Pickering did not follow through; Nigel Little, *Transoceanic Radical, William Duane: National Identity and Empire 1760–1835* (London, Brookfield, VT: Pickering & Chatto, 2008), 153–154; *Hollingsworth v. Duane*, 12 Fed. Case 356, Case No. 6, 615; see naturalization action of William Duane, July 13, 1802, in Filby, *Philadelphia Naturalization Records*.

28. Burk, "Address to the Public."

29. Burk, "Address to the Public."

30. *Polar Star*, November 1, 1796.

31. "Guillotina for 1797," *Hartford Courant*, reprinted in Norwich, Connecticut, *Chelsea Courier*, January 18, 1797; *Polar Star*, January 9, 1797, 3; Bradburn, *Citizenship Revolution*, 229–230.

32. Shulim, "John Daly Burk," 11, 19; John Daly Burk and Brander Matthews, eds., *Bunker-Hill: Or the Death of General Warren: an Historical Tragedy in Five Acts* (New York: Dunlap Society, 1891); letter quoted in William Dunlap and Tice L Miller, *A History of the American Theatre From Its Origins to 1832* (Urbana: University of Illinois Press, 2005), 166. Emphasis original.

33. Shulim, "John Daly Burk," 50–53.

34. Shulim, 55–56.

35. Shulim, 56–57; James T. Callender, *History of the United States for 1796* (Philadelphia, 1797), 279–280, quoted in Durey, "*With the Hammer of Truth*," 56–57.

36. Durey, "*With the Hammer of Truth*," 59–62.

37. Durey, 63–73.

38. *Aurora*, March 2, 1795. Emphasis added. For limiting free speech only to those in the legislature, rather than the public at large, see David S. Bogen, "The Origins of Freedom of Speech and Press," *Maryland Law Review* 42, no. 3 (1983): 431–439, especially 436–437. Another way Federalists (and many Republicans as well) understood free speech was that there should be no censorship prior to publication, but dangerous writings, or writings that maliciously dishonored reputations, could result in public prosecution or private score-settling on matters of personal honor. See Leonard Levy, "The Republicans and the Transformation of Libertarian Thought," in *Major Problems in American Constitutional History*, ed. Kermit L. Hall (Boston: Cengage, 2010), 102–109; Joanne Freeman, "Explaining the Unexplainable: The Cultural Context of the Sedition Act," in *The Democratic Experiment: New Directions in American Political History*, ed. Meg Jacobs, William J. Novak, and Julian E. Zelizer (Princeton, NJ: Princeton University Press, 2003), 20–49.

39. Smith, *Freedom's Fetters*, 206, 210–211; Shulim, "John Daly Burk," 26.

40. Pasley, "*Tyranny of Printers*," 123–124.

41. Waldstreicher, *In the Midst of Perpetual Fetes*.

42. This behavior was limited to printed statements—seditious utterances were prosecuted, as in the last chapter's discussion of the case of Lespinard Colie, but there are no extant cases of federal deportation (or attempts to do so) for spoken seditious utterances.

43. Boston, "Impact of Foreign Liars"; Cleves, *Reign of Terror*, 61–68, 86, 89–90.

44. 8 *Annals of Congress*, 2097.

45. 8 *Annals*, 2102, 599, 2171; *Journal of the House*, 3:379–380 (July 10, 1798); Smith, *Freedom's Fetters*, 105–107, 110–111, 150–152, including quote from John Adams originally appearing in the *Columbian Centinel*, August 18, 1798; See also Pasley, "*Tyranny of Printers*," 118–124.

46. 8 *Annals*, 2095.

47. Pasley, "*Tyranny of Printers*," 111, 118–124. Pasley notes the Federalists' recognition that printers and "partisan newspapers possessed the potential to overturn social and ethnic hierarchy as the organizing principles of political life," and that Federalist extremists feared the spread of revolutionary violence, while Federalist moderates saw the potential for opposition presses to cost them electoral defeats. I build on Pasley to argue that such views also incorporated a Federalist theorization of the operations of the public sphere much along the lines of Brooke's description. The Sedition Act was an attempt at hegemonic gatekeeping and was seen by Federalists as such.

48. US *Statutes at Large*, I, 566–572, 577–578, 596–597.

49. Pickering to Adams, August 1, 1799, in John Adams, *The Works of John Adams, Second President of the United States: With a Life of the Author* (Boston, 1850), ix, 5–7. See also Malone, *Life of Thomas Cooper*, 90–91n 55.

50. Malone, *Life of Thomas Cooper*, 92–95.

51. Malone, 101–104.

52. Malone, 113–119.

53. Malone, 145.

54. Durey, "*With the Hammer of Truth*," 108–111, 114–115; Petition to Naturalize of James Thomson Callender, June 4,1798, Court of Common Pleas, in Filby, *Philadelphia Naturalization Records*.

55. Durey, "*With the Hammer of Truth*," 125–134. The trial itself was a showcase for another point of intersection between citizenship and the public sphere—the powers of jurors. The English common law of seditious libel granted juries the power to determine only the facts of publication—whether the allegedly seditious statement had been written and/or published by the defendant, but not whether the statement itself was seditious. Aware that judge Samuel Chase was likely to find Callender guilty anyway, Callender's defense team chose to bring public attention to a limit of common citizen power and a lack of check on the power of federally appointed judges. Their criticisms of the trial proceedings were further amplified by a jury of handpicked Federalists who, even if they had the power to deliver a verdict, had already decided that Callender was guilty. Although Callender was convicted, fined $200, and sentenced to nine months in prison, his defense team achieved a public relations coup that assisted in the Republican victory in 1800. This experience caused Callender to change his view of libel suits

as a means of policing the public sphere: in his 1795 defense of free speech as a right of citizenship, Callender argued that libel prosecutions could be used to regulate public speech that got out of hand, which he imagined, would be decided by juries—although in such cases guilt or innocence was decided by judges; *Aurora*, March 2, 1795. James T. Callender, *Sedgwick & Co., or a Key to the Six Per Cent Cabinet* (Philadelphia, 1798), 18; Durey, *"With the Hammer of Truth,"* 109, 136, 200n87.

56. Malone, *Life of Thomas Cooper*, 90–91; John Adams to Timothy Pickering, August 13, 1799, in *Works of John Adams*, ix, 14; Smith, *Freedom's Fetters*, 173, 218–219.

57. New York *Time Piece*, June 25, 1798, quoted in Shulim, "John Daly Burk," 29–30.

58. Shulim, "John Daly Burk," 30.

59. Shulim, 31–32.

60. Shulim, 32.

61. Shulim, 35.

62. Pickering was not fully hostile to all British and Irish migrants, only radicals. The English migrant William Cobbett was a Federalist ally in the newspaper wars of the 1790s. Other migrants fulfilled a mercantilist interest: their population fueled the economy, their labor enriched or assisted masters, their land-seeking benefited those political leaders who obtained land expropriated from American Indians.

63. Little, *William Duane*, 18–20. Despite his claims, Duane was actually born in St. John's, Newfoundland, on May 12, 1760, shortly before his parents moved to Vermont; Kim Tousley Phillips, *William Duane, Radical Journalist in the Age of Jefferson* (New York: Garland, 1989), 124–126; *Hollingsworth v. Duane*.

64. Despite this particular victory, quite a number of common law restrictions of free speech remained. Early Republican printers still needed to worry about private libel suits. Unfree people were limited in their access to public speech, while customary restrictions and social norms further placed restrictions on access to presses and what could be said, written, or published. Additionally, Thomas Jefferson, incensed over Federalist opposition presses in 1807, attempted to prosecute them for sedition, but was dissuaded when they threatened to expose his early affair with Mrs. John Walker, as discussed in Joanne Freeman, "Explaining the Unexplainable," 20–49, 40, 49n72, and Dumas Malone, *Jefferson the President, Second Term, 1805–1809* (Boston: Little, Brown, 1974), 372, 377–387. The nineteenth century would see additional conflicts over attempts to suppress abolitionist literature and conflicts over obscene libel. See Helen Lefkowitz Horowitz, *Rereading Sex: Battles Over Sexual Knowledge and Suppression in Nineteenth-Century America* (New York: Knopf, 2002).

65. Shulim, "John Daly Burk," 36–37.

66. Shulim, 37–47.

67. Shulim, 51.

68. The development of a white racial identity among European immigrants, specifically Irish immigrants, is addressed in Noel Ignatiev, *How the Irish Became White* (New York: Routledge, 1995.)

69. Ignatiev, 142–144.

70. Ignatiev, 143–148.

71. Durey, *"With the Hammer of Truth,"* 149–152

72. Durey, 137–138, 153–155.

73. Durey, 153–155.

74. Durey, 156–157.

75. Richmond *Recorder*, September 1, 1802. Reprinted in Baltimore *Republican*, September 6, 1802.

76. Durey, *"With the Hammer of Truth,"* 158–161.

77. Richmond *Examiner*, September 25, 1802, quoted in Durey, *"With the Hammer of Truth,"* 161.

78. Annette Gordon-Reed, *Thomas Jefferson and Sally Hemings: An American Controversy* (University Press of Virginia, 1997) 59–62, and *The Hemingses of Monticello: An American Family* (New York: Norton, 2008), 554–557.

79. Durey, *"With the Hammer of Truth,"* 164–165.

80. Quoted in Durey, *"With the Hammer of Truth,"* 164–165.

81. Durey, 165–167.

82. Durey, 168–171.

83. John Caldwell to Robert Simms, October 18, 1802, in *Irish Emigrants in the Land of Canaan: Letters and Memoirs from Colonial and Revolutionary America, 1675–1815*, ed. Kerby Miller et al. (New York: Oxford University Press, 2003), 636–637. Underlining original. Caldwell is also deploying the term citizen in a local, urban context in this case, while maintaining a national concept of alienship.

84. Rosemarie Zagarri describes the formal side of political organizing, and the ways in which it excluded women while including poorer white men in *Revolutionary Backlash: Women and Politics in the Early American Republic* (Philadelphia: University of Pennsylvania Press, 2007), 157–158.

85. Letter of John Shaw to Robert Tennant, 10 December 1801, D1748/C/1/184/5, Tennent Papers, Public Record Office of Northern Ireland (PRONI).

86. Shaw to Tennant, December 10, 1801.

87. Shaw to Tennant, December 10, 1801.

88. National Archives Record Group 21 (Records of District Courts of the United States, 1685–1991): Landing Reports of Aliens, 1798–1828. US District Court for Eastern Pennsylvania, vol. 1 Hereafter referred to individually as Report No., with name and date.

89. This information has been compiled into a database, along with additional naturalization data from the migrants who appear in the landing reports. A small number of French Royalists who became British subjects appear in the returns.

90. Copy of Oath of Allegiance of Charles Maurice de Talleyrand-Périgord, Miscellaneous Manuscripts Collection, American Philosophical Society, May 19, 1794; John L. Earl, "Talleyrand in America: A Study of His Exile in the United States" (PhD diss., Georgetown University, 1964), 45, 279, 286–289; Stanley M. Elkins and Eric L. McKittrick, *The Age of Federalism* (New York: Oxford University Press, 1993), 567–568, 571–574. It was Talleyrand and his agents who, in attempting to extort a bribe from American commissioners in France, precipitated the XYZ affair and with it the quasi-war with France, leading to the passage of the Alien and Sedition Acts.

91. Alien Landing Report No. 25, Jean Simon Chauvron [Chaudron], December 13, 1798; Naturalization Action of Jean Chaudron, June 21, 1805, in Filby, *Philadelphia Naturalization Records*; *New York Daily Advertiser*, July 30, 1793, 3; *Philadelphia Gazette & Universal Daily Advertiser*, March 8, 1797, 1; March 16, 1797, 2; Thomas Jefferson to Auguste Belin, February 27 and March 6, 1800, in., *The Papers of Thomas Jefferson*, ed. Barbara B. Oberg et al. (Princeton, NJ: Princeton University Press, 2003) vol. 31, 396, 417; Thomas Jefferson to Chaudron and Baralet, April 1, 1802; Jefferson to Chaudron, March 3, 1819, Thomas Jefferson Papers, American Memory, http://memory.loc.gov/ammem/collections/jefferson_papers/index.html.

92. The planter turned umbrella maker is found in Report No. 2, Charles Laurent, June 30, 1798. Laurent had not sunk so low as it might at first appear: the "making or mending of umbrellas," along with "making wooden boxes," hatmaking, and "any thing he could make or execute" while he "endeavor[ed] to support his family" was conducted "with the Help of two Negroes his Wife and his Brother."

93. Ashli White, *Encountering Revolution: Haiti and the Making of the Early Republic* (Baltimore: Johns Hopkins University Press, 2010), 35–37.

94. Baseler, *"Asylum for Mankind,"* 295.

95. An example of the approbation of foreign migrants can be seen in the letter of John Shaw to Robert Tennant, December 10, 1801, PRONI, "now there is no such thing but welcom to all men who Cums here with property or without that is willing to be indousterous." Thomas Jefferson to Auguste Belin, February 27, 1800, and March 6, 1800, in *Papers of Thomas Jefferson*, vol. 31, 396, 417.

96. Henry Bradshaw Fearon, *Sketches of America: A Narrative of a Journey of Five Thousand Miles Through the Eastern and Western States of America, Contained in Eight Reports* (London, 1818), 347–349. The original address, which Bradshaw quotes in his travel narrative, dates from 1809.

97. Fearon.

98. Fearon.

99. Fearon.

100. Fearon.

101. Paul A. Gilje, *The Road to Mobocracy: Popular Disorder in New York City, 1763–1834* (Chapel Hill: Published for the Institute of Early American History and Culture by the University of North Carolina Press, 1987), 130–133; Durey, *Transatlantic Radicals,* 270–272.

102. Durey, *Transatlantic Radicals,* 269–270; Fearon, *Sketches of America,* 19–20, 346–349. Italics original. Emmet probably provided Fearon with the document he quotes.

103. Return of Thomas William Holmes, July 20, 1812. Marshals' Returns of Enemy Aliens and Prisoners of War, 1812–1815, National Archives Record Group 59: General Records of the Department of State, 1756–1999, microfilm publication M588: "War of 1812 Papers" of the Department of State, 1789–1815. Marshals returns have been compiled, except for original "remarks" field, by Kenneth Scott, *British Aliens in the United States during the War of 1812* (Baltimore: Genealogical Publishing Company, 1979).

Chapter 3

Epigraph: Letter of James Mercer to John Minor, 31 March 1813, Letters Received Regarding Enemy Aliens, War of 1812 Papers, NARA Microfilm M588.

1. *The Case of Alien Enemies, Considered and Decided Upon a Writ of Habeas Corpus Allowed on the Petition of Charles Lockington, an Alien Enemy, by the Hon. William Tilghman* (Philadelphia, 1813), i–viii.

2. Return of William Nottingham, July 22, 1812, Marshals' Returns of Enemy Aliens and Prisoners of War, 1812–1815, National Archives Record Group Record Group 59: General Records of the Department of State, 1756–1999, microfilm publication M588: "War of 1812 Papers" of the Department of State, 1789–1815. Marshals' returns have been compiled, excepting the original "remarks" field, in Kenneth Scott, compiler, *British Aliens in the United States during the War of 1812* (Baltimore: Genealogical Publishing Company, 1979). Further marshals' returns of enemy aliens will be referred to by name, e.g. Return of Name. Where my transcriptions differ from Scott's, his transcription appears in parenthesis.

3. Return of William Young, July 24, 1812.

4. *Case of Alien Enemies*, v.

5. Harvey Amani Whitfield has examined the experiences of people who escaped slavery during the War of 1812 by assisting British forces, and their subsequent engagement with subject/citizen status as settlers in Nova Scotia in *Blacks on the Border* (Burlington: University of Vermont Press, 2006), 30–35, 40, 100–104. He has also noted that British military officers evaluated claims of people attempting to escape slavery on their value to British forces as potential soldiers and sources of intelligence. Historians have long noted the differing approaches of American and British peace negotiators to the claims for compensation by former slaveowners and British unwillingness to accept those claims under pressure from the British abolitionist movement. In *The Civil War of 1812: American Citizens, British Subjects, Irish Rebels, and Indian Allies* (New York: Knopf, 2010), 102–113, Alan Taylor has noted that appeals to military patriotism assisted British-born American soldiers in claiming the rights of citizenship, although British treatment of prisoners led to a resurgent nativism among prisoners of war. In *The War of 1812: A Forgotten Conflict* (Urbana: University of Illinois Press, 1989), 175–176, Donald Hickey has noted the measures taken against alien enemies but has not tied them to the significant changes that occurred in citizenship and state power during the war. For a discussion of the disputes over sailors' claims to citizenship and freedom from impressment, and the resulting popular push for war against Britain on the claim of "Free Trade and Sailors' Rights," see Paul A. Gilje, "'Free Trade and Sailors' Rights': The Rhetoric of the War of 1812," *Journal of the Early Republic* 30, no. 1 (2010): 1–23. In *"Asylum for Mankind": America, 1607–1800* (Ithaca, NY: Cornell University Press, 1998), 317–322, Marilyn C. Baseler has discussed the actions of British subjects during the war, and noted the mixed success that demonstrations of patriotism made in obtaining exemptions while pointing to the greater success of petitions in obtaining changes to naturalization law in 1813. Baseler has further noted that no fundamental changes occurred in naturalization

patterns, her chief point of interest in discussing alien enemies, but she has not addressed the significance of changes in law, state power over aliens, and changes in the rights of citizens and penalties of aliens. In *Congress, Courts, and Criminals: The Development of Federal Criminal Law, 1801–1829* (Westport, CT: Greenwood Press, 1985), Dwight Henderson has discussed compulsory registration of alien enemies, as well as the case of *Lockington v. Smith,* which addressed alien enemies' rights to legal agency and ability to petition for a writ of habeas corpus. In *The Development of American Citizenship, 1608–1870* (Chapel Hill: Published for the Omohundro Institute of Early American History and Culture by the University of North Carolina Press, 1978), James H. Kettner addressed the status of alien enemies in Louisiana in the court decision *United States v. Lavery,* which confirmed earlier policies granting citizenship to Louisiana residents prior to statehood regardless of whether they had naturalized. Kettner also noted the aforementioned disputes over prisoners of war, 252, 270; *US Statutes at Large,* I, 577–578. This book focuses on naturalization rather than expatriation, on which there is also a rich body of scholarship.

6. Aristide Zolberg, *A Nation by Design: Immigration Policy in the Fashioning of America* (Cambridge, MA: Harvard University Press, 2006), 19.

7. William J. Novak, "The Legal Transformation of Citizenship in Nineteenth-Century America," in *The Democratic Experiment: New Directions in American Political History,* ed. Meg Jacobs, William J. Novak, and Julian E. Zelizer (Princeton, NJ: Princeton University Press, 2003), 85–119; John C. Torpey, *The Invention of the Passport: Surveillance, Citizenship, and the State* (New York: Cambridge University Press, 2000), 1–2.

8. Hickey, *War of 1812,* 16–20; Taylor, *Civil War of 1812,* 115–119.

9. Hickey, *War of 1812,* 9–13, 17–20.

10. Hickey, *War of 1812,* 20–25, 44–46; more recently, Alan Taylor argues in *Civil War of 1812,* 133–135, that the reasons for the Republican push for war were fourfold: the economic issues (which Taylor argues could still have been renegotiated to prevent war), a push from Western political leaders for attacks upon British-allied Indians, hope for a conquest of Canada, and impressment. I agree with Taylor's analysis, but have chosen to emphasize the commercial aspects of the causes of the war to tie them to the effects of those disputes and fears of British economic power on British subjects residing in the United States during the war.

11. Hickey, *War of 1812,* 9–13, 17–25, 44–46; Herbert Heaton, "The Industrial Immigrant in the United States, 1783–1812," *Proceedings of the American Philosophical Society* 95, no. 5 (1951): 519–527, 520.

12. Torpey, *Invention of the Passport,* 94; *US Statutes at Large,* I, 577–578.

13. Kettner, *Development of American Citizenship,* 245–246; James Morton Smith, *Freedom's Fetters: The Alien and Sedition Laws and American Civil Liberties* (Ithaca, NY: Cornell University Press, 1956), 130, 176. *US Statutes at Large,* I, 570–572, 596–597 (1851). *US Statutes at Large,* II, 781; *US Statutes at Large* VIII, 116–132. Article 3, 117–118, deals specifically with fur trading; New York *Columbian,* July 13, 1812, 3; Hickey, *War of 1812,* 175.

14. *Case of Alien Enemies*, vii. US Marshals received notice of the change in a circular dated April 15, 1813, noting the appointment of Gen. John Mason to the post.

15. *Niles Weekly Register*, May 22 and June 5, 1813, quoted in Heaton, "Industrial Immigrant," 519–527, 520.

16. *Case of Alien Enemies*, iii–iv. This order came after the end of the Congressional session, so the Madison administration may have waited either for Congress to pass legislation like this, or to avoid Federalist objections during the session so that the order was a fait accompli once Congress reconvened in November.

17. Heaton, "Industrial Immigrant," 520.

18. *Poulson's American Daily Advertiser*, August 6, 1812, 4.

19. Hickey, *War of 1812*, 85–86.

20. Smith, *Freedom's Fetters*, 34, 52–54, 160–175. As Smith notes, the original bill of the Alien Act relied even more heavily on the strength of the courts: "It stipulated that no person could 'harbour, entertain, or conceal any alien' without first giving written notice to a federal district judge or Supreme Court justice several days in advance. This was to apply to all citizens, with or without the permits. Every offending 'entertainer,' citizen or alien, would have been subject to an unspecified fine." *Case of Alien Enemies*, v.

21. Elizabeth Sandwith Drinker and Elaine Forman Crane, ed., *The Diary of Elizabeth Drinker* (Boston: Northeastern University Press, 1991), 1424; Return of Frederick Smyth, March 13, 1813; James Robinson and Abraham Shoemaker, *The Philadelphia Directory, City and County Register, for 1803: Containing the Names, Trades and Residence of the Inhabitants of the City, Southwark, Northern Liberties, and Kensington: With Other Useful Tables and Lists: To Which Is Added, An Almanac, Calculated for the Latitude and Meridian of Philadelphia, by A. Shoemaker* (Philadelphia,1802); James Robinson, *The Philadelphia Directory for 1810: Containing the Names, Trades & Residence of the Inhabitants of the City, Southwark, and Northern Liberties: Also, a Calendar, From the 1st of March 1810, to the 1st of March 1811, and Other Useful Information* (Philadelphia, 1810); Smyth is spelled Smith in the 1810 directory. The town of Roxborough is now part of the city of Philadelphia; Larry R. Gerlach, *Prologue to Independence: New Jersey in the Coming of the American Revolution* (New Brunswick, NJ: Rutgers University Press, 1976), 306, 310–311, 321.

22. Return of Peter B. Rindle, September 26, 1812; Timothy Reddy, William McMillan (Scott spells McMillin), September 7–12, 1812; Joseph Moneypenney (Manypenny), August 8–16, 1812; James Richards, September 26, 1812.

23. Return of John C. Gray (Grey), August16–September 26, 1812; Isaiah Thomas et al., *The History of Printing in America* (Worcester, MA, 1874), 297. Joanne Freeman, "Explaining the Unexplainable: The Cultural Context of the Sedition Act," in *The Democratic Experiment: New Directions in American Political History*, ed. Meg Jacobs, William J. Novak, and Julian E. Zelizer (Princeton, NJ: Princeton University Press, 2003), 20–49, 40, 49n72; and Dumas Malone, *Jefferson the President, Second Term, 1805–1809* (Boston: Little, Brown, 1974), 372, 377–387.

24. This was particularly the case for men serving in US forces born in the British dominions, as discussed in Taylor, *Civil War of 1812*, 4–5, 354–355. Among these was

Ned Myers, born in Quebec, and unnaturalized resident of the United States since about 1804. See also Scott, *British Aliens*, vi.

25. *Case of Alien Enemies*, vi–vii. Craig Robertson, *The Passport in America: The History of a Document* (New York: Oxford University Press, 2010), 14–16n33, 264–265; Torpey, *Invention of the Passport*, 21–56; Gaillard Hunt, *The American Passport, Its History and a Digest of Laws, Rulings and Regulations Governing Its Issuance by the Department of State* (Washington, DC: Government Printing Office, 1898), 37–38; see also Adam McKeown, *Melancholy Order: Asian Migration and the Globalization of Borders* (New York: Columbia University Press, 2008), 33. War of 1812 passports bore more similarity to the slave passes of the era and the management of American Indians than to contemporary US passports. Rather than controlling the movements of white people, such as the restrictions on settlement for new arrivals, or restrictions like the passport system (which also existed to control white movement of US citizens in frontier regions), the government now exercised its power to forcibly remove a sedentary white population. In this instance, whiteness counted for less, citizenship for more—and citizenship status mattered more in relations between individuals and the national government, rather than state or local government. The role of race and the color line in citizenship and federal power during the early American republic is discussed in greater detail in the following chapter.

26. Torpey, *Invention of the Passport*, 94.

27. *Case of Alien Enemies*, v.

28. In the 1820s, American working radicals such as William Heighton formulated a more explicit labor theory of value, as described in Bruce Laurie, *Working People of Philadelphia, 1800–1850* (Philadelphia: Temple University Press, 1980), 76. The order, coming from government officials and reflecting the political views of the Virginia dynasty, placed planters safely in the category of productive laborers. The views expressed in the order are somewhat of an expansion of those of Jefferson, Madison, and other Republicans as described in Drew R. McCoy, *The Elusive Republic: Political Economy in Jeffersonian America* (Chapel Hill: Published for the Institute of Early American History and Culture, Williamsburg, Virginia, by the University of North Carolina Press, 1980). McCoy has described the hostility to the mercantile classes as well as Madison's reluctant acceptance of an American merchant marine and commercial export sector in order to combat British economic power. I am proposing that Madison and Republican policymakers viewed wealth made by productive labor as something that needed to be guarded not only as part of the protection against economic and social "decline" reflected in wider European wealth inequalities and reliance on manufacturing, but also as a more immediate problem when dealing with British economic hegemony.

29. Return of Thomas William Holmes, July 20, 1812.

30. Some discussion of the migrant press reaction appears in the later section on migrant resistance in this chapter. Irish immigrants in New York City had access to emerging ethnic newspapers, but Philadelphia lacked such an ethnic press in the early nineteenth century. Although the Irish immigrant press published polemical articles arguing that the Irish and American causes were united against British imperialism, and that Irish

patriots would fight for both causes in the War of 1812 despite their alien status, these papers do not appear to have made direct, strident criticisms of US government alien policy.

31. Job F. Belles, "Informations to Aliens," *The Shamrock*, August 1 and November 14, *1812*. Reprinted from *Savannah Republican*. The commentary was either by the court clerk Job F. Belles or Solicitor-General Thomas U. P. Charlton; New York *Columbian*, July 13, 1812, 3. Reprint from the *Enquirer*; "To British and Irish Aliens," *New York Public Advertiser*, June 27, 1812.

32. New York *Columbian*, July 13, 1812, 3. Reprint from the *Enquirer*. Italics original.

33. Heaton, "Industrial Immigrant."

34. *Concord Gazette*, May 26, 1812, 3. Originally printed in *Keene Sentinel*; *New-Jersey Journal*, May 3, 1814, 2. Emphasis original.

35. Henderson, *Congress, Courts, and Criminals*, 101–102; *Bennington News-Letter*, April 21, 1813, 3.

36. *Bennington News-Letter*, April 21, 1813, 3; *Federal Republican*, April 2, 1813, 2.

37. *Federal Republican*, April 7, 1813, 1.

38. *Case of Alien Enemies*, vi-vii. Italics original. Heaton, "Industrial Immigrant," 520; Henderson, *Congress, Courts, and Criminals*, 102.

39. *Charleston City Gazette*, July 30, 1812; *Saratoga Patriot*, August 19, 1812; a later reminder for newer arrivals appears in *Poulson's American Daily Advertiser*, December 4, 1812. Unable to keep personal tabs on all migrants, Peter Curtenius required boarding-house keepers to assist him in enforcing the passport system and removal order, after the prompting by James Monroe. New York *Spectator*, April 10, 1813.

40. Heaton, "Industrial Immigrant," 524; *Case of Alien Enemies*, vi-vii; Return of Milling Wooley, December 16, 1813.

41. *Case of Alien Enemies*, vi-vii. Italics original. Unfortunately, this source does not include the marshals' responses.

42. The 761 heads of household whose returns are listed account for the extant listings, but the tallies appearing in the original returns indicate a large number of missing records, as noted in the Heaton, "Industrial Immigrant," 519; Return of Thomas Curran July 20, 1812. A Thomas Curran filed a naturalization action in the court of common pleas on March 30, 1813, in P. William Filby, *Philadelphia Naturalization Records: An Index to Records of Aliens' Declarations of Intention And/Or Oaths of Allegiance, 1789-1880, in United States Circuit Court, United States District Court, Supreme Court of Pennsylvania, Quarter Sessions Court, Court of Common Pleas, Philadelphia* (Detroit: Gale Research Company, 1982). Return of Edward Clarke, July 24, 1812. Return of Thomas William Holmes, July 20, 1812. Holmes does not have a corroborating record in Scott, *British Aliens*.

43. *Shamrock*, August 1, 1812, 1; November 14, 1812, 4. "Informations to Aliens" at no time specifically states that the article pertains to Irish people or British subjects generally.

44. Act of 1813, 13th Congress, Session 1, in D. M. Dewey, compiler, *The Naturalization Laws of the United States: Containing Also the Alien Laws of the State of New York: A Synopsis of the Alien Laws of Other States, with the Forms for Naturalizing Aliens, Important Decisions, General Remarks, &c., &c* (Rochester, NY, 1855), 37. The gradualist model was the original plan of many legislators during the debates over the Naturalization Act

of 1790, as discussed in Baseler, *"Asylum for Mankind,"* 257–260; Petition of George Cogghill of the City of New York on behalf of himself and Others, "War of 1812 Papers," reprinted in Baseler, 320–321. A George Coggill, merchant, appears in the alien returns for New York, "age 30, wife & 2 children, corner Broadway & Murray Sts. . . . applied [declared intent to naturalize?] 21 Mar. 1812 ([registered as alien] 7-12 Sept. 1812)," in Scott, *British Aliens.*

45. Return of Robert Dunn, July 20, 1812; Return of William Nottingham, July 22, 1812; Letter of James Mercer to John Minor, March 31, 1813, Letters Received Regarding Enemy Aliens, "War of 1812 Papers," NARA Microfilm M588.

46. Holly Brewer, "The Transformation of Domestic Law," in *The Cambridge History of Law in America*, ed. Michael Grossberg and Christopher Tomlins (New York: Cambridge University Press, 2008), 1: 288–323; Rosemarie Zagarri, *Revolutionary Backlash: Women and Politics in the Early American Republic* (Philadelphia: University of Pennsylvania Press, 2007); Pauline E. Schloesser, *The Fair Sex: White Women and Racial Patriarchy in the Early American Republic* (New York: New York University Press, 2002); Rosemarie Zagarri, "Morals, Manners, and the Republican Mother," *American Quarterly* 44, no. 2 (June 1992); Barbara J. Todd, "Written in Her Heart: Married Women's Separate Allegiance in English Law," in *Married Women and the Law: Coverture in England and the Common Law World*, ed. Tim Stretton and Krista J. Kesselring (Montreal: McGill-Queen's University Press, 2013), 163–191.

47. *Case of Alien Enemies*, v–vi; Also winning exemptions were "owners of real property," or planters and landed elites; Scott, *British Aliens*, 322, 384. Linda K. Kerber, "The Republican Mother: Women and the Enlightenment—An American Perspective," *American Quarterly* 28 (1976): 187–205, 202. Jan Lewis has noted the limits of wives' persuasive, political, and legal power in "The Republican Wife: Virtue and Seduction in the Early Republic," *William and Mary Quarterly* 44 (1987): 689–721. The success of American wives and their British husbands in obtaining exemptions indicates that if such persuasion was presented as having already been achieved, Republican Motherhood could indeed leverage treatment of binational couples into people less foreign regardless of their legal status. Should her British husband not be persuaded of the error of his ways, however, a "patriotic" American-born woman was likely to find herself in more difficult circumstances.

48. Zagarri, "Morals, Manners, and the Republican Mother."

49. Todd, "Written in Her Heart." Additionally, the tug between a woman's loyalty to her husband and her loyalty to the state, and the resulting problems women faced when thinking about citizenship appear in Linda Kerber, *No Constitutional Right to Be Ladies: Women and the Obligations of Citizenship* (New York: Hill and Wang, 1998). Kerber notes the long continuity of women continuing to derive citizen status from their husbands, with its effects on the duties and expectations imposed upon them.

50. This view builds on the concept of citizenship through public celebration and spectacle as laid out in David Waldstreicher, *In the Midst of Perpetual Fetes: The Making of American Nationalism, 1776–1820* (Chapel Hill: Published for the Omohundro

Institute of Early American History and Culture, Williamsburg, Virginia, by the University of North Carolina Press, 1997).

51. Richard L. Bushman, *The Refinement of America: Persons, Houses, Cities* (New York: Vintage, 1993), 90–92, 120–121, 127, 160–162, 440–446. Genteel women in the early republic retained some status as their houses remained, to some degree, places where politics and business were transacted, a loss they would encounter more keenly in the mid-nineteenth century. I have inferred socializing after church services; Dallett C. Hemphill, *Bowing to Necessities: A History of Manners in America, 1620–1860* (New York: Oxford University Press, 1999), 104–126 is mainly concerned with proscriptive etiquette surrounding women's social behavior, but describes the mixed-gender socializing among the emerging middle class in the Revolutionary era; Catherine E. Kelly, *Republic of Taste: Art, Politics, and Everyday Life in Early America* (Philadelphia: University of Pennsylvania Press, 2016).

52. Laurel Thatcher Ulrich, *Good Wives: Image and Reality in the Lives of Women in Northern New England, 1650–1750* (New York: Knopf, 1982), 36–50. Nicole Eustace, *1812: War and the Passions of Patriotism* (Philadelphia: University of Pennsylvania Press), 123, notes that women could expect their husbands to provide them physical and legal protection. Since husbands' alien enemy status prevented them from doing this, the couple could turn to the state for redress.

53. Return of William Young, July 1812; William Lancaster, Jr. 20 July 1812; William Plews, 20 July 1812. Alternatively, we may view William Young's declaration as one of virtual citizenship—all the privileges of citizenship without formal naturalization. Scott, *British Aliens*, 322. Letter of James Mercer, M588.

54. In *British Aliens in the United States*, Scott has transcribed Jackson's passport as follows: "Jackson, George K. age 34, 5ft. 4½ in., florid complex., dark hair, blue eyes, prof. of music, Boston, on 19 Mar. 1812 ordered to Northampton, Hampshire Co. (Mass. Passport No. 3.)." The removal probably dates to 1813, as war had not yet been declared in 1812.

55. Hugh Scott to Gen. John Mason, September 11, 1813, "War of 1812 Papers." Scott, *British Aliens*, 330.

56. Henderson, *Congress, Courts, and Criminals*, 104, 107.

57. Petition of Charles Lockington, *New York Herald*. There is no return for Charles Lockington among the extant Pennsylvania marshal's returns.

58. Petition of Charles Lockington, *New York Herald*. *Case of Alien Enemies*, 3, 15; *Mumford v. Mumford*, 1 Gall. 316. In this case Joseph Mumford, British subject, "resident within the realm thereof," sued Henry Mumford, but was dismissed owing to Joseph's status as an alien enemy. Henry Mumford dissolved a business partnership with a Samuel Warner in December 1811, owned a grocery store in the spring of 1812, which he advertised for sale, and was subsequently a partner in the Union Dying Company, part of the nascent industrial revolution, but it is not clear what specific business matter prompted the suit, nor the exact connection between the two men prior to the dispute, *Rhode-Island American*, January 17, 1812, April 3, 1812, *Providence Gazette*, September 16, 1815; Peter J. Coleman and Penelope K. Majeske, "British Immigrants in Rhode Island

during the War of 1812," *Rhode Island History* 34, 66–75, 67-68; Kim Tousley Phillips, "William Duane, Philadelphia's Democratic Republicans, and the Origins of Modern Politics," *Pennsylvania Magazine of History & Biography* 101 (1977): 365–387, 367–368; Robinson, *Philadelphia Directory for 1810.*

59. *Case of Alien Enemies*, 13–21.

60. Hare is identified only as Mr. Hare in the *Case of Alien Enemies*. First name from listing for Charles W. Hare, Attorney at Law, 9[3] Walnut St., in Robinson and Shoemaker, *Philadelphia Directory for 1803; Case of Alien Enemies*, 13–21; Henderson, *Congress, Courts and Criminals*, 105.

61. Kettner, *Development of American Citizenship*, 249–251.

62. "Extracts from the Report of the Foreign Mission School," Missionary Herald at Home and Abroad, vol. 13 (1817): 517–518.

Chapter 4

Epigraph: National Archives Record Group 21 (Records of District Courts of the United States, 1685–1991): Landing Reports of Aliens, 1798–1828. U.S. District Court for Eastern Pennsylvania, Volume I. Digitized and available through the National Archives and Records Administration Archival Research Catalog: https://catalog.archives.gov/id/279083 . Report No. 74, Desiré, 17 December 1798.

1. *United States Gazette* (Philadelphia), April 25, 1807, 2.

2. James H. Kettner, *The Development of American Citizenship, 1608–1870* (Chapel Hill: Published for the Omohundro Institute of Early American History and Culture, Williamsburg, Virginia, by the University of North Carolina Press, 1978); Rogers M. Smith, *Civic Ideals: Conflicting Visions of Citizenship in U.S. History* (New Haven, CT: Yale University Press, 1997).

3. Lois E. Horton, "From Class to Race in Early America: Northern Post-Emancipation Racial Reconstruction," in *Race and the Early Republic: Racial Consciousness and Nation-Building in the Early Republic,* ed. Michael Morrison and James Brewer Stewart (Lanham, MD: Rowman and Littlefield, 2002).

4. Jeffrey L. Pasley, *"The Tyranny of Printers": Newspaper Politics in the Early American Republic* (Charlottesville: University Press of Virginia, 2001), 123. Of course, this is a view that many (elite) white Americans held, but it was contradicted in many ways. Masters might withhold food and other material needs from slaves to encourage them to fend for themselves, or might be threatened by slaves who dressed in clothing not provided by the master, disrupting the façade of dependence. Economic elites might view themselves as economically independent even as they became enmeshed in a web of debt in the growing global economy.

5. *A Narrative of Five Youth from the Sandwich Islands: Now Receiving an Education in this Country* (New York, 1816), 7, 19, 25–26, 38. Where other scholars have provided a more accurate name transliteration, I have used that version (e.g. Opukuhai'a instead of Obookiah), but where I have not uncovered such a transliteration, I have

used the versions that appear in nineteenth-century missionary accounts. Dates of arrival of the youths are mentioned throughout the work. Thomas Hopoo, "Memoirs of Thomas Hopoo: Written by Himself, a Short Time before he left America," *Hawaiian Journal of History* 2 (1968): 42–54, 45. *The Narrative of Five Youth* described Kanui's removal from the barber shop with approval, as a step in his conversion narrative, while the author cited Carhooa's membership in a brief description that noted his age (twenty-three) and residence of several years in Boston, and that Carhooa was "highly esteemed by his acquaintances." Missionary accounts from this period were often written to argue that nonwhite people were worthy of conversion and that such conversions were possible. Although a Baptist church veered somewhat from Calvinist orthodoxy, in Carhooa's case the author viewed it positively. Douglas Bristol, "From Outposts to Enclaves: A Social History of Black Barbers from 1750 to 1915," *Enterprise & Society* 5, no. 4 (2004): 594–606.

6. E. W. Dwight, *Memoirs of Henry Obookiah: A Native of Owhyhee, and a Member of the Foreign Mission School* (Philadelphia, 1830), 89–94, 101, 110, 120; *Narrative of Five Youth*, 12, estimates Opukahai'a's age at twenty-one at time of writing, which is 1815 or 1816. Opukahai'a died in 1818, making him twenty-three or twenty-four at the time of his death on February 17, 1818.

7. James Fenimore Cooper, *Ned Myers, Or, A Life Before the Mast* (New York: AMS Press, 2009), 121–122. First published 1843.

8. East India Company Court of Directors Minutes, B/ series, August 31, 1737, British Library, quoted in Michael Herbert Fisher, *Counterflows to Colonialism: Indian Travellers and Settlers in Britain, 1600–1857* (Delhi: Distributed by Orient Longman, 2004).

9. Fisher, *Counterflows to Colonialism*, 32–37. As Alan Taylor has noted in *The Civil War of 1812: American Citizens, British Subjects, Irish Rebels, and Indian Allies* (New York: Knopf, 2010), 3, Myers was born a British subject in Quebec but identified as an American after settling in the United States. Cooper, *Ned Myers*; Fisher, *Counterflows to Colonialism*; R. L. Brunhouse, "Lascars in Pennsylvania: A Side-Light on the China Trade," *Pennsylvania History* 7, no. 1 (1940): 20–30.

10. *Maryland Journal and Baltimore Advertiser,* August 12, 1785. "Paltry wages" description is from Brunhouse, "Lascars in Pennsylvania," 23.

11. Sick Keesar et al., "Memorial and Representation of the under written Mr. Sick Keesar first Lieutenant, in behalf of himself and Thirty four others," December 14, 1785, Papers of the Continental Congress, no. 69, vol. 2, 537. Captain John O'Donnell to John Dickinson and Council for the State of Pennsylvania, November 3, 1783, Post Revolutionary Papers, vol. 22, 8, Pennsylvania State Archives, Harrisburg. Both documents are reprinted in Brunhouse, "Lascars in Pennsylvania," although the petition is missing the signatures that appear on the original document. Brunhouse also notes that O'Donnell's letter contained an enclosure, which has been lost, and which may contain a defense of his role in the enslavement of Adam Keesar. More recent scholarship has begun to investigate the South Asian presence in in the early American republic. See Rajender Kaur, "The Curious Case of Sick Keesar: Tracing the Roots of South Asian Presence in the Early American Republic," *Journal of Transnational American Studies* 8, no. 1, 2017.

12. In this chapter, I use the term "people of color" to refer to people of combined European and African ancestry who formed an intermediate racial category between black and white in revolutionary Saint-Domingue. I also refer to people from the colony of Saint-Domingue prior to its 1804 independence as Dominguan, while acknowledging that national identities during the revolutionary period were in a state of flux. White Dominguans almost always ultimately adopted a French identity, while people of color or exclusively of African descent might later have identified as French, Haitian, or African American. I use the term Dominguan primarily to distinguish residents of the colony from residents of metropolitan France. Even here, frequent migration between the two blurred such identities. Paul F. Lachance, "The 1809 Immigration of Saint-Domingue Refugees to New Orleans: Reception, Integration and Impact," *Louisiana History: The Journal of the Louisiana Historical Association* 29, no. 2 (1988): 109–141, 111; Ashli White, email message to author, November 2, 2011.

13. Kettner, *Development of American Citizenship*, 30–36; in pp. 319–320, Kettner notes the attempt to impose denizenship upon African Americans and the legal questions raised. Douglas Bradburn, *The Citizenship Revolution: Politics and the Creation of the American Union, 1774–1804* (Charlottesville: University of Virginia Press, 2009), 238.

14. National Archives Record Group 21 (Records of District Courts of the United States, 1685–1991): Landing Reports of Aliens, 1798–1828. US District Court for Eastern Pennsylvania, vol. 1. (Hereafter referred to individually as Report No., with name and date.) Report No. 74, Desiré, December 17, 1798.

15. Vagrancy report quoted in Susan Branson and Leslie Patrick, "Étrangers Dans un Pays Étrange: Saint-Domingan Refugees of Color in Philadelphia," in *The Impact of the Haitian Revolution in the Atlantic World,* ed. David P. Geggus (Columbia: University of South Carolina, 2001), 193–208, 201

16. Hannah F. Sawyer Lee*, Memoir of Pierre Toussaint, Born a Slave in St. Domingo* (Boston, 1854), 15–21, 27–28, 34; Arthur Jones, *Pierre Toussaint* (New York: Doubleday, 2003), 163, 189–197, 274–277.

17. "Les citoyens de couleur de Philadelphia à l'Assemblée Nationale," September 24, 1793. Unsigned manuscript letter, item 13, vol. 3, Revolution de St. Domingue collection, John Carter Brown Library, Providence, Rhode Island; Ashli White, "'A Flood of Impure Lava': Saint Dominguan Refugees in the United States, 1791–1820" (PhD diss., Columbia University, 2003), 245. The affair of Citizen Genet in the spring of 1793 was the first inkling that revolutionary optimism about a harmonious alliance between republics might be overly optimistic. David Patrick Geggus, "Slavery, War, and Revolution in the Greater Caribbean, 1789–1815," in *A Turbulent Time: The French Revolution in the Greater Caribbean,* ed. David Patrick Geggus and David Barry Gaspar (Bloomington: Indiana University Press, 1997), 1–50, 12–13. Geggus notes that free people of color in particular were involved in distributing a combined revolutionary message along with anticolonialism and antislavery.

18. "Les citoyens de couleur de Philadelphia à l'Assemblée Nationale," *Journal des Revolutions de la partie française de Saint Domingue,* January 6, 1794.

19. *United States Gazette* (Philadelphia), April 15, 1807, 2.

20. *United States Gazette* (Philadelphia), April 15, 1807, 2; Pennsylvania Constitution of 1790, article 3, section 1, in *Laws of the Commonwealth of Pennsylvania*, vol. 3 (Philadelphia, 1810), xxxvi; Kettner, *Development of American Citizenship*, 248–251.

21. Rosemarie Zagarri, *Revolutionary Backlash: Women and Politics in the Early American Republic* (Philadelphia: University of Pennsylvania Press, 2007), 155–157. See Return of William Young, July 24, 1812: "served 9 Years apprenticeship in the City of New York & that he was informed that [coming into] the country while a minor & serving an apprenticeship was sufficient to entitle him to the privileges of a citizen," in Marshals' Returns of Enemy Aliens and Prisoners of War, 1812–1815, National Archives Record Group Record Group 59: General Records of the Department of State, 1756–1999, microfilm publication M588: "War of 1812 Papers" of the Department of State 1789–1815.

22. British subjects at times successfully exercised the franchise as part of their virtual citizenship, and also served in the militia, as evidenced by John Law's militia service, mentioned later in this chapter.

23. Valentin Groebner, *Who Are You?: Identification, Deception, and Surveillance in Early Modern Europe* (New York: Zone Books, 2007), 193. Groebner investigates the development of the modern identity system and its relationship to state surveillance, examining documents from both early modern city-states and emerging nation-states. As modern states were able to devote increasing resources to surveillance, and as literacy became more widespread, early modern states began an attempt to record and document information about all persons within their borders. This is the fictional realm described above, first depicted by Bernhard Siegert in "Pasajeros a Indias. Biographical Writing between the Old World and the New," in *Talleres de la memoria—Reivindicaciones y autoridad en la historiografía indiana de los siglos XVI y XVII,* ed. Robert Folger, Wulf Oesterreicher, and Roland Schmidt-Riese (Hamburg: Lit, 2005), 295–306. Siegert has emphasized the fictionality and fraud inherent in the system, while Groebner has built on Siegert to describe the fictional world created by the record-keeping process. Although they have noted resistance through fraud, neither scholar has shown how individuals could use the identity system, fully aware of its functioning, to their own advantage, as Desiré did.

24. Groebner, *Who Are You*, 193, 201. By the eighteenth century, a transnational surveillance system had functioned for several centuries. Earlier officials examined documents themselves only for authenticity, but authenticity now resided in the body of records against which identity would be checked and verified. The authenticity of the record-keeping system itself was what allowed Desiré to safely document his free status and use it to prevent possible reenslavement.

25. See also Ariela Julie Gross, *What Blood Won't Tell: A History of Race on Trial in America* (Cambridge, MA: Harvard University Press, 2008). Gross's study begins in the antebellum period, when white racial status and citizenship were so closely intertwined as to be almost synonymous. In contrast, the period of the early American republic was more fluid, and migrants had greater room for maneuverability.

26. Extracts from the "Report of the Foreign Mission School," *Missionary Herald at Home and Abroad*, vol. 13 (1817), 517–518.

27. Thomas Law to Mrs. Tucker, July 1, 1829, Thomas Law Papers, University of Virginia Special Collections, MS 2801, Charlottesville, Virginia; thanks to Rosemarie Zagarri for alerting me to this letter. Allen C. Clark, *Greenleaf and Law in the Federal City* (Washington, DC: Press of W .F. Roberts, 1901), 305–312; Robert S. Tilton, *Pocahontas: The Evolution of An American Narrative* (New York: Cambridge University Press, 1994), 45. While Rogers Smith, *Civic Ideals*, 106–110, 144–146, 181–185, has detailed the exclusion of Native Americans from effective citizenship during the era of the early American republic, this view emphasized elite political conceptions of citizenship, along with relations with nations as a collective group outside of regions under full local white administration. Individuals disassociated from a native nation, and with sufficient white ancestry encountered, it seems, a different evaluation of fitness that was tied, as this chapter argues, to other markers of socio-economic status and racial performance.

28. Baptism of John Law, February 10, 1784; Baptism of Edmund Law, December 12, 1788, British Library India Office Family History Search, http://indiafamily.bl.uk/UI/Home.aspx. Thanks again to Rosemarie Zagarri for directing me to sources relating to the Law Family. Clark, *Greenleaf and Law,* 305–312; Naturalization action of Edmund Law, June 1, 1812 [OM], US Naturalization Record Indexes, 1794–1994, vol. 4, 90. Naturalization action of Thomas Law, January 14, 1815 [RB and OM], vol. 5, 67. National Archives Record Group 94: Carded Records Showing Military Service of Soldiers Who Fought in Volunteer Organizations During the War of 1812. Edmund Law is listed as a corporal, serving from July 15–26, 1813, from July 18–26, 1814, and again from August 19–October 8, 1814. John Law is listed as a first sergeant, serving the same dates, but with permitted leave of absence during the last period of service. Both served in Capt. Benjamin Burch's Artillery Company, part of the second regiment of the District of Columbia militia.

29. Lyman F. Hodge, *Photius Fisk: A Biography* (Boston, 1891), 28, 116.

30. Robert J. Allison, *The Crescent Obscured: The United States and the Muslim World, 1776–1815* (New York: Oxford University Press, 1995) 3, 5–7; William Foushee to Patrick Henry, December 6, 1785, in *Calendar of Virginia State Papers and Other Manuscripts*, ed. William Pitt Palmer et al., vol. 4, 1884, 71; James Madison to Thomas Jefferson, January 22, 1786, in *Papers of Thomas Jefferson*, ed. Julian P. Boyd, (Princeton, NJ: Princeton University Press, 1954), vol. 9, 197; US Statutes at Large I (1845), 570–572.

31. Leon Huhner, "Moses Elias Levy: An Early Florida Pioneer and the Father of Florida's First Senator," *Florida Historical Quarterly* 19 (1941): 319–45; C. S. Monaco, *Moses Levy of Florida: Jewish Utopian and Antebellum Reformer* (Baton Rouge: Louisiana State University Press, 2005), 40–47, 58–49, 84–87. Monaco argues that Levy was driven to establish a Jewish colony in the United States by a post-Napoleonic outbreak of anti-Semitism and a belief in American religious liberalism and tolerance. Monaco also notes that Levy was religiously motivated, but similar in views to early-nineteenth-century utopians such as Robert Owen. [Moses Levy], *A Plan for the Abolition of Slavery Consistently with the Interests of All Parties Concerned* (London, 1828), 12–13, 15–19. Levy

cited Puerto Rico and Cuba, where he had lived, as models for interracial marriages, and advocated the export of British convicts to the West Indies for this purpose.

32. Monaco, *Moses Levy of Florida*, 158–160, 164; [Levy], *A Plan for the Abolition of Slavery*. Monaco notes that David Levy Yulee changed his name after his father revealed that Yulee had been the family name in Morocco. Monaco argues that Moses Levy deemphasized or obscured his Moroccan origins, although he clearly stated those origins on his 1821 naturalization document. Monaco also argues that David Levy Yulee adopted his surname in part to be less identifiably Jewish. Laurel Clark, "The Rights of a Florida Wife: Slavery, U.S. Expansion, and Married Women's Property Law," *Journal of Women's History*, 22, no. 4 (Winter 2010), 39–63.

33. John Quincy Adams and Charles Francis Adams, ed., *Memoirs of John Quincy Adams* (Philadelphia, 1876), vol. 10, 483.

34. Monaco, *Moses Levy of Florida*, 132–138, 158–160; [Levy], *A Plan for the Abolition of Slavery*, 12–13, 15–19.

35. Martha M. Umphrey, "The Trouble with Harry Thaw," in *Queer Studies: An Interdisciplinary Reader*, ed. Robert J. Corber and Stephen Valocchi (Malden, MA: Blackwell, 2003), 21–30.

36. Declarations of Intent to Naturalize of Domingo Garcia, March 20, 1812; Antonio Antelo, June 28, 1818, and Antonio Raffelin, November 28, 1817, Alien Landing Reports. The birthdate for Raffelin is given as October 23, 1787, which is ten years before 1798, the date that Alejo Carpentier and Ethel S. Cohen, "Music in Cuba (1523–1900)", *Musical Quarterly* 33, no. 3 (1947): 365–380, list for Raffelin's birth. It is possible that this is another person with the same this name, perhaps a cousin. There are numerous early republican naturalizations for subjects of the king of Spain (and likewise Portugal), but in the absence of a place of birth it is not possible to say whether they are from Iberia, Spanish dominions in the Americas, or elsewhere.

37. Marilyn C. Baseler, "Asylum for Mankind": America, 1607–1800 (Ithaca, NY: Cornell University Press), 298–300.

Chapter 5

Epigraph: Trautmann, Frederic. "Pennsylvania through a German's Eyes: The Travels of Ludwig Gall, 1819–1820." *Pennsylvania Magazine of History and Biography* 105, no. 1 (1981): 35–65.

1. Marietta *American Friend,* December 11, 1818. The announcement itself is dated December 7. The James Brown in question is possibly James Brown, 1766–1835, in between his terms serving as US Senator from Louisiana. "James Brown," in in *Biographical Directory of the United States Congress*, United States Congress, https://bioguider-etro.congress.gov/Home/MemberDetails?memIndex=B000921

2. Douglas Bradburn, *The Citizenship Revolution* (Charlottesville: University of Virginia Press, 2009); David Roediger, *The Wages of Whiteness: Race and the Making of the American Working Class* (New York: Verso, 1991); Alexander Saxton, *The Rise*

and Fall of the White Republic: Class Politics and Mass Culture in Nineteenth-Century America (New York: Verso, 1990); Noel Ignatiev, *How the Irish Became White* (New York: Routledge, 1995); Robert J. Steinfeld, *The Invention of Free Labor: The Employment Relation in English and American Law and Culture, 1350–1870* (Chapel Hill: University of North Carolina Press, 1991); David Waldstreicher, *In the Midst of Perpetual Fetes: The Making of American Nationalism, 1776–1820* (Chapel Hill: Published for the Omohundro Institute of Early American History and Culture, Williamsburg, Virginia, by the University of North Carolina Press, 1997); Simon P. Newman, *Parades and Politics of the Street: Festive Culture in the Early American Republic* (Philadelphia: University of Pennsylvania Press, 1997); John L. Brooke, "Consent, Civil Society, and the Public Sphere in the Age of Revolution and the Early American Republic," in *Beyond the Founders: New Approaches to the Political History of the Early American Republic,* ed. Jeffrey L. Pasley, Andrew W. Robertson, and David Waldstreicher (Chapel Hill: University of North Carolina Press, 2004) 209–50. Indentured servants did participate in festive culture, but this chapter places less emphasis on this aspect of citizenship, as it was clear that this form of political participation was not exclusive to citizens—as further elaborated in John L. Brooke's model of participation in the state relative to hegemony.

3. Gordon S. Wood, *The Radicalism of the American Revolution* (New York: Knopf, 1991).

4. "Proclamation by the Governor of Virginia," November 17, 1775, in Peter Force, ed., *American Archives: Documentary History of the American Revolution*, vol. 3 (https://digital.lib.niu.edu/amarch/toc); see also George Livermore, *An Historical Research Respecting the Opinions of the Founders* (Boston, 1862), 136, for the Philipsburg Proclamation issued by Henry Clinton in 1779; a more extensive discussion of additional proclamations and enslaved peoples' experiences seeking freedom with the British can be found in Gary B. Nash, *The Unknown American Revolution: The Unruly Birth of Democracy and the Struggle to Create America* (New York: Viking, 2005), 161–164, 330–333; *Journal of Continental Congress*, vol. 4, 56, 64 (January 15 and 17, 1776); Virginia *Statutes at Large*, vol. 9 (1821), 275–279 (passed May 20, 1777). See also Sylvia R. Frey, *Water from the Rock: Black Resistance in a Revolutionary Age* (Princeton, NJ: Princeton University Press, 1991), 78–79, for a discussion of the enlistment of African Americans in the Continental Army; Samuel D. McKee Jr., *Labor in Colonial New York, 1664–1776* (New York: Columbia University Press, 1935), 175; Thurlow Weed, printer, *Journals of the Provincial Congress, Provincial Convention, Committee of Safety and Council of Safety of the State of New-York: 1775–1775–1777,* (Albany, NY: 1842), 57, 68.

5. James H. Kettner, *The Development of American Citizenship, 1608–1870* (Chapel Hill: Published for the Omohundro Institute of Early American History and Culture, Williamsburg, Virginia, by the University of North Carolina Press, 1978), 175–209. The idea of a fixed loyalty to the monarch did have some exceptions: while expatriation was tantamount to treason in most cases, the model of citizenship descending from head of household status meant that a British female subject who married an alien would take

her husband's status. Sale of an enslaved person could also bring about a similar change in status.

6. Susan E. Klepp et al., ed., *Souls for Sale: Two German Redemptioners Come to Revolutionary America. The Life Stories of John Frederick Whitehead and Johann Carl Büttner* (University Park: Pennsylvania State University Press, 2006), 189–192, 230–232. This section relies extensively on the two autobiographical narratives written by former indentured servants from Germany, as my research has not uncovered any other extant similar works.

7. *Souls for Sale*, 192–194, 232–251.

8. Ken Miller, *Dangerous Guests: Enemy Captives and Revolutionary Communities during the War for Independence* (Ithaca, NY: Cornell University Press, 2014), 177–180.

9. Miller, *Dangerous Guests*, 180; Rodney Atwood, *The Hessians: Mercenaries from Hessen-Kassel in the American Revolution* (New York: Cambridge University Press, 1980), 186, 192–198, 201–204.

10. Lion G. Miles, *The Hessians of Lewis Miller* (Millville, PA: Johannes Schwalm Historical Association, 1983). Descriptions of tools appear in the accompanying text of each portrait. Miller signed an introduction to his book of watercolor portraits in 1816, when he was twenty years old; the portraits presumably date to a time shortly before then, 12–13, 19, 30, 55; David Waldstreicher, *In the Midst of Perpetual Fetes*, 1–2, 9; Waldstreicher also cites Sean Wilentz, "Artisan Republican Festivals and the Rise of Class Conflict in New York City, 1788-1837," in *Working-Class America*, ed. Michael H. Frisch and Daniel J. Walkowitz (Urbana, Ill., 1983), 37-77.

11. Farley Grubb, *German Immigration and Servitude in America, 1709–1920* (New York: Routledge, 2011), 28, 33; Miller, *Dangerous Guests*, 179–183; Marilyn C. Baseler, *"Asylum for Mankind": America, 1607–1800* (Ithaca, NY: Cornell University Press, 1998), 229; Bradburn, *Citizenship Revolution*, 242; Robert William Fogel and Stanley L. Engerman, "Philanthropy at Bargain Prices: Notes on the Economics of Gradual Emancipation" *Journal of Legal Studies* 3, no. 2 (1974): 377–401; Gary B. Nash and Jean R. Soderlund, *Freedom by Degrees: Emancipation in Pennsylvania and Its Aftermath* (New York: Oxford University Press, 1991), and Joanne Pope Melish, *Disowning Slavery: Gradual Emancipation and "Race" in New England, 1780–1860* (Ithaca, NY: Cornell University Press, 1998) also note the continuation of bondage in Northern states during this time.

12. *South Carolina Gazette*, December 6, 1783, quoted in Baseler, *"Asylum for Mankind,"* 231; see also Steinfeld, *Invention of Free Labor*, 199.

13. New York *Independent Gazette*, January 24, 1784.

14. Location of slave market from William Offutt, *Patriots, Loyalists, and Revolution in New York City, 1775–1776* (New York: Norton, 2015), 11.

15. Hoang Gia Phan, *Bonds of Citizenship: Law and the Labors of Emancipation* (New York: New York University Press, 2013), 32–36; J. Hector St. John Crèvecoeur, *Letters from an American Farmer* (New York: Fox, Duffield, 1904 [first published 1782]), 48–91; John Murrin, "Fundamental Values, the Founding Fathers, and the Constitution," in

To Form a More Perfect Union: The Critical Ideas of the Constitution, ed. Herman Belz et al. (Charlottesville: University Press of Virginia, 1992), 1–37.

16. Phan, *Bonds of Citizenship,* 24; *Records of the Federal Convention of 1787,* ed. Max Ferrand (New Haven, CT: Yale University Press, 1911), 222.

17. Phan, *Bonds of Citizenship,* 27–29; for debaters' ideologies at this time; see also Murrin, "Fundamental Values." See Chapter 3 for a discussion of the labor theory of value, as well as Bruce Laurie, *Working People of Philadelphia, 1800–1850* (Philadelphia: Temple University Press, 1980), 76.

18. Phan, *Bonds of Citizenship,* 32; US Constitution, article 1, section 2, clause 3; *Debates in the Federal Convention of 1787,* August 8, 1787.

19. See Chapter 2 for a more extensive discussion of the Federalist conception of citizenship. *Souls for Sale,* 38–39, 45.

20. *Souls for Sale,* 124, 151–152, discusses the demographics of Whitehead's Pennsylvania community, 35–39. Writing decades later about the militia in eastern North Carolina immediately prior to Nat Turner's rebellion, Harriet Jacobs describes citizenship functioning in a similar fashion, assigning citizen status only to the elite of the North Carolina community where she had been enslaved: "It was always the custom to have a muster every year. On that occasion every white man shouldered his musket. The citizens and the so-called country gentlemen wore military uniforms. The poor whites took their places in the ranks in every-day dress, some without shoes, some without hats." Harriet Ann Jacobs, *Incidents in the Life of a Slave Girl* (Boston, 1861), 97.

21. Sharon Braslaw Sundue, "Class Stratification and Children's Work in Post-Revolutionary Urban America," in *Class Matters: Early North America and the Atlantic World,* ed. Simon Middleton and Billy G. Smith (Philadelphia: University of Pennsylvania Press, 2008), 198–212. Holly Brewer, *By Birth or Consent: Children, Law, and the Anglo-American Revolution in Authority* (Chapel Hill: University of North Carolina Press, 2005), 230–287; G. S. Rowe, *Embattled Bench: The Pennsylvania Supreme Court and the Forging of a Democratic Society, 1684–1809* (Newark: University of Delaware Press, 1994), 209–213. *Respublica v. Keppele,* 2 Dallas 197 and 1 Yeates 233 (Pennsylvania, 1793).

22. *By Birth or Consent,* 230–287; Sundue, "Class Stratification;" Rowe, *Embattled Bench,* 209–213. Sundue and Rowe offer differing interpretations of the effects of the Hannis case, with Sundue arguing that it did little to improve the lives of Philadelphia's child servants, while Rowe argues for substantial court access and scrutiny of contracts for white servants. Sundue does note the growing push for children's education as part of a program to develop a public of educated citizens. Education stipulations were a standard provision in children and family redemptioner contracts, though limited usually to six weeks' schooling per year. See Farley Grubb, *German Immigrant Servant Contracts Registered at the Port of Philadelphia, 1817–1831* (Baltimore: Genealogical Publishing Company, 1994).

23. Rowe, *Embattled Bench,* 209–213; 2 *Dallas* 227; 1 *Yeates* 480–483. Rowe discusses the growing racial disparity in judicial attitudes and rulings, while noting some

abolitionist successes in *Republica v. Aberilla Blackmore*, which liberated people brought to Pennsylvania after 1780, and in limiting extremely long indentures for formerly enslaved people. "Republica v. Gaoler of Philadelphia County," 1 *Yeates* 368; 4 *Yeates* 82–83, 204–205.

24. *Souls for Sale*, 17–19.

25. Rowe, *Embattled Bench*, 209–213; *Republica v. Keeper of the Prison of the City and County of Philadelphia*, 2 Yeates 257. These cases are from Pennsylvania, a state with a large number of indentured servants. Other states, such as Ohio, prohibited indentures entirely, as did Indiana after an 1821 court case. In an 1856 case in Massachusetts, *Parsons v. Trask*, 73 Mass. (7 Gray) 473 (1856), the court viewed an indenture as invalid when a suit was brought for enticing the indentee away to another employer. See Steinfeld, *Invention of Free Labor*, 135, 173, 178.

26. John Gilbert McCurdy, *Citizen Bachelors: Manhood and the Creation of the United States* (Ithaca, NY: Cornell University Press, 2009); Steinfeld, *Invention of Free Labor*, 157, 160; Walter S. Sanderlin, *The Great National Project: A History of the Chesapeake and Ohio Canal* (Baltimore: Johns Hopkins University Press, 1946), 71–77, discusses the inability of C&O Canal Company to effectively retain control of the indentured servants whose passage the company paid for to work on the canal's construction.

27. Christoph C. Raible et al., "Tambora 1815 as a test case for high impact volcanic eruptions: Earth system effects," *WIREs Climate Change* 7, no. 4 (2016): 569–589, https//doi.org/ 10.1002/wcc.407; Renate Auchmann et al., "Extreme climate, not extreme weather: the summer of 1816 in Geneva, Switzerland," *Climate of the Past* 8, (2012) 325–335, https://doi: 10.5194/cp-8-325-2012; Farley Grubb, *German Immigration and Servitude in America*, 311–312, 343, 361–362n16; John Bailey, *The Lost German Slave Girl: The Extraordinary True Story of Sally Miller and Her Fight for Freedom in Old New Orleans* (New York: Atlantic Monthly Press, 2003), 20–28.

28. Moritz von Fürstenwarther, *The German in North America,* ed. H. C. von Gagern, trans. Siegmar Muehl (Iowa City, IA: The Translator), 1–6. [First published 1818.]

29. Fürstenwärther, *The German in North America.*

30. Fürstenwärther.

31. Fürstenwärther, 21–24, 26–27.

32. Fürstenwärther, 27–28.

33. Fürstenwärther, 28–29.

34. Fürstenwärther, 15, 21, 23

35. *World Messenger*, December 3, 1817; *True American Commercial Advertiser*, June 18, 1817; *Freedom's Messenger*, October 30, 1817; all quoted in Fürstenwärther, 56.

36. Fürstenwärther, 17; Bailey, *Lost German Slave Girl*, 45.

37. Fürstenwärther, 48.

38. Fürstenwärther, 42, 48. Fürstenwärther briefly addressed other aspects and conceptions of citizenship, p. 37. He noted the role of formal, legal status, and the barriers to property ownership that aliens faced, while noting that an oath of allegiance could circumvent this issue. He also noted the lack of restrictions on occupations open to aliens.

39. *Daily National Intelligencer,* June 2, 1817.

40. James Brown, Memorial to United States Senate for Change of Venue, December 28, 1819. *American State Papers*, class 10, "Miscellaneous," vol. 2, 550–554, http://memory.loc.gov/cgi-bin/ampage?collId=llsp&fileName=038/llsp038.db&Page=550. The specific runaways Brown listed by name appear in Book C of Redemptioners, October 30, 1818, reprinted in Grubb, *German Immigrant Servant Contracts*. Linda Showalter, "The German Redemptioners at Marietta, or How an Entire Town Conspired to Rescue 22 Immigrants from a Cruel Fate," *Tallow Light* 49, no. 4 (2018): 98–103, contains a brief account of the events.

41. Deposition of James Brown; Caleb Emerson, "For the American Friend," Marietta *American Friend*, January 1, 1819.

42. Deposition of James Brown; Emerson, "For the American Friend."

43. Deposition of James Brown.

44. Deposition of James Brown.

45. Deposition of James Brown.

46. Deposition of James Brown; Emerson, "For the American Friend."

47. Deposition of James Brown.

48. Deposition of James Brown.

49. James Brown, "Caution," Marietta *American Friend,* December 11, 1818.

50. Marietta *American Friend*, December 11 and 18, 1819.

51. Marietta *American Friend*, December 11 and 18, 1819; An Act Respecting Fugitives from Justice, and Persons Escaping Service from their Masters, 1793, 1 Stat. 302. The migrants' worthiness of kindness, charity, and freedom can also be viewed as part of their assertion of status associated with race and potential citizenship. I have yet to find these migrants in local census or other records, but suspect that they changed their names after their escape.

52. Emerson, "For the American Friend."

53. Gautham Rao, "The Federal Posse Comitatus Doctrine: Slavery, Compulsion, and Statecraft in Mid-Nineteenth Century America," *Law and History Review* 26, no. 1 (January 2008). Rao notes the use of the posse in enforcing the Fugitive Slave Law of 1851, as well as a variety of matters in the early American republic. The term "Dutch slaves" appears in Fürstenwärther's report as follows: "The indenture contracts described above contrast with slavery which is a true injustice. The contracts are voluntary and the term of service is limited in time. However, it may well cast a shadow on the German name and contribute to making it scorned, if not in theory then in practice, when the arrangement is not free from many abuses and illegalities which make it hateful. The common expression is not 'bind and serve' but 'buy and sell.' Indeed in southern states one calls indentured persons 'Dutch' or 'white slaves.'" Fürstenwärther, 27n. In reviewing Fürstenwarther's original published report, the *North-American Review* expressed skepticism, stating that "We are more inclined to doubt a part of this anecdote, as we have observed our southern and western brethren to be very sparing in the word slave, even when applied to the blacks." *The North-American Review and Miscellaneous Journal* 11, no. 28 (1820): 1–19, 7.

54. Deposition of James Brown.

55. Deposition of James Brown.

56. Deposition of James Brown; "Guide to the Caleb Emerson Collection," Slack Research Collections, Marietta College Library. http://lib2.marietta.edu/spc/FindingAids/Emerson%20-%20Caleb%20Emerson%20Collection.pdf; Showalter, "German Redemptioners at Marietta."

57. Deposition of James Brown

58. Virginia law had, since the 1660s, granted masters absolute power over enslaved people. An Act About the Casuall Killing of Slaves, 1669, *Statutes at Large; Being a Collection of all the Laws of Virginia,* ed. William Waller Hening (Richmond, VA, 1809–1823), vol. 2, 270.

59. Deposition of William Eastham, March 23, 1819; Deposition of Roderick Osborn, March 23, 1819; Deposition of James Brown, November 8, 1819. All depositions accompany Brown's memorial to Congress.

60. Frederic Trautmann, "Pennsylvania through a German's Eyes: The Travels of Ludwig Gall, 1819–1820," *Pennsylvania Magazine of History and Biography* 105, no. 1 (1981): 35–65; unsigned review of *Versuch über den politischen Zustand der Vereinigten Staaten von Nord America, &c. (Essay on the Political Condition of the US of North America),* by Frederic Schmidt; *Meine Auswanderung nach den Vereinigten Staaten in Nord America, &c.; (My Emigration to the U.S. of N. America in the Spring of 1819), and My Return Home in the Winter of 1820,* by Ludwig Gall, *North-American Review* 17, no. 40, (July 1823): 103.

61. Trautmann, "Gall"; Rosemarie Zagarri, "Morals, Manners, and the Republican Mother," *American Quarterly* 44, no. 2 (1992): 192; W. J. Rorabaugh, *The Craft Apprentice: From Franklin to the Machine Age in America* (New York: Oxford University Press, 1986), 52–53.

62. Frances Trollope, *Domestic Manners of the Americans* (New York: Penguin Classics, 1997), 45–48, 294. [First published 1832.]

63. Xenophobic attitudes from the 1790s still lingered: the Irish emigrant Thomas Addis Emmet found those views hampered his political rise in New York. The English visitor Henry Bradshaw Fearon wrote that despite Emmet's successful legal career, "native Americans speak of him with great jealousy" because he "was guilty of two unpardonable crimes," being "a foreigner" and the "second and greatest of all, in being an Irish rebel!" Fearon noted the widespread distinctions between "citizens of native and foreign birth" and attended a debate where the audience cheered a speaker who advocated the exclusion of the foreign-born from all political offices. Henry Bradshaw Fearon, *Sketches of America: A Narrative of a Journey of Five Thousand Miles through the Eastern and Western States of America* (London, 1819), 19–20, 346–349. Italics original.

64. I am thinking of works such as Cathy Davidson, *Revolution and the Word: The Rise of the Novel in America* (New York: Oxford University Press, 2004); Rachel Hope Cleves, *Reign of Terror in America: Visions of Violence from Anti-Jacobinism to Anti-slavery* (New York: Cambridge University Press, 2009), and primary sources such as

Susanna Rowson, *Charlotte. A Tale of Truth* (London, 1791) and Leonara Sansay's *Secret History; or the Horrors of St. Domingo* (Philadelphia, 1808). My claim is merely a venture into reconceptualizing citizenship in the early American republic, rather than a comprehensive assertion.

65. Levi Coffin, *Reminiscences of Levi Coffin* (Cincinnati, OH, 1880), 557–560. Toni Morrison, *Beloved* (New York: Knopf, 1987).

66. Coffin, 560.

67. Coffin, 567.

Conclusion

1. Aristide Zolberg, *A Nation by Design: Immigration Policy in the Fashioning of America* (Cambridge, MA: Harvard University Press, 2006), 110–113, 120–124; James H. Kettner, *The Development of American Citizenship, 1608–1870* (Chapel Hill: Published for the Omohundro Institute of Early American History and Culture by the University of North Carolina Press, 1978), 250–251; William J. Novak, "The Legal Transformation of Citizenship in Nineteenth-Century America," in *The Democratic Experiment: New Directions in American Political History*, ed. Meg Jacob, William J. Novak, and Julian E. Zelizer (Princeton, NJ: Princeton University Press, 2003), 85–119; US Constitution, amendment XIV, amendment XV; Siobhan B. Somerville, "Notes toward a Queer History of Naturalization," *American Quarterly* 57, no. 3 (2005): 659–675; National Archives and Records Administration (NARA), "Records of the Immigration and Naturalization Service [INS]," http://www.archives.gov/research/guide-fed-records/groups/085.html.

2. US Law Code, title 50, chapter 3, paragraph 21.

3. Muzaffar Chishti, Sarah Pierce, and Jessica Bolter, "The Obama Record on Deportations: Deporter in Chief or Not?" Migration Policy Institute, January 26, 2017.

4. Somerville, "Toward a Queer History of Naturalization"; DOMA Project, "Victory for Monica & Cristina! Government Closes Deportation Case Against Married Lesbian Couple in New York," blog entry, December 6, 2011, http://www.stopthede-portations.com/blog/2011/12/victory-for-monica-cristina-government-closes-deporta-tion-case-against-married-lesbian-couple-in-new-york.html. The success in this case did not at that time lead to blanket equal treatment of same-sex couples on a par with heterosexual couples by the federal government. On the contrary, under pre-*Obergefell* US policy, binational same-sex couples could not petition for permanent residency for the noncitizen partner. See Craig J. Konnoth and Gary J. Gates, "Same-sex Couples and Immigration in the United States," Williams Institute, UCLA School of Law, November 2011. http://williamsinstitute.law.ucla.edu/wp-content/uploads/Gates-Konnoth-Bina-tional-Report-Nov-2011.pdf.; *Obergefell v. Hodges*, 576 U.S. ___ (2015); Jackie Yodashkin et al., "Immigration Equality and Sullivan & Cromwell LLP File Two Lawsuits Against US State Department for Discriminating Against Married Same-Sex Couples and Their Children," Immigration Equality, January 22, 2018, https://www.immigrationequality.

org/fightforfamiliespressrelease/; Jackie Yodashkin, "Immigration Equality Statement on the Death of Roxsana Hernandez in Immigration and Customs Enforcement Custody," May 31, 2018, https://www.immigrationequality.org/immigration-equality-statement-on-death-of-roxsana-hernandez-in-ice-custody/; Gallup, "In Depth: Topics A to Z: Marriage," https://news.gallup.com/poll/117328/marriage.aspx, in a May 2018 poll, 78 percent of respondents stated that they viewed polygamy as "morally wrong." The poll did not ask about legal recognition.

5. DREAM Act of 2009, S.729.IS; Yolanda Gonzalez Gomez, "Undocumented Youth Lobby for Dream Act," *Huffington Post*, November 21, 2011, http://www.huffingtonpost.com/2011/11/21/dream-act-step-up-fight-for-dream-act-2012_n_1102033.html. "United We Dream," http://unitedwedream.org/about/history/. Mae Ngai, "Impossible Subjects: A Problem of Law and History," keynote address presented at Living on the Margins: "Illegality," Statelessness, and the Politics of Removal in Twentieth-Century Europe and the United States, February 9–11, 2012, German Historical Institute, Washington, DC.

6. "Attorney General Eric Holder Speaks at Northwestern University School of Law," March 5, 2012, http://www.justice.gov/iso/opa/ag/speeches/2012/ag-speech-1203051.html (includes text of remarks "as prepared for delivery").

7. "Attorney General Eric Holder Speaks"; James Morton Smith, *Freedom's Fetters: The Alien and Sedition Laws and American Civil Liberties* (Ithaca, NY: Cornell University Press, 1956), 162–169.

8. Most notably, Trump's campaign speech that described immigrants as disproportionately criminal: "When Mexico sends its people, they're not sending their best. . . . They're sending people that have lots of problems, and they're bringing those problems with us. They're bringing drugs. They're bringing crime. They're rapists. And some, I assume, are good people." Tal Kopan, "What Donald Trump has said about Mexico and vice versa," CNN, August 31, 2016, https://www.cnn.com/2016/08/31/politics/donald-trump-mexico-statements/index.html; Jason Stanley, *How Fascism Works: The Politics of Us and Them* (New York: Random House, 2018), xiii–xiv, 132–134; Emanuella Grinberg and Eliott C. McLaughlin, "Travel ban protests stretch into third day from US to UK" CNN, January 31, 2017, https://www.cnn.com/2017/01/30/politics/travel-ban-protests-immigration/; Lara Putnam and Theda Skocpol, "Middle America Reboots Democracy," *Democracy*, February 20, 2018, https://democracyjournal.org/arguments/middle-america-reboots-democracy/; Jeremy Pressman and Erica Chenoweth, "Crowd Estimates, 1.21.2017," https://docs.google.com/spreadsheets/u/1/d/1x-aoiLqYKz8x9Yc_rfhtmSOJQ2EGgeUVjvV4A8LsIaxY/htmlview?sle=true#gid=0; Matt Broomfield, "Women's March against Donald Trump is the largest day of protests in US history, say political scientists," *The Independent*, January 23, 1017, http://www.independent.co.uk/news/world/americas/womens-march-anti-donald-trump-womens-rights-largest-protest-demonstration-us-history-political-a7541081.html.

9. "It's Time to End Chain Migration," December 15, 2017, https://www.whitehouse.gov/articles/time-end-chain-migration/; "National Security Threats—Chain Migration and the Visa Lottery System," February 1, 2018, https://www.whitehouse.gov/articles/

national-security-threats-chain-migration-visa-lottery-system/; "President Donald J. Trump Taking Action Against Illegal Immigration," June 28, 2017, https://www.white-house.gov/briefings-statements/president-donald-j-trump-taking-action-illegal-im-migration/; Mae Ngai, "Immigration's Border-Enforcement Myth," *New York Times*, January 28, 2018, https://www.nytimes.com/2018/01/28/opinion/immigrations-bor-der-enforcement-myth.html; Mae Ngai, "The Dark History of Defining 'Family'" *New York Time*s, July 19, 2017, https://www.nytimes.com/2017/07/19/opinion/travel-ban-upheld-supreme-court.html; Mae Ngai, "The Strange Career of the Illegal Alien: Immigration Restriction and Deportation Policy in the United States, 1921–1965," *Law and History Review* 21 no. 1 (Spring 2003): 69–107.

10. It is further worth noting that the original controversy concerned unqualified voters in the sheriff's election in Philadelphia: bringing in voters from out of state and encouraging underage voters to vote fraudulently; nonwhite immigrants received the most attention in the original article. Mike Huckabee, "Nancy Pelosi introduces her campaign committee for the take back of the House," Twitter, June 23, 2018, 5:19 a.m. The tweet is accompanied by an image of men with tattoos and flashing signs, whom Huckabee presumably intends to represent MS-13. https://twitter.com/govmikehucka-bee/status/1010497564435730434?lang=en; See also The Hill, "Mike Huckabee tweets apparent photo of MS-13 gang members, calls them Pelosi's 'campaign committee'" Twitter, June 23, 2028, 5:01 p.m. for reproduction of the image. Stanley, *How Fascism Works*, 26–27, 144–146, 200n5; Kate Manne, *Down Girl: The Logic of Misogyny* (New York: Oxford University Press, 2018), 234–235n17; Arlie Russell Hochschild, *Strangers in Their Own Land: Anger and Mourning on the American Right* (New York: New Press, 2016), 221–222, quoted in Manne. See also Peter Beinart, "Why Trump Supporters Believe He Is Not Corrupt," *The Atlantic*, August 22, 2018, https://www.theatlantic.com/ideas/archive/2018/08/what-trumps-supporters-think-of-corruption/568147/.

11. Erika Lee et al., "#ImmigrationSyllabus," January 26, 2017, http://editions.lib.umn.edu/immigrationsyllabus/; George Yancy, *Backlash: What Happens When We Talk Honestly about Racism in America* (Lanham, MD: Rowman & Littlefield, 2018); Dorothy Kim, "Medieval Studies Since Charlottesville," *Inside Higher Ed*, August 30, 2018, https://www.insidehighered.com/views/2018/08/30/scholar-describes-being-conditionally-accepted-medieval-studies-opinion.

12. Daniel Hunter, *Building a Movement to End the New Jim Crow: An Organizing Guide* (Denver: Hyrax Publishing, 2015.) The rise of mass incarceration from 1980s onward has coincided with the criminalization of undocumented migration, and a growing share of people in prison for immigration-related reasons, as detailed in Torrie Hester, "Deportability and the Carceral State," *Journal of American History* 102, no. 1 (June 2015): 141–151.

13. "Nation's Foreign-Born Population Nears 37 Million," US Census Bureau, October 19, 2010, http://www.census.gov/newsroom/releases/archives/foreignborn_popula-tion/cb10-159.html.

Lightning Source UK Ltd.
Milton Keynes UK
UKHW011552021221
394963UK00004B/196